INCLUDES
1 CD

THE COMPLETE IDIOT'S GUIDE® TO

Web Animation

by Marc Campbell

ALPHA
A Pearson Education Company

International Standard Book Number: 0-02-864420-4
Library of Congress Catalog Card Number: 2002113239

04   03   02   8   7   6   5   4   3   2   1

Interpretation of the printing code: The rightmost number of the first series of numbers is the year of the book's printing; the rightmost number of the second series of numbers is the number of the book's printing. For example, a printing code of 02-1 shows that the first printing occurred in 2002.

Printed in the United States of America

Note: This publication contains the opinions and ideas of its author. It is intended to provide helpful and informative material on the subject matter covered. It is sold with the understanding that the author and publisher are not engaged in rendering professional services in the book. If the reader requires personal assistance or advice, a competent professional should be consulted.

Publisher: *Marie Butler-Knight*
Product Manager: *Phil Kitchel*
Managing Editor: *Jennifer Chisholm*
Acquisitions Editor: *Eric Heagy*
Development Editor: *Michael Koch*
Production Editor: *Katherin Bidwell*
Copy Editor: *Susan Aufheimer*
Illustrator: *Chris Eliopoulos*
Cover/Book Designer: *Trina Wurst*
Indexer: *Julie Bess*
Layout/Proofreading: *Angela Calvert, Megan Douglass, Brad Lenser*

Contents at a Glance

Contents

Introduction

Web surfers don't like static pages. They demand images, not just plain text, and they like a certain amount of graphic design. They also want animation. Sit them down in front of something that looks like a TV set, and they expect at least some of the images to move. Blame it on too many Saturday morning cartoons.

Web builders have slowly come around to giving their audience what they want. It started with small, looped sequences and brightly flashing banners. It progressed to more adventurous animations with short narrative storylines and better, more compact graphics. Then came the sound tracks and the interactive elements, the buttons and clickable hotspots. Animations became longer and more involved. Some played more like games. Others watched more like animated shorts, just as good if not better than most of the commercial stuff. Nowadays, the commercial stuff looks like it came off the web—I'm thinking particularly of those flying, laser-blasting preschoolers—while web animation veers into territories such as application server and multiuser platform.

I like web animation, and you're going to like it, too. I say this not in my capacity as taskmaster and despot but as a fellow enthusiast of moving illustrations. Web animation is easy to learn but a challenge to master. In some respects, it's exceedingly demanding. You have to get into its rhythm and play by its rules, or your animations simply won't work, leaving you to figure out why. In other respects, it's completely flexible. It allows you to mix and match media more easily than any other form of animation. It has its limitations, but they encourage you to be innovative.

I should also mention that building web animation is fun. Once you learn the basics and get a feel for the process, you'll start looking for excuses to deploy a new creation on the job, at school, or in your free time. Who can blame you? The process ends with something for you and others to watch and enjoy.

Learning web animation is also a great way to train for more advanced forms like the 3-D stuff that appears in movies and TV. Many proven techniques in 3-D animation compare favorably to the same stupid tricks you'll pick up in this book. What's more, some web animation *is* 3-D animation in the truest sense, and I'll spend the latter part of this book helping to bridge the gap between there and here.

Who Should Read This Book

If computer animation intrigues you, this book is for you. It assumes no previous animation experience. You don't need it! All you need is your latent creativity, a spirit of adventure, and a desire to learn. It helps if you can bluff your way through your computer's operating system, of course, but you don't need to know anything more sophisticated than how to open a folder or where to find a saved file.

Since the focus of this book is building animation, I've supplied much of the art for the example projects on the CD-ROM. You don't need to be an illustrator to be an animator. If you just happen to be an illustrator, too, then I encourage you wholeheartedly to produce your own artwork. If you'd rather not, that's fine, too—my stuff is there if you need it.

How This Book Is Organized

This book is organized into five parts:

Part 1, "Computer Animation at a Glance," presents a bird's-eye view of the proceedings, giving you some history and some comparisons to mull over. Here you'll receive your first introduction to the tools and techniques of web animation.

Part 2, "Creating Animated GIFs," shows you how to use Macromedia Fireworks MX to assemble animated GIFs, the original and most ubiquitous form of web animation.

Part 3, "Creating Flash Movies," spends seven chapters discussing the finer points of making movies in Macromedia Flash MX.

Part 4, "Creating Shockwave Movies," explores the web animation side of Macromedia Director 8.5 and introduces you to the possibilities of Shockwave 3D.

Part 5, "Where to Go from Here," develops some of the themes in Shockwave 3D and applies them to full-fledged 3-D modeling and animation.

Hardware Requirements

The CD-ROM that comes with this book contains trial versions of Fireworks, Flash, Director, and Tabuleiro ShapeShifter3D 1.5 (a 3-D modeling plug-in for Director), in addition to the free QuickTime 6 player. To install and run these applications, your Windows system needs to meet the following requirements:

- ◆ Windows 98 SE or better
- ◆ 400MHz processor
- ◆ 64MB RAM (128MB recommended)

♦ 279MB free hard drive space

♦ 1024 × 768 display resolution

♦ 3-D accelerator

For your Mac system, you need:

♦ OS 9.1 or OS X 10.1

♦ Power Macintosh G3 Processor

♦ 64MB RAM (128MB recommended)

♦ 279MB free hard drive space

♦ 1024 × 768 display resolution

♦ 3-D accelerator

Extras

Page through this book, and you'll find sidebars and margin notes that come in four varieties. They are:

Animation Advice _____

These notes offer tips, tricks, and shortcuts. May you benefit from my many mistakes over the years!

Shop Talk _____

These notes provide plain-language definitions for technical jargon.

Cut! _____

These notes alert you to common problems and pitfalls and offer practical solutions.

The Big Picture

These notes sum up, clarify, or amplify the current discussion. They also go off on tangents.

Acknowledgments

This book was a team effort. If it succeeds in instructing you, entertaining you, or helping you, I hope you'll join me in thanking the following parties.

Thank you, Neil Salkind, Jessica Richards, Stacey Barone, and the rest of you go-getters at Studio B. Thank you, Eric Heagy, for blazing the trail. Thank you, Michael Koch, for making it work. Thank you, Katherin Bidwell, for a fine production. Thank you, Susan Aufheimer, for making sense of it all. Thank you, Michael Hunter, for your work on the CD-ROM. Thank you, Greg Ross, for your expert advice. An especially hearty thank you goes out to everyone at Alpha who helped to make this book happen.

Thank you, Bobbi Jo, for seeing me through.

Special Thanks to the Technical Reviewer

The Complete Idiot's Guide to Web Animation was reviewed by an expert who double-checked the accuracy of what you will learn here to help us ensure that this book gives you everything you need to know about the basics of web animation. Special thanks are extended to James Dean Conklin.

Trademarks

All terms mentioned in this book that are known to be or are suspected of being trademarks or service marks have been appropriately capitalized. Alpha Books and Pearson Education, Inc., cannot attest to the accuracy of this information. Use of a term in this book should not be regarded as affecting the validity of any trademark or service mark.

Part 1

Computer Animation at a Glance

Before you get your hands dirty, why not sit back, relax, and soak up a little context for your animation excursions? This part compares and contrasts traditional animation with its computerized counterpart and introduces you to the tools and techniques you'll use to liven up the web.

Introducing Computer Animation

In This Chapter

◆ Comparing computer animation with traditional animation

◆ Comparing vector graphics with raster graphics

◆ Setting up your animation studio

◆ Exploring hardware and software

For all its sophistication, computer animation is essentially a simple procedure. You take the special reagent, which is a viscous, luminescent green substance, and inject it directly into the computer. In a few moments, the computer begins to walk about the room on its own. The main trick is controlling the computer after you animate it, because it tends to become violent, even homicidal. Keeping a healthy assortment of tranquilizers on hand is always a good idea.

Just kidding with you. Computer animation is really nothing of the sort. Please don't inject your computer with any kind of reagent without the supervision of a trained technician.

All kidding aside, this chapter provides a quick introduction to the world of computer animation and tells you what you need to get started.

Welcome to the Picture Show

It's funny when you think about it. Not too long ago, the world was abuzz about movies like *Tron* and music videos like Dire Straits's "Money for Nothing." It wasn't that they were always particularly good—especially in the case of *Tron.* Yet critics hailed them as innovative, and editors threw ink and columns at them, and television viewers could watch hour-long specials about their creation. Why? Because of a new-fangled device called a computer and a technique called computer animation, where-by computer-generated material replaced traditional special effects and even human actors.

Advocates of this new technique announced that the future had arrived, and they predicted that computer animation would get only bigger and more encompassing. The detractors didn't even try to challenge this claim, because they knew that it was true. Instead, they kept their criticisms on the artistic level, arguing that advances in technology don't make up for weak material.

The field of computer animation has grown indeed since the days of mediocre science fiction movies. It's hard to find a movie, television show, or commercial that doesn't use computer animation in one form or another. In fact, when you consider recent offerings like the *Star Wars* prequels and *The Lord of the Rings,* you're hard-pressed to find 10 scenes that don't have computer animation in them.

It seems there's no going back to the good old days. Computer animation is faster and cheaper than its predecessors. It's also digital, which makes it compatible with every other piece of equipment in the modern editing room and production studio. Producers and directors can blend live action with animation more seamlessly than ever.

Shop Talk

Animation is the process of taking something that doesn't move by itself and making it appear to move.

What Is Computer Animation?

Maybe a better question to start is, "What is animation?"

Animation is the process of taking something that doesn't move by itself, like a puppet of a giant ape, a clay sculpture of a winged horse, a drawing of a screwy rabbit, or a construction-paper cutout that looks something like a kid, and making it appear to move. Animators use various techniques like stop-motion photography and cel animation to create the illusion of motion.

If animation is the process of making something motionless appear to move, then, in computer animation, that something motionless is a digital image—a computer graphic—and the animation studio is the computer itself. Computer animation is an animation technique in its own right, an approach to bringing life to inanimate things. It's not necessarily a substitute for traditional approaches, although it allows animators to attempt feats of great complexity that would be too costly or too time-consuming otherwise.

Computer animation has much in common with its forerunners, including some of the same technical vocabulary, but it also has many important differences. To bring these out, it'll be helpful to take a quick look at traditional animation.

What Is Traditional Animation?

Traditional animation isn't really a useful category unless you need something to compare with computer animation. What has come to be called traditional animation is actually a collection of different techniques that share two important points.

First, traditional animation doesn't use a computer to create the illusion of motion. Instead, it uses a camera. Imagine, if you will, a reel of movie film. Unroll the film and hold it up to the light, and you see a number of individual photographs called frames. When a movie projector plays back the film at a high speed—usually 24 frames per second—the human eye blends the rapid series of still photographs together, and your favorite actors appear to move across the screen.

> **The Big Picture**
>
> The first full-length animated feature film was Disney's *Snow White and the Seven Dwarfs* (1937).

Traditional animation works on the same principle, only it doesn't start with live action. It starts with the individual frames themselves. The animator takes a series of still photographs, each slightly different from the next. When threaded together and projected on a screen at high speed, the human eye interprets motion where originally there was none.

Take, for instance, the traditional technique of stop-motion photography. In stop-motion photography, the animator makes almost imperceptible adjustments to the pose of a model and shoots a few frames of film on the camera. Then the animator makes a few more tiny adjustments and shoots a few more frames of film. The process goes on for weeks just to complete a single scene. But when the animator finally finishes and plays back the film, the tiny adjustments add up, and a perfectly inanimate object appears to move of its own accord.

Shop Talk

A **cel** is a single drawing on a piece of transparent acetate. The transparency of the acetate allows the static background painting underneath the cel to show through.

Cel animation happens in a similar way. The animator draws a series of slightly different poses of a particular character, each on a different piece of acetate or *cel*. The animator superimposes these cels against a static background image and shoots a frame (or more) of film for each. The process isn't very exciting to watch, but the result often is. The drawings appear to come to life, as if the movie camera had photographed the character in motion, when in fact the animator built the motion from the ground up.

The second trait that all traditional animation techniques share is that the subject of the animation is always a physical thing. The object that appears to move on screen has a real-world equivalent that doesn't move at all, like a series of animation cels or a three-dimensional model. This makes sense if you think about how traditional animation works. In order for a camera to photograph something, something has to be in front of the camera. In computer animation, the image is created directly on the computer and there is no cel or three-dimensional image involved.

How Are They the Same?

Computer animation and traditional animation have the same goal: taking something motionless and making it appear to move. The process of achieving this goal is similar, at least in broad strokes. Computer animators start with motionless computer images, just like traditional animators start with models, puppets, or cels. Computer animators manipulate these images with software to create the illusion of motion, just like traditional animators use the camera to shoot a few frames of film at a time.

To do so, computer animators borrow many of the same tricks from traditional animators. In cel animation, for instance, animators draw the moving characters on clear pieces of acetate and then superimpose the characters on a static background illustration. This way, the animator doesn't have to redraw the entire background in every single cel. In computer animation, you find the same modus operandi. The computer animator places a moving character on its own layer, which is like a virtual piece of acetate. Underneath the character layer is the static background image. The character moves across its layer without disturbing the background at all.

The language of traditional animation also finds its way into computer animation. Cels that represent the starting and ending positions of a character's movement are called keyframes. The lead animator on a project usually produces these. Drawing all the cels of in-between motion is called tweening, a thankless, tedious task that usually falls to junior members of the team.

Computer animation works with similar concepts. Keyframes become the starting and ending points for a particular image in motion. The animator sets these up in the animation software. But instead of passing the animation file to a junior staffer or intern for tweening, the computer animator executes a single command in the software, and the computer automatically fills in all the intermediate steps.

> **CAUTION Cut!**
>
> A common misconception is that, in computer animation, the computer does all the work. While the computer helps to automate tedious tasks like camera position and creating certain movements, computers aren't sophisticated enough to figure out how to animate a scene. You still need intelligent, creative, talented humans at the controls.

How Are They Different?

Unlike traditional animation, computer animation is entirely digital. That is to say, it's entirely virtual. There is nothing actual in front of the camera. In fact, there is no camera. At every stage of production, from the initial static art to the final product, the animator manipulates digital information instead of a model or a series of cels.

Because everything is digital from start to finish in computer animation, the process of creating the art and the process of animating it are more closely related to each other than they are in traditional animation. In stop-motion photography, as you'll recall, a team of model builders creates the puppet or clay sculpture and then hands it off to the animators, who photograph it. But when you work in a digital environment, animation becomes more a natural extension of the production process, like a branch of the same tree. In fact, you can start with *any* digital image—a photo of your boss, a piece of clip art, a sales forecast—and animate it. Import the image into the animation software, and it's good to go. The process of bringing it to life isn't always easy, but it's never impossible. You might say that any computer graphic is an animation waiting to happen.

Traditional animation is also by nature a group effort. The sheer amount of work that comes with an animation project makes it hard for single-person outfits to get anything done. It takes three years to produce the average animated feature film, even with a dedicated team of seasoned professionals in a state-of-the-art studio.

Computers help to streamline the production process to such an extent that computer animators can achieve satisfying results by themselves in less time using the PCs that they already own. Not that computer animation is necessarily a discipline for lone wolves: Put a team of computer animators in a state-of-the-art studio and give them three years to do something, and they create photorealistic worlds that mesh so convincingly with live actors and settings that most viewers can't tell what's actual and what's virtual. But the fact remains that, if you want to get started in animation, computer animation is the best and most economical way to do it.

The Big Picture

In the 1930s and 1940s, American animators shot their work at 30 cels per second—1 cel for each frame of film. This is why the motion in classic cartoons seems so fluid and natural. The more cels per second you have, the more realistic the motion. These days, American consumers settle for 24 cels per second in the movies and 12 cels per second on TV, while Japanese animation uses 12 and even 8 cels per second.

Introducing Computer Graphics

If computer animation and computer graphics are so closely related (and they are), it's hard to discuss one without the other. In this book, you'll deal with two types of computer graphics: raster graphics (also called bitmaps) and vector graphics.

About Raster Graphics

Raster or *bitmap graphics* are computer images composed of rows and columns of *pixels*, which are very small, colored squares. The pixels are so small that you can't distinguish them individually. Your eye blends them together, and you see a continuous image.

Shop Talk

A **raster** or **bitmap graphic** is a computer image composed of **pixels**, which are very small, colored squares.

A similar principle applies to photos in a newspaper. When you look at a picture on the front page, you see a continuous image of the president giving a press conference. But if you look at the same picture under a magnifying glass, you notice hundreds of individual dots of different colors or varying shades of gray. Likewise, if you magnify a raster graphic with imaging software, you begin to see the individual pixels, as Figure 1.1 shows.

Figure 1.1

Magnify a raster graphic, and you begin to see the individual pixels that make it up.

Rasters are the most common graphics for home computer users. If you've worked with computers before, you're probably familiar with graphic file formats like GIF, JPEG, and BMP. (For those just starting out, your computer stores an image as a file, a collection of digital data, and the file format determines how the computer stores the information.) All three of these formats are raster formats. Rasters are convenient and easy to use, and many different software applications support them, which means that you can open and view them with everything from image editors to word processors to desktop publishing programs to web browsers. Also, rasters are everywhere. The icons on your computer desktop are rasters. Go to the web, and virtually all the images you see are rasters. Even most of the animation on the web is raster based. You won't be surprised to learn that you spend Chapters 3 through 7 in this book creating raster-based animation.

The Big Picture

GIF, JPEG, and BMP are different file formats for raster graphics. GIF stands for Graphics Interchange Format. This is a good format for line art or images with comparatively little color information. JPEG stands for Joint Photographic Experts Group. This is a good format for photographs or images with large amounts of color information. BMP stands for Windows Bitmap. It's a good all-purpose format, although BMP files tend to be larger in size than GIFs or JPEGs.

However, for all their popularity, raster graphics aren't terribly bright. The information that a raster image contains amounts to what color pixel goes where. When a human being looks at a raster, a photo of Mars, a pie graph, or a corporate logo appears. But when the computer looks at a raster, all it sees are rows and columns of differently colored squares. The computer doesn't interpret the grid of pixels as anything other than pixels. In other words, it doesn't comprehend the content of the image.

This lack of comprehension is not without its consequences. Imagine that you want to take a photograph of a bird in flight, remove the bird from the background, and animate it. This poses some interesting (but not insurmountable) challenges.

First, since the computer doesn't comprehend the content of a raster image, you can't just load the photo into the animation software, click the bird, drag it away from the sky, and begin animating. The computer doesn't understand where the sky ends and the bird begins. All it understands is that some of the pixels are blue, while others are white, gray, black, and other bird colors. As I said, this is an interesting but not an insurmountable challenge. To proceed, you need to blow the picture up to giant size so that you can see the individual pixels better, select all the bird pixels, exclude all the sky pixels, and then extract the bird.

Before you animate, though, you have to explain to the computer where the bird's wings are. Just like you had to differentiate the bird from the sky, you have to differentiate the parts of the bird, since the raster image contains only information about the colors of pixels. Once again, you need to zoom in, collect all the wing pixels, and extract them. This can be a tedious process.

Editing the size and shape of raster images poses another interesting challenge. Rasters are resolution dependent, meaning that they display at a set number of pixels per inch. Therefore, if you double the size of the raster, you need twice as many pixels to render the image. Where do you get this extra information? The computer literally makes it up. It analyzes the image and produces an identical twin for every pixel it detects. The result is precisely the same as looking at the original image through a 2× magnifying glass. The image quality begins to deteriorate.

About Vector Graphics

Vector graphics address many of the challenges that raster graphics pose, particularly when it comes to computer animation. *Vector graphics* contain no pixels. Instead, a vector expresses an image in terms of the shapes the image contains.

Shop Talk

A **vector graphic** is an image expressed in terms of the shapes that the image contains. There are no pixels in a vector graphic.

Take, for example, an illustration of a red ball against a white background. A raster graphic stores this image as a grid of pixels. It tells the computer that some pixels are white, while others are red, yet it doesn't explain the roundness of the shape to the computer. A vector graphic, on the other hand, informs the computer that there is a round, red shape in the middle of a white background. It lets the computer know where the red shape begins and the background ends. If you move the ball to a different location on the screen, the vector informs the computer that there's supposed to be white where the red shape used to be. The vector allows the computer to perceive the image similar to the way a human being perceives it, only on a much more rudimentary level. The vector doesn't realize that the shape is a ball, and it doesn't know that the ball should bounce when it hits the ground, but it can distinguish one object (the ball) from another (the background).

This increase in intelligence brings a number of advantages. Since the vector provides shape information about its content, the computer can change the vector's size with

mathematical precision. If you double the size of a vector image, the computer doesn't have to invent information to fill in the gaps. It simply doubles the proportions of the various shapes that make up the image. The result is as crisp and clean as the original. There is absolutely no loss of image quality.

> ### The Big Picture
>
> Vectors are composed of paths, which are mathematical representations of the shapes in the image.

Not only can you change the size of vector graphics with confidence, you can stretch them, compress them, contort them, distort them, and otherwise transform them to your heart's content. They are remarkably resilient, as Figure 1.2 shows, which bodes well for the prospect of animating them. Before this book is through, you'll know the joy of working with vectors, and you'll see how much easier it is to animate them than their pixel-based counterparts.

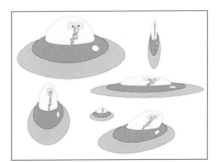

Figure 1.2

You can put a vector image through some serious changes, and it always comes out looking as crisp and clean as the original.

While vector graphics meet the editing challenges that face raster graphics, vectors come with an interesting set of challenges of their own. You'll recall that raster graphics enjoy the wide support of all kinds of software applications. Vector graphics don't have the same level of support. You can't just open any old piece of software and load up a vector the same way you can a raster. More often than not, you need dedicated graphics software to do the job. Consequently, if you choose a vector-based animation format, you need to make sure that your audience has the appropriate software for viewing it. Thankfully, the vector-enabled formats you use in this book, namely Flash and Shockwave, are popular ones, and the Flash Player and Shockwave Player are standard pieces of equipment on most computers.

Animation Advice

With decent graphics software, you can easily change a vector image into a raster. This gives you the best of both worlds: You can create the image in the editing-friendly vector environment and distribute the image in the viewing-friendly raster environment.

Another drawback with vectors is that they're really good for illustrations like cartoon characters, technical diagrams, and pie charts, but that's really all they're good for. Rasters are much more versatile. A raster can be a photograph or a still from a movie as well as an illustration, while a vector can be only an illustration. This doesn't matter so much if you want to animate cartoon characters, technical diagrams, and pie charts, but if you want to animate that photo of the bird in flight, there's no better alternative than to blow up the picture and start grouping pixels.

Building an Animation Studio

The great thing about computer animation is that you don't need to buy a movie camera, hire a bunch of animators, or rent six months of studio time. You can do it all from the comfort of your computer workstation. It may be helpful, though, to upgrade some of your older equipment or acquire some specialized hardware and software.

Getting the Right Hardware

To do beginning computer animation like the kind in this book, you need the following hardware, which you probably have already:

- A computer
- A monitor
- A mouse

Your computer should have at least 128MB RAM, although 256MB or 512MB wouldn't hurt, especially if you want to run dedicated graphics software with your animation software at the same time. Also, it's helpful if your hard drive has plenty of free space. Animation files and graphics can add up in a hurry.

There's a common misconception that you need a Macintosh system to do graphics work like computer animation. It's certainly true that many creative types prefer Macintosh computers (or the Mac) to Microsoft Windows-based systems, and there was a time in the past when Macintosh systems beat Windows systems in graphics applications, but that time is no more. All the software you use in this book comes in Windows and Mac OS versions. Even high-end software for creating animation for TV and the movies supports Windows as well as Mac OS (or the new OS X). So, when it comes to choosing a computer, pick the system that you prefer. There's no need to rush out and buy a Macintosh just to do computer animation if you already have a perfectly good Windows system.

If your monitor is on the small side, you might think about upgrading to a larger screen. When you're doing graphics work, it's helpful to have plenty of screen space. The average monitor screen size is 17 inches, which is sufficient for the animation you create in this book. If you get into more advanced graphics work, you'll find a high-end 21-inch display indispensable.

CAUTION **Cut!**

You don't need a Macintosh computer to do computer animation, even serious 3-D computer animation. This is old thinking. Nowadays, a Windows system performs just as well in graphics applications.

Thin LCD (liquid quartz display) monitors are all the rage these days. They look sleeker, they flicker less, and they take up less space than the old, fat, dusty CRT (cathode ray tube) monitors, the ones that look like TV sets. But thin isn't usually the best choice for graphics work. LCD monitors give you less resolution than CRTs, and the lower-end models don't always display subtle differences in color accurately. If you want a thin monitor, choose a higher-end TFT (thin film transistor), and make it big. Otherwise, save yourself a bundle and go with a decent CRT.

You'll use a mouse for drawing as well as interacting with the animation software, so make sure your mouse feels right in your hand. It's usually the case that your computer came with the worst mouse imaginable. There are plenty of deluxe models out there, so splurge a little and upgrade.

After you collect the essentials, you might think about additional pieces of hardware, such as the following:

◆ A drawing tablet

◆ External storage

A drawing tablet is useful if you plan on creating your own art for animation. It's a flat piece of hardware with a pressure-sensitive area on which to draw, and it comes with a stylus. Many artists prefer drawing tablets to the mouse, since it's easier and more natural to use.

Shop Talk _____

Archiving means to put a finished project into more or less permanent storage.

External storage is handy for *archiving* your work. Animation and graphics files can take up a good amount of space on your hard drive, especially for large projects. When you finish, you can free up that space by copying the project folder to a CD-R, Zip disk, or Jaz disk. You can even use standard 3½-inch floppy disks for modest projects, including many of the ones in this book.

Getting the Right Software

Professional animation software is readily available at a wide variety of prices. At one end of the scale, the GIF Construction Set from Alchemy Mindworks is the cost of a new CD. At the other, Maya Complete from Alias|Wavefront is the cost of a good used car. What you want to do with computer animation determines the kind of software you need.

If you're creating simple animations to post on the web or attach to the bottom of your e-mail messages, you need a good animated GIF program. A GIF (pronounced "jiff" like the peanut butter or "giff" with a hard G) is a kind of raster file that supports animation. Making animated GIFs is easy and fun, and it doesn't cost much. I mentioned GIF Construction Set by Alchemy Mindworks already—this is the most popular software for creating animated GIFs, and it's extremely affordable. Macromedia Fireworks MX is more expensive than GIF Construction Set, but it provides several advanced features for GIF animation, and it's also a fine image-editing program in its own right. You use Fireworks in Part 2 of this book.

If you want to create more involved, more interactive web animations, you need software that produces SWF files. SWFs, commonly called Flash files, are vector-based animation files. They are generally very compact, which makes them excellent for web use. Macromedia Flash MX is the obvious choice for SWF software, and it's the software that you use in Part 3 of this book. But Macromedia Flash isn't the only choice. LiveMotion software from Adobe also produces SWFs, as does Corel RAVE, Macromedia Fireworks, Adobe After Effects, Poser from Curios Lab, and even Macromedia Dreamweaver, a website authoring and management tool. All of these software titles come with reasonable price tags.

Animation Advice _____

If you use other Adobe products like Photoshop and Illustrator, you might find that you prefer the interface of LiveMotion.

If you want to create advanced interactive web animations and multimedia, you need Macromedia Director. Director produces Shockwave files. The Shockwave and Flash formats have much in common, as you'll learn in Chapter 2 and in Part 4. One of the really exciting features of Director is that the most recent version, 8.5, allows you to create 3-D animation. SWFs and animated GIFs are notoriously 2-D. Working with Director provides an excellent introduction to more sophisticated concepts in computer animation. Director is more advanced than Flash, and it's also more expensive.

If you want to create full-blown 3-D computer animation like the kind that appears in the movies and TV, you need software like 3ds max from Discreet or Maya from Alias|Wavefront. While you can run these applications on better personal computers, the sheer cost of the software is prohibitive to all but professional animators and extremely serious animation enthusiasts. The process for creating high-end 3-D animation is also much more advanced. I'll talk about it in Part 5.

The CD-ROM that comes with this book contains all the animation software you need to get started. Unfortunately, it doesn't come with 3ds max or Maya, but it does come with 30-day trial versions of Macromedia Fireworks MX, Macromedia Flash MX, and Macromedia Director 8.5.

These animation programs are development tools. That is, they take static images and allow you to animate them. They also come with drawing tools so that you can create the art that you're going to animate. However, to create more sophisticated art, you're usually better off using a dedicated image editor or illustration program. Creating the art in the graphics software and then importing it into the development environment is the usual flow of production in a professional setting.

An *image editor* is a software application that creates and edits raster graphics. Adobe Photoshop is the monarch of image editors. It's the industry standard, and it's a fine piece of software by anyone's definition. Photoshop should be your first choice when you go to buy an image editor. Other respectable image editors include Corel PHOTO-PAINT and Jasc Paint Shop Pro.

Shop Talk

An **image editor** is a piece of software for creating and editing raster graphics. An **illustration program** is a piece of software for creating and editing vector graphics.

An *illustration program* is software that creates and edits vector graphics. If you're building Flash or Shockwave animations, Macromedia FreeHand is a smart choice for your illustration program. Aside from being a first-rate piece of software, FreeHand integrates especially well with the animation applications in Macromedia. Those who read *The Complete Idiot's Guide to Computer Illustration* (Alpha Books, 2002), the companion volume to this book you now have in hand, know only too well my preference for Adobe Illustrator. It's an excellent illustration program, an industry favorite, and it plays nicely—if not perfectly—with Flash. CorelDRAW and Deneba Canvas also come highly recommended.

The Least You Need to Know

- Computer animation is an approach or strategy to creating animation in a digital environment.

- Computer animation has much in common with traditional animation, but it also has several important differences.

- Raster or bitmap graphics are computer images composed of pixels.

- Vector graphics contain mathematical information about the shapes that compose the image.

- To do computer animation, you need a computer, a monitor, a mouse, and animation software.

- Animation software varies widely in complexity and price, depending on the type of animation you want to create.

Chapter 2

Animating the Web

In This Chapter

- ◆ Exploring web animation
- ◆ Understanding different web animation formats
- ◆ Knowing when to use which format
- ◆ Looking at web animation software

You saw in Chapter 1 that computer animation is a broad field. It starts with simple raster-based formats like animated GIFs and progresses through multimedia formats like Flash and Shockwave to the advanced 3-D world like you get in the movies. What's the best way to approach so diverse a topic?

When you're learning computer animation, you want to start with something easy and then work your way up, because the high-end 3-D stuff can be incredibly complex. You want something that lets you produce satisfying animations quickly. You also want a popular format so you can share your work with the world without software compatibility issues.

All roads point to web animation. It's quick, easy, remarkably robust, fantastically popular, surprisingly versatile, and inherently portable. Simply put, it's the best way to start animating on the computer. This chapter introduces you to web animation as a major subset of computer animation and gets you up to speed on the essentials.

What Is Web Animation?

Web animation comes in the form of a computer file, and you view the animation by opening the file in a software player. The player you use depends on the type of animation file you want to view.

In theory, any kind of computer animation is potentially web animation. All you have to do is upload the animation file to the web. But in practice, the most successful web animation meets two requirements.

First, web animation files tend to be small in size and short in duration. They range from 1 or 2K to 10 or 12MB in size, and they provide anywhere from a few seconds to a few minutes of animation. Modest file sizes make for easier downloading. You don't want to force your audience to wait an hour or two to see your animation. In fact, if your animation takes more than a few minutes to load, you'll lose all but your most dedicated viewers. Faster modems and inexpensive high-speed Internet access mean that web animation files can be larger and longer than they were even a year ago, but most web animations are still closer in spirit to a Sunday newspaper comic strip than to a half-hour TV show.

Shop Talk

Web animation is computer animation designed and optimized for distribution on the web.

Second, web animation relies on the support of popular and readily available players. Web animation isn't like TV in this regard. When you turn on the TV, you can view any channel as long as your antenna picks it up or your cable provider offers it. But on the web, your audience needs to have the right kind of TV, so to speak. Your viewers can't enjoy your work unless they have the player that opens the type of animation file you created.

Understanding Web Animation Formats

Three animation formats meet the requirements of the web with characteristic flair: animated GIFs, Flash, and Shockwave. These formats are compact enough for web delivery yet versatile enough for all kinds of applications, everything from advertisements and eye candy to full-blown multimedia and 3-D animation. Better still, the players for these formats are widely distributed. You (and your audience) probably have the right players on your computer already.

About Animated GIFs

The animated GIF is the old standby in web animation. The GIF, or Graphics Interchange Format, has been around since 1987, and it has supported animation since 1996. The animated GIF and the web came of age at around the same time. While the web has expanded enormously in terms of size and complexity, animated GIFs are pretty much the same and still going strong, blinking and sputtering through their looped sequences of action.

Most of the animation you see on the web is the animated-GIF variety. The ads you ignore when you visit web pages are almost always animated GIFs, as are the little signs, pinwheels, logos, icons, and cartoon characters that do the same thing over and over again. Not that annoyance is a necessary characteristic—some truly effective web animations succeed in this format. It's a solid solution for short, direct pieces of work. As far as ubiquity, how's this for player penetration: Anyone who owns a web browser like Microsoft Internet Explorer, Netscape, or Opera can view animated GIFs.

The Big Picture

CompuServe owns the GIF format.

GIF is a raster graphics format. Likewise, animated GIFs are raster based. An animated GIF is actually a collection of several raster images packaged together and played in sequence. Each image occupies a frame in the animation. The animator controls the order of the frames and the amount of time each one appears on screen.

To illustrate the idea, imagine, if you will, a stack of playing cards sitting faceup on a table. Each card in the stack represents a frame of the animated GIF. When the animation begins, the viewer sees the first frame, which is like the card at the top of the stack. After the specified amount of time elapses, the computer switches to the next frame, which is like you removing the top card and putting it at the bottom of the stack. The computer progresses frame by frame until it reaches the last one in the sequence, and then it usually starts over again at the top, looping ad infinitum (and sometimes ad nauseum), just as you might go through the cards one by one, putting each one at the bottom of the stack. If the computer switches frames fast enough, your eye blends them together, and you perceive continuous motion instead of a series of still images. A movie works on the same principle. So does a flipbook.

Animation Advice

GIF images have a built-in palette of up to 256 colors. If your animation doesn't use that many colors, you can decrease its file size by setting up the GIF for a smaller palette.

But since each frame in an animated GIF is a separate image, the more frames you have, the larger the total file size becomes. An animated GIF with too many frames can clog up a slow modem connection. For this reason, the best animated GIFs use only a few frames, and those frames are web optimized—that is, the images are processed in such a way as to minimize their file size while retaining image quality. The Fireworks software you use in Part 2 of this book automatically optimizes each frame, making the total file size as small as possible while retaining the overall quality of the image.

About Flash

The Flash format is the second most abundant kind of animation on the web, and its presence is growing. Not only does it supply more sophisticated animations than animated GIFs, it's beginning to creep into the traditional domain of animated GIFs: advertisements, animated logos, and the like.

Unlike the animated GIF format, Flash provides interactivity as well as animation. Your audience can participate fully in your Flash movie, as it's called. You can add buttons to the movie and then program them to respond in certain ways when the user clicks them. You can control the flow of your movie with short scripts. Flash gives you so much interactivity, in fact, that you can use this format to create an entire website interface, not just an animation on the site.

The Flash format also provides *multimedia* capabilities, by which you can embed different kinds of information in the movie file. You can add sound effects, dialog, and musical scores, as well as art files from image editors and illustration programs.

Shop Talk

Multimedia means using different kinds of media files in the same project.

The Big Picture

The Flash file format uses the extension SWF. SWF stands for Shockwave Flash or Small Web File.

How can Flash provide so much more than animated GIFs while maintaining comparable file sizes? The reason, in a nutshell, is that Flash is a vector-based format. Remember from Chapter 1 that a vector graphic provides information about the shapes that make up the image. The same holds true in a Flash movie. Flash keeps track of the position and shape of the objects you want to animate. A Flash movie has logic built into it, you might say. Where an animated GIF is just a series of still images with a few brief instructions to the computer about how long to present each frame, a Flash movie is more like a collection of vector images with a complete set of instructions about how to animate them. The computer executes these instructions each time the movie plays.

Assume that you want to move a red ball from the top of the screen to the bottom. In an animated GIF, you would create a frame for each position of the ball. The first frame has the ball at the top of the screen. The second frame shows the ball a bit lower, the third frame has the ball lower still, and so on, until the last frame, when the ball reaches the bottom. This gets the job done, but it isn't terribly efficient. Flash transmits the same information to the computer in a more intelligent way. Since Flash records the position of the object, the computer knows where the ball starts out and where it should end. And since Flash records the shape of the object, the computer knows what the ball looks like. The computer simply calculates the number of in-between steps and redraws the shape of the ball automatically at each step. Where an animated GIF requires, say, 8 or 12 frames to create the dropping motion, the Flash movie requires only two keyframes: one with the ball at its start point, and one with the ball at its end point. The computer figures out the in-between steps as the movie plays.

Larger Flash projects have much larger file sizes than the typical animated GIF, especially once you start adding audio clips and sound effects. If an animated GIF exceeds 100K, I would strongly caution you against its use. But I start to get nervous about Flash files only when they approach 10MB. I can get away with this disparity because Flash offers streaming. That is, you can set up a Flash movie so that it starts to play as soon as the Flash Player begins downloading it. This way, the user doesn't have to sit and wait for the entire movie file to download. The action starts almost instantaneously.

The only drawback to streaming is that, if the Flash Player plays the movie faster than the Internet connection downloads it, your audience sees pauses in the action. The movie simply halts. It stops in its tracks until the Flash Player receives the next shipment of movie data, as it were. This is a concern only with slower Internet connections or congested websites. Still, it's a concern that you can't dismiss outright, because much of your audience views your movie over a standard dial-up connection. Always test your movie over a regular modem to sample the quality of the streaming. If you can live with occasional pauses and hiccups, let it stand. If you can't, consider trimming down the file size of the movie.

> ### The Big Picture
>
> Macromedia Flash began life as FutureSplash Animator, the product of another company. The story goes that Macromedia acquired FutureSplash as a strategy for reducing competition against its own Shockwave format. Instead of burying FutureSplash, though, Macromedia promoted it vigorously alongside Shockwave. Flash is now the predominant form of plug-in-based computer animation.

Creating Flash Animation

To create Flash animations, you need software, like Macromedia Flash, Adobe LiveMotion, or Corel RAVE, that exports the SWF file format. But to view Flash animations, you need the Flash Player from Macromedia. The Flash Player comes as a plug-in, or a separate piece of optional software, for your web browser. You can download the Flash Player plug-in for free on the web, but you probably don't have to. Macromedia reports that more than 98 percent of all computer users online have Flash Player installed. That's more than 436 million installations! Even if you're not one of these 436 million, the Flash Player installs automatically when you set up Macromedia Flash MX, which comes as a free 30-day trial on the CD-ROM in this book.

Now is a good time to point out a potential ambiguity: Don't confuse Flash MX, the animation software, with Flash Player, the browser plug-in, both of which are referred to as "Flash." These are two entirely different pieces of software. Flash MX is a commercial development environment for *creating* SWF files, while the Flash Player is a free browser plug-in for *viewing* SWF files. Your audience doesn't need to buy the Flash development environment just to view Flash animation.

The Flash format is compact, intelligent, and ubiquitous. So why isn't there more Flash animation on the web? Part of the reason is that potential Flash creators need to buy the animation software, and while the software is easy to use once you get the hang of it, you need certain skills that aren't necessarily intuitive. (Not to worry—this book teaches all the skills you need to get started.) There is a financial commitment as well as a time commitment for training and practice, but these aren't the only sticking points. Like most types of multimedia content, most Flash animation isn't very accessible or usable by people with certain disabilities. Accessibility is a timely concern on the web. Governments in many countries including the United States require that their websites be accessible, and many businesses are following suit.

Animation Advice

A Flash movie can detect whether a browser has the correct version of the Flash Player plug-in. If not, the movie can instruct the browser to download the Flash Player automatically.

Accessibility hinges on the concept of comparable user experience. That is, a website is accessible if it offers the same information to people with disabilities as it offers everyone else. In the case of static images, which sight-impaired people can't see, the usual solution is to provide a detailed textual description of the image which screen-reading software converts to audio. That way, people who can't see the image can hear its description and get more or less the same information. But how do you provide text equivalence for a complex multimedia presentation? Compounding the difficulty is that many kinds of accessibility software don't support animation formats like Flash, and those that do support only the latest version of Flash. Even if you came up with equivalent text, you might have problems implementing it.

The World Wide Web Consortium (W3C), an organization that promotes universal access to the web, recommends that, until accessibility software supports multimedia content, the best way to make accessible multimedia is to include a separate audio track that narrates the presentation. This seems like a drastic solution for many designers. It incurs additional expense and design time, and it isn't always easy to implement for existing productions. For this reason, those who need accessible websites often shy away from multimedia content entirely, including Flash.

As I mentioned before, the most recent version of Flash offers a kind of qualified support for text equivalence. While not a perfect solution, it's certainly a step in the right direction. See Appendix A for a quick tour of Flash MX accessibility features.

About Shockwave

You'll notice at once many similarities between Shockwave and Flash. In fact, many computer animators regard Shockwave as the older sibling of Flash, and rightly so. Like Flash, Shockwave is a compact and intelligent format, and, like Flash, Shockwave supports interactive movies with streaming capabilities. Shockwave requires a browser plug-in for viewing, just like Flash, and it shares the same accessibility drawbacks.

You get much more than just animation with Flash, and that goes doubly for Shockwave. Interactive animation is the strong suit of Shockwave. It's more robust than Flash in delivering rich multimedia. That is, you can incorporate many different types of media, including video and audio clips, static images of vector and raster types, and even other Flash and Shockwave movies, into Shockwave presentations. You can use Shockwave to deploy multiuser applications like games and chat rooms, and the latest version of Shockwave also supports 3-D animation.

Macromedia's free Shockwave Player plug-in isn't quite as ubiquitous as the Flash Player among online computer users. Macromedia

The Big Picture

Shockwave began as a format for CD-ROMs and kiosk presentations. When the web came to prominence in the late 1990s, the market for CD-ROMs almost completely disappeared, but Shockwave hung on as a viable form of web animation, particularly for applications that require a high degree of interactivity. Developers also use Shockwave to create animated menus for DVDs.

estimates that over 300 million users have downloaded and installed Shockwave Player compared to Flash's 436 million. Even so, 300 million is a very respectable number. If you want to develop Shockwave animations, you can do so with confidence. Incidentally, when you download the Shockwave Player, you also get the Flash Player automatically.

When to Use What

Animated GIFs, Flash, and Shockwave all give you web animation. Which format should you use for your project?

If you're building a small animation, especially one that loops, your best bet is the animated GIF. The animated GIF is the best supported web animation format by browsers, so this format makes the most sense if you're creating an advertisement banner for a web page. You should also consider the animated GIF for animated interface controls on a website, like animated buttons or navigation bars. Animated GIFs supply most of the nuts-and-bolts animation on the web.

If you're building something more advanced for the web such as a short feature or an interactive presentation, Flash makes the most sense. Flash achieves more sophisticated animation than GIF in a more compact, intelligent way, and since the Flash Player is nearly as common as Microsoft Internet Explorer, you don't have to worry so much about your audience not having the right plug-in. The Flash multimedia and interactive capabilities are good enough for most general-purpose applications. You can easily add audio and interface controls such as buttons.

> **CAUTION**
>
> **Cut!**
>
> Web animators want to animate. It's in their blood. But before you jump headlong into a project, make sure that you plan adequately. Choose the right format for your audience and the right format for your animation. Hopefully, these formats will be the same. If not, rethink your project so that it makes sense for your audience.

If you require richer multimedia or more robust interactivity, Shockwave is the way to go. Use Shockwave to build sophisticated games and demanding applications. Remember also that Shockwave is the only major format that offers native 3-D animation for the web. Pick Shockwave if you need 3-D, even if your animation is quick and simple.

Introducing the Software

In this book, you explore three pieces of software, one for each of the three web animation formats: Macromedia Fireworks MX for animated GIFs, Macromedia Flash MX for Flash animation, and Macromedia Director 8.5 for Shockwave animation.

Fireworks for Animated GIFs

Macromedia Fireworks MX is an image editor for web graphics (see Figure 2.1). You'll use it to create animated GIFs, but this is just one of its many capabilities. Fireworks gives you several interesting techniques for creating animated GIFs that smaller, more dedicated programs like GIF Construction Set (from Alchemy Mindworks) don't offer. The concepts you pick up from creating animated GIFs in the Fireworks environment will serve you well when you tackle Flash. In fact, you can export simple Flash animations from Fireworks as well as animated GIFs.

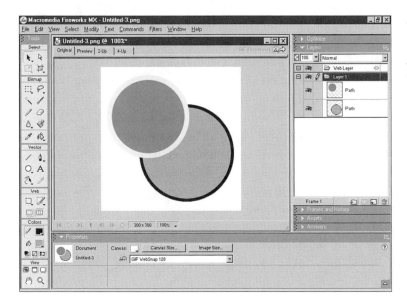

Figure 2.1

Use Macromedia Fireworks MX for all your web-graphic needs, including animated GIFs.

Fireworks has been around since 1998, which makes Fireworks MX the fifth release of the software in five years. Fireworks is the comrade in arms of Macromedia Dreamweaver, a very popular and powerful tool for developing and managing websites.

Flash for Flash Animation

Macromedia Flash MX is a tool for creating SWF files (see Figure 2.2). It's the best known and the most widely used application of its kind, but it isn't the only one. Adobe LiveMotion and Corel RAVE are popular alternatives for developing Flash content.

The Big Picture

You can even use Macromedia Fireworks to export SWF files, although these animations aren't as sophisticated as the ones that you get from Macromedia Flash.

Figure 2.2

Use Macromedia Flash MX to create Flash animations.

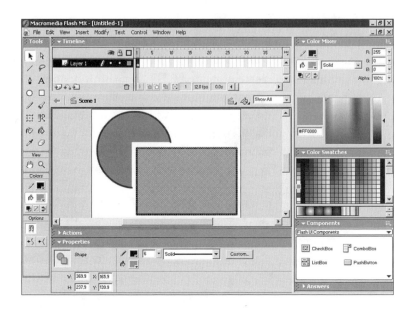

Flash first appeared in 1997 as the successor to FutureSplash Animator, which came out in 1996. Flash MX is the sixth release of the software in six years (or the seventh in seven years if you count FutureSplash Animator).

Director for Shockwave Movies

Macromedia Director 8.5 is the tool for creating Shockwave files (see Figure 2.3). You can create SWF files from many different software applications, but only Director allows you to create Shockwave files.

Director first appeared in 1985 as a Macintosh-only application called VideoWorks from Macromind, the company that would become Macromedia. The software has evolved more slowly than Flash or Fireworks, weathering fads and trends with perhaps more class.

Shockwave as such didn't appear until 1995, when Macromedia tested the waters of porting Director animation in a compressed, web-ready format. That there was even an audience for this kind of content on the web wasn't a proven concept in 1995. Now, there are more web surfers with the Shockwave Player plug-in than without it.

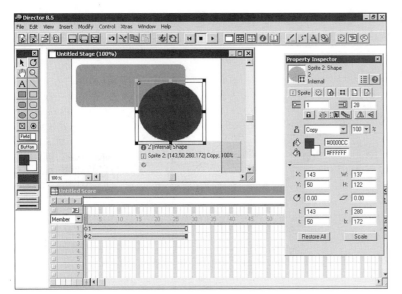

Figure 2.3

Use Macromedia Director 8.5 to create Shockwave animations.

The Least You Need to Know

◆ Web animation is computer animation designed for the rigors of online distribution.

◆ There are three major formats for web animation: the animated GIF, Flash, and Shockwave.

◆ Animated GIFs work best for short, looping animations.

◆ Flash is the best all-around format for longer-form animations with basic multimedia and interactivity.

◆ Shockwave is the best format for animations with complex interactivity, rich multimedia, and 3-D rendering.

◆ Use Macromedia Fireworks MX to create animated GIFs, Macromedia Flash MX to create Flash movies, and Macromedia Director 8.5 to create Shockwave movies.

Part 2

Creating Animated GIFs

Enough history! It's time to start animating the web. This part shows you how to use Macromedia Fireworks MX to create animated GIFs. Along the way, you'll pick up the skills that you need to tackle Flash and Director later in this book.

Introducing Fireworks

In This Chapter

◆ Exploring the Fireworks interface

◆ Creating a canvas

◆ Using the drawing and editing tools

◆ Saving your work

You learned in Chapter 2 that Macromedia Fireworks MX is the software to use for creating animated GIFs.

Fireworks has many other uses besides. I'll touch on a few of these in this chapter, although I'll concentrate mostly on the functions that help you to create convincing web animations.

Exploring the Interface

If you haven't already installed the trial version of Fireworks from the CD-ROM, now would be the time to do so. The procedure is quick and painless. See Appendix B for instructions.

After you install the software, launch it. The software loads up, and the Fireworks interface appears, as in Figure 3.1. The *interface* of a piece of software is its outward appearance, including its buttons, fields, menus, tools, dialog boxes, and work areas. The interface is the way that a human communicates with the computer programs that make the software work. Everything you see in the Fireworks window is part of the interface. Don't be alarmed if your screen doesn't match the figure exactly. Part of the beauty of the interface is that you can customize it to suit your work preferences.

Figure 3.1

Launch the software, and the Fireworks interface appears.

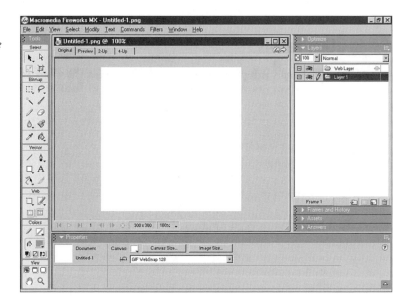

The default Fireworks interface has three main areas: the Tools panel, which occupies the left side of the screen; the other panel groups and panels, which sit on the right side of the screen and along the bottom; and the work area, which is the large gray space in the center.

Using the Tools Panel

Shop Talk

Tools in Fireworks are the drawing and editing commands that appear in the **Tools** panel.

Glance at the Tools panel, and you see that it contains several sets of icons. These icons represent drawing and editing commands, which Fireworks calls *tools*. The tools appear grayed out right now because you don't have an active document window or canvas in the work area. You'll remedy this situation shortly. For now, just know that, to pick a tool from the Tools panel, all you have to do is click the appropriate icon.

Some of the tool icons have a small black triangle in the lower right corner. The Pointer tool—the one in the upper left of the Tools panel—is just such a tool. The triangle signifies that there are hidden tools underneath the current icon. The hidden tools have similar functions to the tool that shows in the panel, but the people at Macromedia figured that you wouldn't need to use them as often, so they hid the icons instead of cluttering up the Tools panel.

Using Other Panels

The Fireworks interface gives you more panels than just the Tools panel. You don't have to look hard for them. The Properties panel sits along the bottom of the screen, and a number of others occupy the right side.

Fireworks organizes the panels into collapsible and expandable panel groups. A panel group is collapsed when the triangle next to its name points to the right, and the panel group is expanded when the triangle points down. To collapse or expand a panel group, click the triangle.

Panel groups like Optimize and Layers have only one panel inside them, while panel groups like Frames and History and Assets contain a few panels represented by tabs, as in Figure 3.2. As you might expect, the Frames and History panel group contains the Frames panel and the History panel. Click the tab of the panel to cause that panel to appear in front.

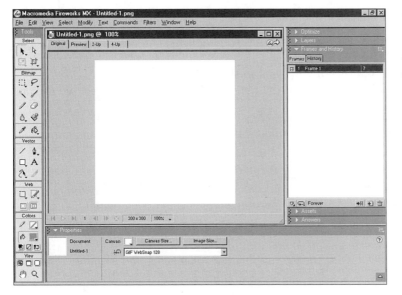

Figure 3.2

The Frames and History panel group contains two panels: one for Frames and one for History. Click the tab of the panel to call that panel to the front of the group.

Creating a New Canvas

Playing around with tools and panels is more productive after you open a canvas. To do so, choose File → New. The New Document dialog box appears, as in Figure 3.3.

Figure 3.3

Set up a new canvas with the New Document dialog box.

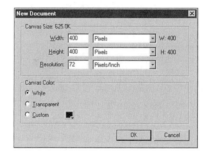

The New Document dialog box is easy to use. The top portion of the dialog box gives the physical dimensions of the canvas. Type the desired width of the canvas in the Width field, and type the height in the Height field. By default, Fireworks measures in pixels, but you can change the units of measurement by selecting inches or centimeters from the dropdown menus next to these fields. Stick with pixels for now, and specify **400** for the width as well as the height. This creates a decent-sized canvas.

The Big Picture

Screen resolution is commonly regarded as 72 pixels per inch, although Windows PCs generally display at 96 pixels per inch.

The Resolution field is an important one. Since raster graphics like GIFs are resolution dependent, you want to make sure that you set up the canvas to display at the correct resolution. Fireworks makes the resolution 72 ppi (pixels per inch) by default. You should always use this value for animated GIFs. Seventy-two pixels per inch is screen resolution, or the resolution that many computer monitor screens use. (To be precise about it, Macintosh computers display at 72 ppi. Monitors for Windows PCs usually display at 96 ppi, but in the interest of cross-platform compatibility, use the lower Macintosh value.) Type **72** into the Resolution field if you see some other value.

Now, set the background color for the canvas. You may choose white, transparent, or a custom color. If you want a custom color, click the color box next to the Custom option and pick from the set of swatches that appears. For now, go with white.

Click the OK button, and Fireworks opens a new canvas to your specifications. Notice that the tools become active as soon as the document window appears. You might take this opportunity to try out one of the hidden tools in Fireworks since you couldn't when I brought up the subject earlier. Go to the Tools panel, and hold down the mouse button on a tool icon with a triangle. After a second or so, a menu of hidden tools appears, as in Figure 3.4. Choose a hidden tool from the menu and release the mouse button. The hidden tool's icon replaces the original tool's icon in the Tools panel. To put the original tool back in the panel, simply open the menu of hidden tools again and select the original tool.

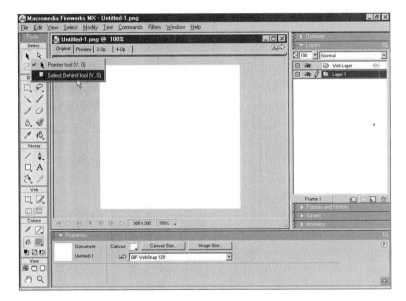

Figure 3.4

By holding down the mouse button on a tool with a triangle in the lower right corner, the tool's hidden toolset appears.

You may modify the size and color of the canvas at any time. To do so, choose Modify → Canvas from the menu. Change the width and height of the canvas under Canvas Size. Set a new background color under Canvas Color.

Using the Drawing Tools

Now that you have a canvas, you can test out the drawing tools. Note that the Tools panel gives you two types: bitmap and vector. The bitmap tools create raster graphics on the canvas, and the vector tools create vector graphics. You are free to use both types of tools. Even though animated GIFs are raster images, Fireworks allows you to build them using vectors, since vectors are easier to edit. However, once you export the canvas as an animated GIF, all the vectors change into raster graphics. I'll talk more about this a little later in this chapter.

To begin, select the Brush tool in the Tools panel. (This is the second tool on the right in the Bitmap category.) Look at the Properties panel at the bottom of the screen, and notice that the panel shows options for the brush, as in Figure 3.5. Change the color, size, style, and texture of the brush by setting the values of the various fields. Then go into the canvas, hold down the mouse button, and paint with the brush. Release the mouse button to lift the brush from the canvas. Reposition the mouse pointer and hold down again to paint some more.

Animation Advice

Always keep the Properties panel open. This panel shows various options for changing the characteristics of the selected graphic.

Figure 3.5

Select the Brush tool, and the Properties panel shows options for the brush.

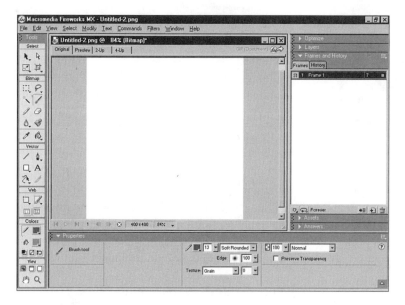

Now go to the panel groups on the right side of the screen and open the Layers panel. The Layers panel shows two folders: one called Web Layer and one called Layer 1. Underneath the Layer 1 folder should be an item called Bitmap with a thumbnail of the lines you just painted. This is the way Fireworks tells you that you added a bitmap graphic to the canvas, which makes sense, since the Brush tool is one of the bitmap drawing tools.

Go back to the Tools panel, and this time find the Rectangle tool, the second tool on the left in the Vector category. Notice the triangle in the corner of the icon—this tells you that the Rectangle tool has a hidden toolset. Click the Rectangle tool, and hold down the mouse button until the hidden toolset appears. Choose the Ellipse tool from the menu. The Properties panel reconfigures itself to show the options for the Ellipse tool, as in Figure 3.6.

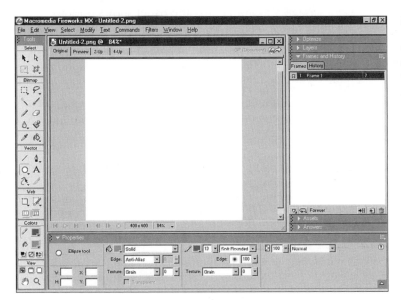

Figure 3.6

Now select the Ellipse tool, and the Properties panel reconfigures itself for ellipse options.

If you look closely at the Properties panel, you see two color squares instead of just one. If you infer from this that vector graphics have two color properties while raster graphics have only one, you're absolutely correct. Vectors have color values for the *stroke* of the shape as well as the *fill*. To create a solid green ellipse with a blue outline, then, you would set the fill color to green and the stroke color to blue.

Shop Talk

The **stroke** color is the color of the outline or contour of a vector graphic. The **fill** color is the color of the interior region.

Which color is which on the Properties panel? Look closely again, and you'll find a paint-bucket icon and a paintbrush icon. The color square next to the paint bucket represents the fill color of the vector, and the color square next to the paintbrush represents the stroke color. Click the color square for the fill, and choose a shade of green from the swatches. Then pick a shade of blue for the stroke. Set the size and style of the stroke by playing with the other fields.

Move into the canvas, position the pointer where you want to start drawing, hold down the mouse button, and drag the ellipse (holding down the Shift key while you draw changes the ellipse to a perfect circle). Release the mouse button to finish.

Glance back at the Layers panel, and you see that Fireworks has added a new item under the Layer 1 folder. This one says Path, and it shows a thumbnail of the ellipse or circle you just drew. A path is a vector shape.

So far, so good. Now grab the Pencil tool, the third tool on the left in the Bitmap category. The Properties panel shows you options for the Pencil, which you may tweak as you require. You can set the color of the pencil but not the size of the tip or the style.

Before you start drawing, take a look at the Layers palette. Fireworks automatically highlights the Bitmap graphic under Layer 1. If you draw with the Pencil tool now, you will add pencil lines to the currently existing raster graphic, the one you created previously with the Brush tool.

> ### The Big Picture
>
> A layer is a drawing surface on the canvas. You'll use layers extensively in Chapter 5.

You can also create a new bitmap graphic for the pencil lines. This is usually the best way to proceed. By creating separate bitmaps, you make editing easier, as you'll see shortly.

To add the pencil lines to a new bitmap graphic, go to the bottom of the Layers panel and click the icon to the left of the trashcan. This is the New Bitmap Image button. When you click it, Fireworks adds a blank bitmap graphic to Layer 1 and highlights it.

Move back to the canvas, and draw with the Pencil. The lines go into the new bitmap graphic, just like you wanted. To add pencil lines to the original bitmap graphic, click its thumbnail in the Layers panel.

After you finish with the Pencil, grab the Line tool, the top left tool under the Vector category. Set the properties of the tool in the Properties panel, and start drawing, keeping your eye on the Layers panel. Notice that each vector shape automatically gets its own entry in the list under Layer 1. This is because each vector is a separate, independent graphic on the Fireworks canvas, unlike rasters, which, as you know, are much dumber by comparison. You have to create new raster objects manually by clicking the New Bitmap Image button.

Keep going with the drawing tools. (Table 3.1 supplies a comprehensive list.) You have two goals at this point: to have fun, and to get comfortable with drawing in Fireworks. Don't be afraid to play with the options in the Properties panel! You can create some interesting effects with the arsenal of styles and textures that Fireworks gives you.

Table 3.1   Fireworks Drawing Tools

Tool	Category	Effect
Brush	Bitmap	Makes freeform shapes with various tips and styles
Ellipse	Vector	Makes ellipses and circles
Line	Vector	Makes straight lines
Pen	Vector	Plots anchor points
Pencil	Bitmap	Makes freeform shapes with a pencil tip
Polygon	Vector	Makes multisided shapes
Rectangle	Vector	Makes rectangles and squares
Rounded Rectangle	Vector	Makes rectangles and squares with rounded corners
Vector Path	Vector	Makes freeform shapes with various tips and styles

Animation Advice

The Pen tool can be misleading for newcomers to vector graphics. It doesn't draw lines in the same way as the bitmap Brush or Pencil tools. Instead, the Pen plots anchor points, which are the mathematical coordinates that determine the shape of a path. To create a straight line with the Pen, click the mouse button once and release—this sets an anchor point. Move the mouse pointer, and click and release again to set another anchor point. A straight line appears between the two anchors. To create a curved line, click and hold down the mouse button, and drag a pair of direction handles, which control the slope and direction of the line. Release, and reposition the mouse pointer. Then, to complete the curved line, either click the button once and release or hold the button down and drag another pair of direction handles. Curved paths in vector graphics go by many names, depending on the software you use to create them. Fireworks calls them Bezier paths or Bezier curves after Pierre Bézier, a French mathematician and computer graphics pioneer.

Inserting Text

To add text to the canvas, use the Text tool. This is the second tool on the right in the Vector category. Click this tool, and the Properties panel changes to show you various options for text, as in Figure 3.7. Set the font, style, color, and formatting of the text with these options.

Figure 3.7

When you select the Text tool, the Properties panel gives you options for adding text to the canvas.

In Fireworks, there are two ways to use the Text tool. You can click the mouse button once and release, which creates a *variable-width* text object, or you can hold down the mouse button and drag, which creates a *fixed-width* text object. Fireworks adds the new text object to the Layers palette, and a flashing cursor appears in the canvas. Start typing!

> **Animation Advice**
>
> A **variable-width** text object is a text object with no set right margin. A **fixed-width** text object is a text object with a set right margin.

The behavior of the text depends on the type of text object you created. A variable-width text object has no set right margin. This kind of text object gets wider as you type. The text will disappear off the edge of the canvas if you type enough of it, and you have to press Enter or Return to start a new line. By comparison, a fixed-width text object has a set right margin. The text automatically wraps at the end of the margin. There's no need to press Enter or Return, unless you want to force a carriage return.

Variable-width text objects work best for small pieces of text like labels or short captions. Fixed-width text objects are better for longer pieces of text like paragraphs or lists.

To edit the content of a text object, grab the Text tool, and then drag the mouse pointer to highlight the letters or words that you want to change.

Modifying Your Art

An image editor is only as good as its editing tools. Fortunately, Fireworks offers several excellent tools of this kind. The right tool for the job depends on what type of graphic you want to edit.

Erasing and Cutting

Erasing and cutting are two of the most common procedures for editing graphics. Erasing applies to raster graphics, and cutting applies to bitmaps. Not surprisingly, you find the Eraser tool in the Bitmap category of the Tools panel and the Knife tool in the Vector category.

The Big Picture

Those of you who have used Adobe Photoshop before may notice some key differences between the two applications. In Photoshop, each layer is, in essence, a single raster graphic. Photoshop doesn't differentiate the pixels of the layer so that, if you drag the eraser tool in Photoshop across the layer, you erase everything in the tool's path. But in Fireworks, each layer can contain multiple raster graphics. You can erase one bitmap and leave the other untouched, even if they're on the same layer. In this respect, Fireworks is more like Adobe Illustrator.

To erase a portion of a raster graphic, grab the Eraser tool, which is the third tool on the right under Bitmap. Set the size and shape of the Eraser in the Properties panel if you desire. Then, go to the Layers panel, and click the bitmap image that you want to erase. Now, simply bring the mouse pointer into the canvas, position it, and hold down the mouse button. Drag the mouse to erase. Notice that, if the current raster image overlaps another raster image, you erase only the pixels in the currently selected raster. This is the advantage to adding new bitmaps to the canvas. You don't have to be as precise with the Eraser tool. If your hand slips, you don't have to worry about erasing pixels in another bitmap.

You can't use the Eraser tool if you select a vector from the Layers panel, since erasing is a raster-graphics thing. For vector graphics, use the Knife tool instead. This is the third tool on the right in the Vector category.

The way the Knife works is different from the way the Eraser works. Imagine that the vector is a piece of construction paper, and you want to change its shape. Which would you use: an eraser or a knife? Erasing it doesn't do much good, unless you press so hard that you burn through the construction paper. It's better to get out the knife and make a few precision cuts.

CAUTION

Cut!

Don't confuse the Knife tool in the Vector category with the Slice tool in the Web category. Web designers use the Slice tool to divide up a web interface into separate, smaller graphics. This allows the web page to load faster. The Slice tool doesn't help you at all to cut a vector graphic.

Animation Advice _____

When you use the Eraser, it's generally a good idea to zoom in on the part of the image that you want to erase, just to make sure that you pick up all the stray pixels. You can set the magnification of the canvas by holding down the mouse button on the percentage value at the bottom right of the document window and choosing a new magnification from the menu that slides out. The View menu also has several commands for changing the magnification of the canvas.

Before you grab the Knife tool, though, select the vector image that you want to cut. You can click the thumbnail of the image in the Layers panel, or you can use the Pointer tool, which is the first tool on the left at the top of the Tools panel. Select the Pointer, and then click once on the vector image that you want to cut to select this image. Now, pull out the Knife, hold down the mouse button, and drag the mouse pointer all the way through the shape to make a clean cut. Make sure the Knife starts and ends outside the boundaries of the shape. Release the mouse button to finish.

If you glance at the Layers palette, you'll see that Fireworks has split the vector image you cut into two separate paths. To prove it, grab the Pointer tool again, and click a blank area of the canvas, deselecting everything. Then, with the Pointer, click one of the pieces of the cut path. Hold down the mouse button, and you can drag the piece away. Press the Delete key or click the trashcan icon on the Layers palette to delete the snippet.

Admittedly, the Knife isn't as direct as the Eraser. If you want to use the Eraser on a vector graphic, you must first change the vector into a raster, which is easy enough to do. Select the vector in question with the Pointer tool, and choose Modify → Flatten Selection. The vector becomes a raster, as the Layers panel reveals—the name of the graphic changes from Path to Bitmap in the list. You may now use the Eraser tool to tidy up the image, but be warned! Once you change a vector into a raster, there's no going back.

Adjusting Vector Images

Is it so bad, changing a vector into a raster? Perhaps not, but then again, perhaps! As I mentioned in Chapter 1, vectors are eminently editable. You can demonstrate this concept for yourself in Fireworks.

Using the Pointer tool, select the vector image of your choice. Then, grab the Freeform tool. This is the third tool on the left in the Vector category. The Freeform tool allows you to reshape a vector image as if you were molding a piece of clay.

Position the Freeform tool outside the vector image, hold down the mouse button, and drag the tool into the image, and then press in on the contour of the shape. Drag the tool from the stroke of the vector, and you can poke the shape in or out. Drag from inside the vector, and you press out on the shape. You can change a simple shape into virtually anything, as Figure 3.8 shows.

Animation Advice _____

After you play with the Freeform tool, check out the Reshape Area tool, which hides under the Freeform tool in the Tools panel. The Reshape Area tool reshapes a vector graphic more dramatically than even the Freeform tool.

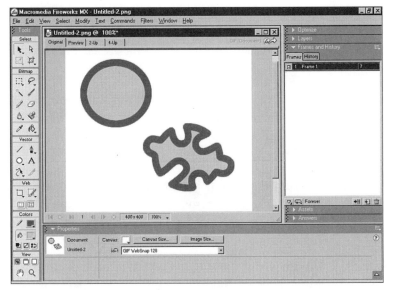

Figure 3.8

With the Freeform tool, you can change a simple vector graphic into virtually anything, as if you were molding a piece of clay.

For more precise adjustments, use the Subselection tool. This is the tool to the right of the Pointer in the Tools panel. The Subselection tool allows you to reposition the anchor points of a vector graphic. The *anchor points* are the points that define the vector's shape. It stands to reason, then, that if you change the position of the anchor points, you change the shape of the vector graphic.

You can put this theory to the test easily enough. Grab the Subselection tool from the Tools panel, and click a vector graphic. The anchor points turn white. Now, move the mouse pointer to one of the anchor points, hold down the mouse button, and drag. The anchor point drags with you, and the shape of the path changes as a result, as in Figure 3.9.

Figure 3.9

The Subselection tool lets you reposition the anchor points of a vector, thus changing the vector's shape.

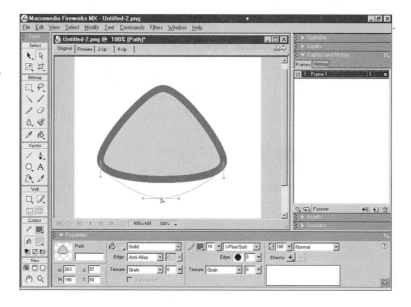

Processing Raster Images

You might not be able to use vector-editing tools on raster images, but Fireworks provides some handy image-processing tools that work only on bitmaps. These are the Blur tool and its hidden toolset. The Blur tool is the fourth tool on the left in the Bitmap category of the Tools panel. Reveal the hidden toolset by holding down the mouse button on the Blur tool's icon.

Animation Advice

If your raster image has less than perfect image quality, like a grainy old photograph, use the Blur tool to cover up the blemishes.

To use one of these tools, first select a raster graphic by clicking the thumbnail on the Layers panel or clicking the raster image itself with the Pointer tool. Then, grab the image-processing tool of your choice from the Tools panel, set the options in the Properties panel, position the mouse pointer where you want to begin processing, and hold down the mouse button. Drag the mouse across the pixels of the raster image to process them. Table 3.2 lists the image-processing tools and their effects.

Table 3.2   Fireworks Image-Processing Tools

Tool	Effect
Blur	Softens lines and corners
Burn	Darkens colors

Tool	Effect
Dodge	Lightens colors
Sharpen	Intensifies lines and corners
Smudge	Smears colors

Saving Your Work

When you're done creating or editing a canvas, you can save your work as a computer file. You can also export your work as a web-optimized image.

What's the difference between the two? Plenty! Saving as a computer file retains all the vector information as well as the layers and frames of the canvas. (You'll use layers and frames to create animated GIFs starting in Chapter 4.) Fireworks uses the PNG (Portable Network Graphic) format for saved files. By comparison, exporting as a web-optimized image flattens the image. That is, it compresses all the special infor-mation into a web-ready graphic format like GIF or JPEG. Incidentally, you can also export to the PNG format. However, an exported PNG file is flattened, unlike the version you get when you save.

The saved version, the Fireworks PNG, is your work file. This is the one that you open in Fireworks when you want to edit or make changes. The exported version, the GIF, JPEG, or flattened PNG, is the live file. This is the one that you post on the web or attach to an e-mail. Of course, nothing prevents you from opening the exported version of a file in Fireworks for editing. However, because the exported version is flat, it's more difficult to work with. It doesn't retain any of the vector or layer information that the Fireworks PNG version keeps. Making two versions of the same file is a concept that will appear again in Parts 3 and 4.

The Big Picture

PNG (pronounced *ping*) is a web graphics format similar to a GIF. In fact, it owes its existence to the GIF. In late 1994, CompuServe decided to charge for the use of its proprietary GIF format, so that software makers whose programs export to GIF owe CompuServe a royalty. One group's response to this was to develop the PNG format: like a GIF in many ways, but in many ways better, and completely free. The PNG is robust enough to serve as Fireworks' native format, and many web browsers support it, but GIFs still dominate the web—in part because GIFs offer animation and PNGs do not!

For now, don't bother exporting the canvas, because you haven't created any animation. Save a PNG work file instead. To do so, choose File → Save from the menu. Since this is the first time you saved the canvas, the Save As dialog box appears. (In the future, if you want to save the canvas using the same file name, choose File → Save. You skip the Save As dialog box this way. If you want to save the canvas in a different location or under a different file name, choose File → Save As, and you get the Save As dialog box.) Navigate to a convenient location on your hard drive, specify a name for the file in the File Name field, and click the Save button.

The Least You Need to Know

- Create a new canvas by choosing File → New and setting its resolution to 72 dpi.

- Use bitmap tools for raster graphics and vector tools for vector graphics.

- Add new raster graphics to the canvas by clicking the New Bitmap Image button.

- To change a vector image into a raster, select the image and choose Modify → Flatten Selection.

- Adjust the shape of vector images with the Freeform and Subselection tools, and process pixels in raster images with the Blur tool and its hidden toolset.

- Saving the canvas creates a PNG work file, suitable for editing, while exporting the canvas creates a web-ready version of the file.

Chapter 4

Animating GIFs

In This Chapter

- ◆ Opening a new canvas
- ◆ Using frames to create animation
- ◆ Adjusting the animation
- ◆ Troubleshooting the animation

You know your way around the Fireworks interface well enough. It's time to open a new canvas, draw some graphics, and set up some frames. In short, it's time to start building animated GIFs.

This chapter takes you through the process of creating an animated GIF from start to finish.

Opening the Canvas

To create an animated GIF, you need something to animate. Fortunately, this book comes complete with all kinds of animation projects. To start you off, allow me to share one of my best-loved short pieces, the critically acclaimed *Bouncing Red Ball*. By deconstructing this classic work and showing you how to build it step by step, you'll see why 66 percent of those surveyed prefer watching *Bouncing Red Ball* to getting a root canal.

Begin by launching Fireworks, and choose File → New. This calls up the New Document dialog box. Type **300** for the width and **350** for the height. (Make sure that pixels are the units of measurement for each field.) Keep the resolution at 72 ppi, and make the canvas color white. Click OK, and Fireworks opens a new canvas.

You have the workspace. Now you need the graphic to animate. The main character of *Bouncing Red Ball* is a red circle, so go to the Tools panel and grab the Ellipse tool, which is one of the hidden tools under the rectangle icon. Then go to the Properties panel and set the fill color to your choice of red. The fill color is the color square next to the paint bucket. Finally, turn off the stroke color entirely by clicking the stroke-color square—the one next to the pencil icon—and selecting the transparency swatch, which is the white swatch with a red line through it at the top of the pop-up window.

You're ready to draw. Bring the mouse pointer into the canvas, and drag an ellipse. As you draw, hold down the Shift key to change the ellipse into a perfect circle. (This is an old trick that works with just about every graphics program on the planet.) Release the mouse button when you have a decent-sized shape. Then, grab the Pointer tool, the very first tool on the left, and select the circle. Go to the Properties panel, and type **25** in the X field and **10** in the Y field to position the shape in the upper left corner of the canvas. These values are arbitrary, but, as you'll discover when you begin to animate, precise measurements help you to create smoother animation.

When you finish, your canvas should look much like Figure 4.1.

Figure 4.1

Begin Bouncing Red Ball *by drawing a circle on the canvas.*

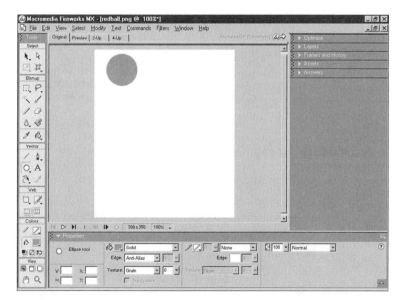

Setting Up the Frames

You have a static graphic. If you choose File → Export now, you can save this image for the web. You don't want to create a static graphic, though. You want an animated GIF.

In Chapter 2 you learned that an animated GIF is really a collection of separate raster images packaged together as a single GIF file. These separate images are called the *frames* of the animation. The animated GIF file also contains information about how long each frame should appear on screen, which is the *frame delay*. You won't be surprised to learn that, when you build an animated GIF in Fireworks, the next step is to set the default frame delay and create the frames.

To work with frames, you want the Frames panel ready at hand (see Figure 4.2). Open the Frames and History panel group and click the Frames tab, or choose Window → Frames.

Shop Talk

In Fireworks, a **frame** represents a single image in the GIF animation. The **frame delay** is the amount of time that the frame appears on screen.

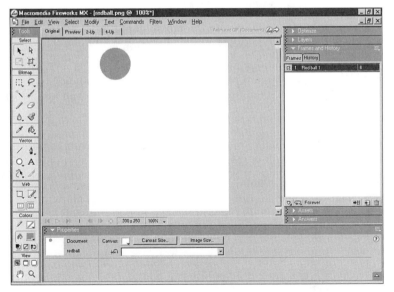

Figure 4.2

Open the Frames panel under the Frames and History panel group whenever you want to work with frames.

Notice that there's one frame in the Frames panel already: the default frame, Frame 1. It's often useful to rename the default frame to something more suited to your animation, something like Red ball 1, since this is going to be the starting frame of the animation. To change the name of the frame, double-click the existing name, type **Red ball 1** into the field that pops up, and press Enter or Return.

The number in the column to the right of the name represents the frame delay, which is, as you know, the amount of time that the frame appears on screen before the animation switches to the next frame in the sequence. The default frame delay in Fireworks is seven, or seven one-hundredths of a second. This probably seems like an extraordinarily short amount of time, and in the physical world, it is. I wouldn't want to hear that I had seven one-hundredths of a second to get to the airport terminal, for instance. Let me warn you, though, that time in animation works differently. It's often the case that seven one-hundredths of a second is way too much time.

> **Animation Advice**
>
> A default frame delay of six or seven is sufficient for most animated GIFs. You may prefer a shorter frame delay for extremely fast motion, but this can result in unconvincing work. The animated object may appear to blink in and out of existence instead of move.

Think of it like this: If an animated movie flickers by at 24 frames per second, it means that each frame appears on screen for one twenty-fourth of a second, which is a little more than four one-hundredths of a second. Already default frame delay in Fireworks is nearly double that of a movie.

I recommend building *Bouncing Red Ball* at a rate of 16 frames per second, which isn't the movies, but it's good enough for an animated GIF. Sixteen frames a second works out to a frame delay of roughly six one-hundredths of a second, so click the 7 in the Frames panel, type **6** in the pop-up window that appears, and make sure there's a check in the box for retaining the frame-delay value when you export the file. If you don't check this box, the final animation will play at its own speed.

You set the default frame delay. Now, create some frames. Notice the button to the left of the trashcan icon in the Frames panel. This is the New/Duplicate Frame button. If you click this button, you insert a blank frame into the canvas, but don't click the button just yet! It's smarter to duplicate the current frame instead of inserting a brand new one. Why? Consider the next frame in the sequence. It'll look much like the first frame, only the red ball will be a few pixels lower on the canvas. Since each frame in the animation is a separate image, inserting a new, blank frame means that you have to redraw the red ball or at least copy it from the first frame and paste it into the second. This sounds too much like work. It's easier just to duplicate the current frame. That way, your new frame already contains a red ball.

To duplicate a frame, click its name in the Frames panel, hold down the mouse button, drag the frame into the New/Duplicate Frame icon and release. Fireworks adds an identical copy of the current frame, right down to the name, to the canvas. Double-click the name of the second frame and type **Red ball 2.** Don't worry about positioning the red ball in the second frame just yet.

Recall that you're designing *Bouncing Red Ball* to play at roughly 16 frames per second. To cut down on the amount of work, assume that *Bouncing Red Ball*, from start to finish, lasts one second. Again, one second may not seem like a lot of time in the everyday world, but it'll feel much longer in the animation. Sixteen frames per second for a one-second animation works out to sixteen frames, of which you have two. You need to create 14 more duplicate frames.

The best way to do this is to hold down Ctrl (Windows) or Command (Mac) and select the unselected frame, which is probably the first frame in the Frames panel. Holding down Ctrl or Command allows you to select multiple frames. Drag the selection to the New/ Duplicate Frame button. Fireworks duplicates both selected frames, and you now have four frames total in the Frames panel.

> ### The Big Picture
>
> Creating bouncing balls is something of a time-honored tradition in computer graphics. Perhaps the most famous bouncing-ball demo is *Boing*, a short animation that showcased the power of the Amiga personal computer. *Boing* was revolutionary for its time. It spawned countless imitations. The year was 1984.

Now, select the fourth frame if it isn't already selected, hold down Shift this time, and select the first frame. Holding down Shift automatically selects all the frames between the current selection and the frame that you click. Since the current frame is the last and the frame that you click is the first, Fireworks selects all four frames. Drag this selection to the New/Duplicate Frame button, and you get eight frames total in the Frames panel. Repeat this procedure one more time, and you get 16 total frames.

Animation Advice

If duplicating frames by hand seems like a tedious job, you'll be happy to learn that Fireworks gives you an excellent shortcut (which I'll tell you about in Chapter 6). However, it's important to build at least one or two animated GIFs the long way, so pretend I didn't bring up the subject of the shortcut for now. Other tools for creating animated GIFs don't offer any shortcuts, so you'll be a better, more versatile creator of animated GIFs if you go through the full process a few times.

The only bothersome part is changing all the names of the frames to correspond to their actual numbers. You have a bunch of Red ball 1s and Red ball 2s. Double-click the name of each frame and change it to match its position. When you finish, your Frames panel should look something like the one in Figure 4.3.

Figure 4.3

If your animation plays at roughly 16 frames per second, make 15 duplicates of the first frame for a 1-second animation.

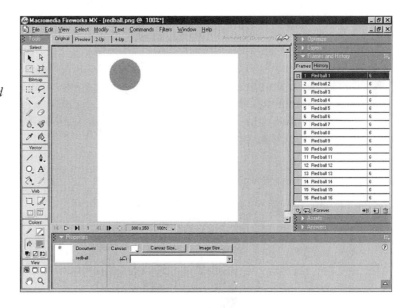

Setting Up the Motion

You have a canvas with 16 frames. You set each frame to appear for six one-hundredths of a second. All you need to do now is create the illusion of motion.

In general terms, here's how you proceed. Select the second frame in the canvas and move the red circle a few pixels toward the bottom. Then select the third frame in the canvas and move the red circle a few more pixels toward the bottom. Continue like this until you reach the bottom of the canvas. Then, in the next frame, move the circle a few pixels above the position of the bottommost circle in the previous frame. Finally, by Frame 16, position the circle a few pixels above the position of the uppermost circle in Frame 1. When you play back the animation at last, the computer steps through the frames one by one, pausing six one-hundredths of a second between each, and 16 separate drawings of the red ball appear to become one, and that red ball appears to bounce, hence my famous *Bouncing Red Ball*.

Shop Talk

Eyeballing means to adjust the position of a graphic on the canvas by relying on what looks correct to your eye.

You can accomplish this at least two ways. You can select each frame of the canvas and, using the Pointer tool, drag the red ball to what feels like an appropriate position. This is the *eyeballing* technique, which works fine if you have no other options. Fireworks gives you a more precise method: selecting each red ball with the Pointer tool and entering numerical coordinates in the Properties panel. You used this method already when you positioned the red ball in Frame 1.

Since the subject of this animation is a bouncing ball, being mathematical about the positions of the shapes creates a better, more realistic animation. You probably remember from physics class that an object doesn't maintain the same speed as it falls. Gravity accelerates it as it goes, so that its speed doubles every second. You probably also remember from physics class that, for every action, there is an equal but opposite reaction. This means that, once the ball hits the floor, it bounces upward at a rate similar to its speed at the time of impact. Gravity gets hold of it again, and its speed gradually slows, until the force of gravity over-comes the ball's momentum and pulls it back down, and the process repeats. In terms of your animation, this means that the ball should go faster and faster until it reaches the bottom of the canvas, then gradually slower and slower until it reaches the top of the canvas again.

> ### The Big Picture
>
> On planet Earth, the rate of acceleration of a falling object is 9.8 meters per second.

You have 16 frames to complete a single bounce. It makes sense to divide these frames in half: Give eight frames to the ball dropping down and eight frames to the ball bouncing back up. Now, your ball starts in Frame 1 at the coordinates (25, 10). To check this, select the first frame, click the circle with the Pointer tool, and look at the X and Y values in the Properties panel. If you assume that the ball drops 2 pixels between Frames 1 and 2, the coordinates for the circle in the second frame become (25, 12), because 10 + 2 = 12. Because the object accelerates at twice its current speed, the ball drops 4 pixels between Frames 2 and 3, making the coordinates of the circle in the third frame (25, 16), because 12 + 4 = 16. The ball drops 8 pixels between Frames 3 and 4, giving the coordinates (25, 24), and so on. Given this rate of acceleration, Table 4.1 provides the coordinates for the circles in Frames 1 through 8.

Table 4.1   Coordinates for the First Eight Frames of *Bouncing Red Ball*

Frame	Coordinates
1	(25, 10)
2	(25, 12)
3	(25, 16)
4	(25, 24)
5	(25, 40)

continues

Table 4.1   continued

Frame	Coordinates
6	(25, 72)
7	(25, 136)
8	(25, 264)

Animation Advice

One of the tricks to creating a successful animation is to strive for natural-looking motion. Break open your high school physics textbook and reacquaint yourself with Newtonian concepts!

To set the coordinates of the circle in Frame 2, select the second frame in the Frames panel, grab the Pointer tool, and click the circle. Go to the Properties panel, and type **12** in the Y field. Repeat this procedure for the circles in Frames 3 through 8, increasing the Y value each time according to the coordinates in Table 4.1.

Now, for the return leg of the journey, use the same values in the opposite direction. This gets you to Frame 15. For Frame 16, make the Y value one pixel less than in the fifteenth frame. Table 4.2 shows the coordinates for the circles in Frames 9 through 16.

Table 4.2   Coordinates for the Second Eight Frames of *Bouncing Red Ball*

Frame	Coordinates
9	(25, 136)
10	(25, 72)
11	(25, 40)
12	(25, 24)
13	(25, 16)
14	(25, 12)
15	(25, 10)
16	(25, 9)

Use the Pointer tool and the Properties panel to set the Y values for the circles in these frames. When you finish, you're ready to test the animation.

Previewing Your Work

If you look at the bottom of the document window, you'll find a series of icons that look like the playback buttons on a CD player or VCR. These are exactly what they appear to be. They don't activate your CD player or VCR, of course, but they do allow you to play your animation for a preview before you export the final animated GIF file.

To begin, click the first button on the left. This resets the animation to the first frame. Then click the Play button, which is the second button from the left. Sit back and watch your animation play. The Frames panel highlights the current frame.

The playback is a bit slower on the canvas than in the actual animated GIF, but never mind that. The preview feature in Fireworks gives you more than a good idea about what the finished animation will look like. Click the Stop button, which replaces the Play button, to freeze the animation at the current frame. Use the Previous Frame and Next Frame buttons, the last buttons in the series, to step through the frames one at a time.

Adjusting the Animation

Hit Play again, and take another look at the animation. You may notice some *strobing*, or afterimages, in the vicinity of Frames 7, 8, 9, and 10. Strobing happens when you move an object too great a distance in too short a time. Sure enough, if you look back at Tables 4.1 and 4.2, you see that Frames 7 through 10 have the largest jumps in the positions of the red ball.

Strobing in animated GIFs is quite common, but you should try to eliminate it whenever possible. There are two ways to cut down on strobing: lengthen the frame delay or shorten the distances. You know from previewing the animation that the speed feels just about right, so lengthening the frame delay in this case doesn't seem like the best solution. But you also took great pains to make the distances accurate for a realistic animation. Changing the distances may cut down on strobing, but it does so at the expense of the goal of the animation. There doesn't seem to be a reasonable solution for reducing the strobing in *Bouncing Red Ball*. Or is there?

One way to shorten the distances is to shrink the entire canvas and everything in it. To do so,

Shop Talk

When an animation **strobes,** the viewer's eye appears to see two or more frames on the screen at the same time.

choose Modify → Canvas → Image Size. This calls up the Image Size dialog box, as in Figure 4.4. Look under the Pixel Dimensions section, and you find the width and height of the canvas exactly as you specified earlier. Change the units of measurement from pixels to percent for both fields. Now, shrink the canvas to a quarter of its original size by typing 25 in the field for the width. The field for the height automatically changes to 25 percent to maintain the proportions of the image as long as you check the Constrain Proportions option at the bottom of the dialog box. Click OK to resize the image.

Figure 4.4

Use the Image Size dialog box to change the size of the canvas and everything in it.

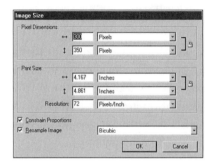

The canvas is now a quarter of its original size. But when you press Play, the strobing isn't nearly as noticeable.

Looping the Loop

When you preview your animation in Fireworks, the animation always loops continuously until you hit the Stop button. However, for the final animated GIF file, you can specify different looping instructions.

CAUTION

Cut!

Remember that the looping instructions affect only the final animated GIF file. The animation always loops forever in Fireworks until you press the Stop button, no matter what you set for the looping.

Go back to the Frames panel, and find the second button from the left at the bottom of the panel. This is the GIF Animation Looping button. Next to the button is a label that says Forever by default, which indicates that, when you export the animated GIF, the sequence of frames repeats over and over again, indefinitely. To specify different looping, click this button, and a menu slides up, as in Figure 4.5.

For the purposes of *Bouncing Red Ball*, keep the looping on the setting for forever, but feel free to experiment with different looping schemes for your own animations.

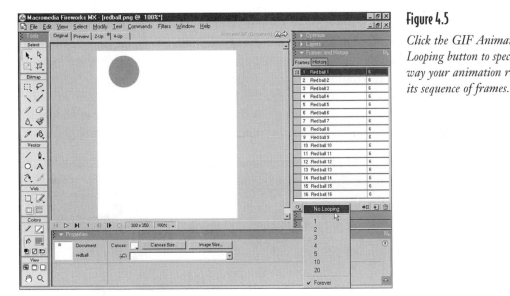

Using Onion Skinning

Bouncing Red Ball plays pretty well as it is because you calculated the precise coordinates of the ball for each frame. Assume for a moment that you had used the eyeball method to position each shape and you needed to tweak the positions for some of the frames. It would be handy to see the positions of the balls in neighboring frames to help you make the proper adjustments.

Fireworks provides a feature called *onion skinning* that does exactly this. Onion skinning shows multiple frames on the canvas simultaneously. The term "onion skinning" is a holdover from traditional animation, back in the days when animators would work on a lightbox. In traditional onion skinning, the animator would place a thin sheet of paper over the most recent frame to use as a reference for the next frame. The light from the lightbox would shine through both pages, allowing the animator to see the art underneath. You can duplicate the effect by drawing something on a sheet of printer paper, placing a blank sheet of paper on top of it, and holding both up to your monitor screen.

To use the digital version of onion skinning in Fireworks, go to the Frames panel, and find the first column on the left, the one with the

Shop Talk

When you **onion skin,** you set the canvas to display multiple frames simultaneously. This allows you to troubleshoot a motion sequence.

strange icon. This is the icon for onion skinning. To show a range of frames, select the first frame in the range by clicking in the name column of the desired frame—don't click in the onion-skinning column just yet. Notice that the onion-skinning icon jumps to the selected frame. Now, select the last frame in the range by clicking in the onion-skinning column of that frame, and Fireworks presents the contents of all the frames in the range. The first frame in the series appears at full opacity, while the onion-skinned frames show as partially transparent, as you see in Figure 4.6.

Figure 4.6

With onion skinning, you see the contents of multiple frames on the canvas simultaneously.

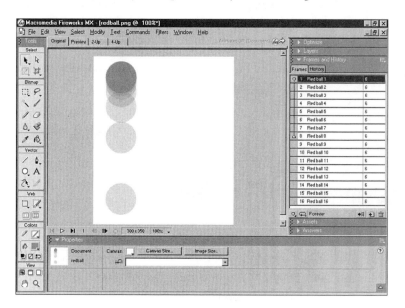

To reset the ending frame, click in the onion-skinning column of a different frame. To see the same number of frames from a different starting point, click in the name column of a different frame. To choose a new starting and ending point entirely, first click in the onion-skinning column of the current starting frame. Then, select a new starting frame by clicking in the name column of that frame, and select a new ending frame by clicking in the onion-skinning column. To turn onion skinning off, click in the onion-skinning column of the starting frame.

The Big Picture

Onion skinning disappears temporarily when you press the Play button in the document window, but it returns when you press the Stop button.

Onion skinning isn't just for looks. You can manipulate the contents of any onion-skinned frame by clicking the desired item with the Pointer tool. This is what makes onion skinning useful for tweaking the positions of objects in different frames.

Exporting the File

I promised you that, by the end of this chapter, you would have created an animated GIF. All you have to do now is export the file, and a promise made is a promise kept.

Before you do that, though, save a work copy of the animation as a Fireworks PNG file. Remember from Chapter 3 that you want to create two files of every animation: a work file and a live file. The work version is the Fireworks PNG that you keep on your hard drive for editing purposes. The live version is the animated GIF that goes on the web or in your e-mail. So, choose File → Save, navigate to a convenient spot on your hard drive, and save your work as *redball.png*.

Now, export the animated GIF. Open the Optimize panel group, and look for the drop-down list to the left of the Matte color square. This list shows the format of the exported file. Choose Animated GIF from this list, as in Figure 4.7. Then, choose File → Export from the Fireworks menu, and the Export dialog box appears, as in Figure 4.8.

Animation Advice

If you want to save *Bouncing Red Ball* as a Flash file, choose Macromedia Flash SWF from the Save As Type list on the Export dialog box.

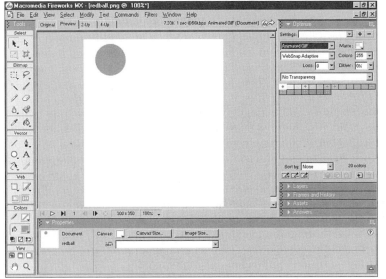

Figure 4.7

When you want to export an animated GIF from Fireworks, make sure that the dropdown list to the left of the Matte color square in the Optimize panel shows the Animated GIF option.

The File Name field of the Export dialog box should automatically provide the name redball or redball.gif. If it doesn't, erase whatever Fireworks filled in and type **redball.** Set the Save As Type list to the option for images only and click the Save button. Fireworks creates an animated GIF of your image.

Figure 4.8

Save your animation as an animated GIF with the Export dialog box.

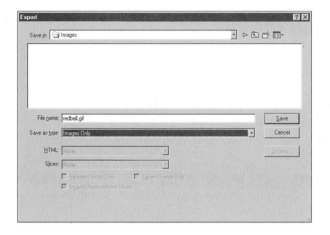

To prove it, choose File → Open, and double-click the redball.gif file. Fireworks opens your animated GIF in a new document window. You can play the animated GIF with the playback buttons at the bottom of the document window, just like you can with the Fireworks PNG version you saved. However, if you look at the Frames panel, you see that the names you gave to the frames are gone. Further, if you try to edit the position of the red ball in any one of the frames, you find that you can't, not without moving the entire background with it! This is a perfect illustration of the difference between the live version of the animation and the work version of the animation. The work version retains the vector information of the shapes and the names of the frames, while the live version is a completely flattened, rasterized, web-ready animated GIF.

Not to worry, though. You already saved a work version of your file, so, when you want to add more to *Bouncing Red Ball* (as you should, because I was only joking when I said that it was internationally acclaimed), you can do so with complete confidence.

The Least You Need to Know

- ◆ To create a new canvas in Fireworks, choose File → New from the menu.

- ◆ For animated GIFs, always set the resolution of the canvas to 72 pixels per inch.

- ◆ To save you from redrawing artwork, duplicate existing frames instead of creating new ones.

- ◆ Cut down on strobing by increasing the frame delay or reducing the distance between moving images.

- ◆ Set looping to determine how many times an animated GIF repeats.

- ◆ Use onion skinning to view multiple frames simultaneously.

Chapter 5

Animating with Layers

In This Chapter

◆ Using layers for more complex animations

◆ Managing layers

◆ Sharing layers across frames

◆ Adding special effects

Bouncing Red Ball is a simple animation. It has a single moving object and no background. Its storyline is also rather weak.

Animated GIFs don't have to be this simple. You can easily create multiple moving images against a colorful background. The secret to achieving this is to use multiple layers.

This chapter shows you how to create and manage layers and to leverage their power for more ambitious animations. In the process, I demonstrate how to add special visual effects to your work.

Setting Up Layers

One of the advantages to using Fireworks to create animated GIFs is that Fireworks gives you the ability to add multiple layers to the canvas. A *layer* is like a sheet of transparent acetate that you place on top of the canvas.

The layer is a separate drawing surface, if you will. You can add bitmap and vector graphics to it. But because the layer is perfectly transparent, you can see the graphics underneath it.

In the context of creating an animated GIF, layers offer some interesting possibilities. Put one set of drawings on one layer and another set of drawings on another layer, and you get two separate animations playing simultaneously. Add a static background image in the bottommost layer, and you can share it across frames. You don't have to recreate the background for every frame of the animation.

Using layers is easy. It's so easy, in fact, that you've been doing it all along, only you may not have realized it. When you created the acclaimed *Bouncing Red Ball* in Chapter 4, you drew a round red vector graphic on the canvas. Fireworks added this vector to the canvas's first layer by default. Don't believe me? Launch Fireworks and choose File → Open. Load up *redball.png*, and then open the Layers panel group. Notice that the graphic of the red ball is in the folder called Layer 1, as shown in Figure 5.1.

Shop Talk

A **layer** is a transparent drawing surface on the canvas.

Figure 5.1

Notice that the red circle of Bouncing Red Ball *is in Layer 1 of the canvas.*

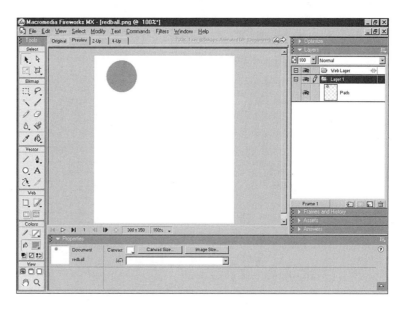

The upshot of this is that you could create a new layer—call it Layer 2. You could draw a green circle on this layer, copy the new layer across all 16 frames of the animation, change the position of the green circle in each of the 16 frames, and turn out a sequel, *Bouncing Red and Green Balls*. It'll be more fun, though, to leave bouncing balls behind for the time being and experiment with layers on a new project: *The Robot Is Frustrated*, another of my runaway international box-office successes. In this animation, the alien life form from my book, *The Complete Idiot's Guide to Computer Illustration* (Alpha Books, 2002), uses the mailbox from the same book to torment a robot, as Figure 5.2 shows.

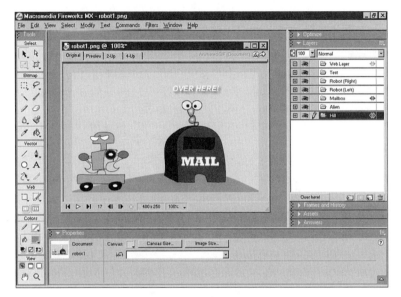

Figure 5.2

This still from The Robot Is Frustrated *captures the essence of the animation.*

This animation requires five illustrations. You can find them on the CD-ROM that comes with this book. The first step is to load the graphics files into the animation software, so launch Fireworks if you haven't already done so, and pop the CD-ROM into your computer. Choose File → Open from main menu in Fireworks, and navigate to the Chapter 5 folder. Inside this folder are five files: *alien.png, hill.png, mailbox.png, robot_left.png,* and *robot_right.png.*

Hold down Ctrl (Windows) or Command (Mac), and click all five files. Then click the Open button. Fireworks opens all five images in separate document windows. Notice that the bottom half of the alien life form is missing. This is because you don't need the bottom half of it—it never pokes more than its upper body above the top of the mailbox.

Animation Advice

If you prefer to supply your own art for the animation, by all means, do so! You don't have to use the files on the CD-ROM.

You have the pieces of the animation. Now you need the canvas on which to animate. Choose File → New, and specify a canvas 400 pixels wide and 250 pixels high. Keep the resolution at 72 pixels per inch, as always. Select the Custom option for the canvas color, and click the color square. Choose a color of blue for the background to represent the sky. I chose a light shade of slightly purplish blue, #CCCCFF, but you can pick whatever color suits your fancy. Click OK to create the canvas.

Creating New Layers

The next step is to copy the images from the CD-ROM files into the canvas you just created. I also recommend that you put each image in its own layer. This makes managing the animation easier and more straightforward. You could conceivably put all the images in the same layer, but it can cause headaches later on.

Click one of the images you loaded from the CD-ROM, and choose Edit → Copy. Now click the canvas you just created, and choose Edit → Paste. Fireworks pastes an exact replica of the graphic into the first layer of the new canvas. Double-click the name of the layer, and type a descriptive label such as Hill if you copied and pasted the hill or Robot (Left) if you copied and pasted the left-facing robot.

So much for the first layer. Now, create a new layer for the next image. Click the folder icon at the bottom of the Layers panel. This is the New/Duplicate Layer button. Fireworks inserts a new layer immediately above the current one. Remember, this is like pulling a sheet of acetate over the canvas.

Close the document window of the image you just copied and pasted, and pick another image. Copy its contents. Click the animation canvas, and make sure that the new layer is highlighted in the Layers panel. If it isn't, click it. Choose Edit → Paste, and the new layer acquires its piece of art. Notice that the art on the new layer sits on top of the art in the lower layer but that you can still see the lower layer in the areas where the two pieces of art don't overlap. Rename the new layer to something descriptive, and add a third layer to the canvas. Don't forget to close the document window of the art you just copied.

CAUTION

Cut!

Don't try to paste art into the Web Layer! Fireworks uses the Web Layer to store information about other types of web images, not animated GIFs. If you try to put art in the Web Layer, Fireworks files it in the second lowest layer in the Layers panel instead.

Copy and paste the remaining illustrations into the animation canvas, putting each illustration on its own layer and giving each layer a descriptive name. When you finish, you should have only one open document window—the animation canvas—and this canvas should have five layers with the following labels (or something like them) in no particular order: Hill,

Robot (Left), Robot (Right), Mailbox, and Alien. There's also a sixth layer, another Fireworks default called Web Layer. You use this layer frequently when you build web interfaces with Fireworks, but you don't use it at all in animation. Feel free to ignore the Web Layer completely. I'd suggest that you delete it, but Fireworks doesn't allow you. Just pretend as if it doesn't exist.

Reordering Layers

The next step is to order the layers correctly. This just means figuring out what image should sit on top of which other images. I could have told you the correct order of the layers from the start, but I didn't on purpose so that I could show you one of the more useful features in Fireworks. I mentioned before that, when you organize your canvas into layers, managing your animation becomes much easier. This is part of what I was talking about. Go to the Layers panel, and click the Hill Layer. The hill is part of the background. You want all the other pieces of art to sit on top of the hill. Therefore, the Hill Layer belongs at the bottom of the Layers panel. Hold down the mouse button on this layer, drag the layer to the bottom, and release. As if by magic, the art in all the other layers moves in front of the hill.

The layer second from the bottom should be the one with the alien. You may have guessed the Mailbox Layer, thinking that it was part of the background, but the alien hides behind the mailbox, as you saw in Figure 5.2. Therefore, the Mailbox Layer should be above the Alien Layer in the Layers panel. Drag the Alien Layer to the position just above the Hill Layer in the Layers panel, and then drag the Mailbox Layer to the position just above the Alien Layer, leaving the two Robot Layers on top. It doesn't matter the order of the Robot Layers. As you'll see when you set up the animation, the Robot Layers don't appear at the same time. When the left-facing robot is visible, the right-facing one is hidden, and vice versa. As long as both Robot Layers are higher in the Layers panel than the ones with the mailbox, alien, and hill, you're in good shape.

> **The Big Picture**
>
> Layers stack from top to bottom in Fireworks. In other words, the uppermost layer in the Layers panel is at the top of the canvas.

You need one last layer to complete this animation: the layer with the alien's line of dialog, "Over here!" Select the uppermost layer in your animation, the one directly under the Web Layer, and click the New/Duplicate Layer button on the Layers panel. Double-click this layer's name, and type Text in the field that pops up. Leave this layer for now. You'll create the text for it a bit later in this chapter.

Before you continue, make sure the Layers panel for your canvas shows the following order, from top to bottom: Web Layer, Text, the two Robot Layers, Mailbox, Alien, and Hill. If your Layers panel doesn't show this particular order, drag and drop layers accordingly.

Now, position the various pieces of art in their starting positions. You may have begun to do this already with the Pointer tool by eyeballing it. This is fine for getting a feel for the composition of the scene, but I recommend the more mathematically precise method of typing values into the X and Y fields of the Properties panel, just like you did in *Bouncing Red Ball*.

Grab the Pointer tool and select the hill graphic. Type **0** in the X field of the Properties panel, and type **208** in the Y field. This positions the hill at the bottom of the canvas. Click the alien, and type **236** for X and **114** for Y. Click the mailbox, and type **198** for X and **111** for Y. Click the left-facing robot, and type **115** for X and **109** for Y. Finally, click the right-facing robot, and type **10** for X and **124** for Y. Your canvas should look like the one in Figure 5.3.

Animation Advice _____

If you want to select a graphic that another graphic completely obscures, simply go to the Layers panel and click with the Pointer tool the item in the list that corresponds to the graphic you want to select.

Figure 5.3

After you create and order the layers for this animation, set up the starting positions for the different pieces of art.

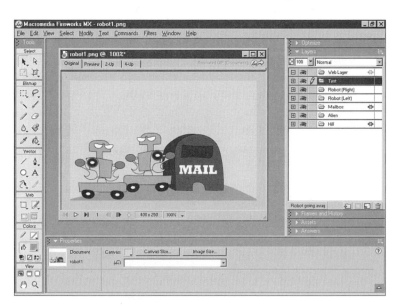

Showing and Hiding Layers

I mentioned before that the left and right robots don't appear on screen at the same time. When one is visible, the other is hidden. Right now, both robots are visible, but you can easily change this. Go back to the Layers panel, and click the eye icon to the left of the right-facing robot's layer. The eye icon disappears, as does the right-facing robot. You haven't deleted the robot. It's still there. Click the empty block to get the eye icon back, and the robot reappears in its old position.

As you can see (or not see, as the case may be), the eye icon controls visibility. When the eye shows, the item beside it in the Layers panel shows. When the eye is missing, the item beside it disappears. Notice that the layer itself has an eye icon as well as the art inside the layer. When you poke the eye of the layer, the entire content of the layer vanishes. But when you poke the eye of an individual graphic inside the layer, only that graphic disappears. In this case, of course, it doesn't matter which eye icon you poke, since each layer has only one graphic each. The effect is identical. But keep this in mind when you build animations of your own. If you have more than one graphic in a layer, you can hide individual images by clicking their personal eye icons, or you can hide everything in the layer by clicking the layer's eye icon.

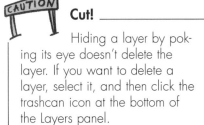

Cut! _____

Hiding a layer by poking its eye doesn't delete the layer. If you want to delete a layer, select it, and then click the trashcan icon at the bottom of the Layers panel.

Hide the right-facing robot again, and compare your canvas to the one in Figure 5.4.

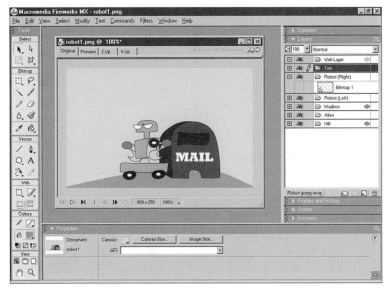

Figure 5.4

By poking an eye icon in the Layers panel, you make the corresponding graphic disappear. Click again to restore visibility.

Animating Multiple Layers

You're ready to start animating.

There are three moving images in *The Robot Is Frustrated.* The first is the robot, which paces back and forth. The second is the alien life form, which pops up behind the mailbox and crouches down behind it again. The third is the alien's line of dialog, which disappears off the top of canvas, fading out as it goes.

There are two static images in this animation: the hill and the mailbox. Neither illustration moves. The X and Y values for these illustrations remain constant throughout.

When you have an animation with some moving images and other static images, it helps you in the long run if you share the layers of the static images across frames.

Sharing Layers Across Frames

Sharing a layer creates a single version of the layer for all the frames in the animation. That is, the contents of a shared layer always appear in the same position with the same properties, no matter how many frames you add to the animation. If you don't share a layer, as you'll soon see, you can change the position and properties of the contents of the layer from frame to frame.

The beauty of using shared layers is this: Assume that you want to tweak the position of the mailbox in *The Robot Is Frustrated.* If you share the Mailbox Layer across frames, all you have to do is move the mailbox once, and this image changes position automatically in every frame of the animation. If you don't share the Mailbox Layer, you have to go into every frame individually and reposition the stupid mailbox—a pain by anyone's definition.

Animation Advice

Don't share the layers of moving images in the animation. You should share the layers only of static images. Since a shared layer looks the same in all frames, the X and Y properties of its contents don't change, so there's no illusion of movement when you play back the frames at high speed.

Of all the layers on the canvas, only the Mailbox Layer and the Hill Layer are completely static. The other layers contain moving images. The static layers are the ones you should share across frames.

Double-click the Hill Layer, and the Layer Name field pops up as before. Notice below the field a check box for sharing the layer across frames, as in Figure 5.5. Check this box, and close the popup window by clicking anywhere outside it. Now look at the Hill Layer on the Layers panel, and you notice a new icon to the right of the name. The Web Layer has a similar icon. This icon indicates that the Hill Layer shares its contents across frames. Follow the same procedure for the Mailbox Layer, and you're ready to continue.

Figure 5.5

Check the box under the Layer Name field to share a layer across frames.

Getting Down to Business

Set up the default frame delay. Open the Frames and History panel group, click the Frames tab for the Frames panel, double-click the frame-delay value, and type **6** in the field. This is the same frame delay you used in *Bouncing Red Ball*. It's equivalent to six one-hundredths of a second, which gives you roughly 16 frames per second.

The Robot Is Frustrated has 33 frames from start to finish. Frames 1 through 16 show the left-facing robot moving toward the lower left corner of the canvas while the alien life form comes up from behind the mailbox. Frame 17 has the alien giving its line of dialog. Frames 18 through 33 show the right-facing robot heading back up the hill to the source of the commotion, but the alien has ducked back down behind the mailbox. Hence, the robot is frustrated. The animation starts again at Frame 1 and plays through for as long as you can stomach watching it.

Double-click the first frame in the Frames panel, and rename it "Robot going away" or something to that effect. Drag this frame to the New/Duplicate Frame button. Select both frames, and drag them to the New/Duplicate Frame button, and so on, until you have the first 16 frames. Stop for now—you'll create the rest of the frames later.

Now, change the position of the left-facing robot for each of the 15 new frames. Here's how the process works: Select the second frame in the Frames panel, and click the left-facing robot in the canvas. Go to the Properties panel, and type **108** in the X field and **110** in the Y field. Go back to the Frames panel, and select the third frame. Click the robot in the canvas, and type **101** in the X field and **111** in the Y field. As you can see, the robot moves slowly down the hill. The X value drops seven pixels between each frame, and the Y value increases by one pixel.

The Big Picture

Professional animators almost always create storyboards, or visual breakdowns of the animation, before animating. These storyboards look and read much like a comic strip, and they serve as the blueprint for the production. Even for a short animated GIF, you may find it helpful to sketch out a few story panels on a piece of paper.

Continue this process for the rest of the frames. Table 5.1 shows the proper X and Y coordinates. After you finish, click the play button at the bottom of the document window to test the animation.

Table 5.1 Coordinates for the Robot in *The Robot Is Frustrated* (Frames 1–16)

Frame	Coordinates	Frame	Coordinates
1	(115, 109)	9	(59, 117)
2	(108, 110)	10	(52, 118)
3	(101, 111)	11	(45, 119)
4	(94, 112)	12	(38, 120)
5	(87, 113)	13	(31, 121)
6	(80, 114)	14	(24, 122)
7	(73, 115)	15	(17, 123)
8	(66, 116)	16	(10, 124)

So far, so good. Now animate the alien life form. The alien doesn't emerge until the eighth frame of the sequence, so click the eighth frame in the Frames panel. Since the mailbox completely covers the alien, you have to select the alien graphic in the Layers panel. Look under the Alien Layer, and click the alien's bitmap graphic with the Pointer tool. This does the trick. Go to the Properties panel, and type **114** in the Y field. (The value of 236 in the X field remains constant.) Then select the ninth frame, click the alien's bitmap in the Layers panel, and type **107** in the Y field. You can just see the tops of the alien's eyes poking out behind the mailbox. Continue until Frame 16, subtracting 7 from the Y value in each successive frame. Table 5.2 gives the proper coordinates. Play the animation again when you're done to make sure everything works correctly.

Animation Advice

Don't forget that you can step through the animation frame by frame by clicking the Next Frame and Previous Frame buttons at the bottom of the document window.

Table 5.2   Coordinates for the Alien in *The Robot Is Frustrated* (Frames 1–16)

Frame	Coordinates	Frame	Coordinates
1	(236, 114)	9	(236, 107)
2	(236, 114)	10	(236, 100)
3	(236, 114)	11	(236, 93)
4	(236, 114)	12	(236, 86)
5	(236, 114)	13	(236, 79)
6	(236, 114)	14	(236, 72)
7	(236, 114)	15	(236, 65)
8	(236, 114)	16	(236, 58)

Adding Effects

Next comes Frame 17, where the alien gives its line of dialog, "Over here!" Select the sixteenth frame in the Frames panel, and drag it to the New/Duplicate Frame button. Rename this frame Over here! The positions of the robot and the alien are the same in this frame. You need to create the text for the line of dialog, though, in the Text Layer.

Animation Advice

If you're using a Mac, you might not have the Arial font. You probably have Helvetica, though, which is a perfectly good substitute.

Go to the Layers panel, and select the Text Layer. Now grab the Text tool from the Tools panel, move into the canvas, and click. This inserts a new text object into the selected layer. In the Properties panel, choose a font (I'm using Arial), make the font size 16, make the color white (#FFFFFF), and click the buttons for both boldface and italic. Type **Over here!** to create the dialog. Go back to the Properties panel, and set the X value to **212** and the Y value to **22.** This positions the text above the alien's head.

The white text against the blue background color doesn't have enough contrast, in my opinion. You can improve the contrast by adding a drop-shadow effect to the text.

Applying a Drop Shadow

On the right side of the Properties panel, you find a plus and a minus button next to the label Effects. Click the plus button, and a context menu appears, as in Figure 5.6. This menu allows you to add any combination of special visual effects to the selected graphic.

Figure 5.6

Click the plus button on the Properties panel to open the Effects menu.

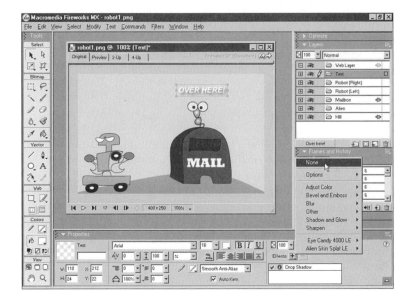

You want a drop shadow for the text object, so choose Shadow and Glow → Drop Shadow. Fireworks adds a drop shadow to the text, helping it to stand out better against the blue background. If you look under the Effects label in the Properties panel, you see an entry for the drop-shadow effect you just applied, as in Figure 5.7. Adjust the settings of the drop shadow by double-clicking the name of the effect or clicking the I icon to the left of the effect's name. To hide the effect temporarily, click the check mark to the left of the effects name. (Click again to restore the effect.) To remove the effect entirely, click its name, and then click the minus button.

Figure 5.7

The Effects list on the Properties panel shows you the effects you applied to a graphic.

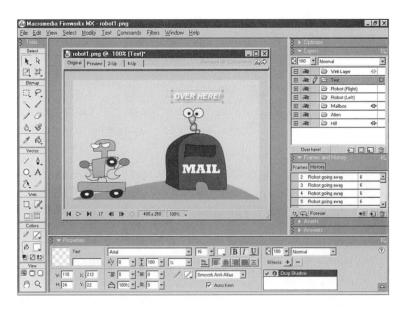

Feel free to tinker with the drop shadow until it looks the way you like. I opted for default drop-shadow settings, because I think they look fine. Make one final edit to this frame: Set the delay to 50 instead of 6. This pauses the animation for half a second.

Now, create the final frames of the animation. Make a duplicate of the Over Here frame for the eighteenth frame of the sequence, and call this one Robot Coming Back. Set the frame delay to 6 again.

> **The Big Picture**
>
> You can add as many effects to a graphic as you like. Keep in mind, though, that the more effects a graphic has, the worse it tends to look. You rarely ever want to use more than two effects on any one graphic. In most cases, you can (and should) get away with just one.

This segment of the animation shows the robot coming back up the hill. You want to use the right-facing robot for this leg of the journey. Go to the Layers panel, and poke the eye icon of the left-facing robot to hide this graphic. Activate the eye icon for the right-facing robot to reveal this graphic.

You're ready to duplicate the frames. Select the eighteenth frame in the Frames panel, and drag it to the New/Duplicate Frame button. Select Frames 18 and 19, drag them to the New/Duplicate Frame button, and so on, until you have 33 frames total.

> **The Big Picture**
>
> Science fiction writer Isaac Asimov developed three laws for robotics in the early 1940s. The first law states that a robot must not injure a human being, either by action or inaction. The second law states that a robot must obey the orders of a human being, as long as these orders don't violate the first law. The third law states that a robot must protect itself, as long as doing so doesn't violate the first law. Although these laws originated in fiction, many modern robotics engineers use them as a kind of guiding light.

Position the robot and alien graphics for the remainder of the frames. Table 5.3 gives the coordinates.

Table 5.3 Coordinates for the Robot and Alien in *The Robot Is Frustrated* (Frames 18–33)

Frame	Robot Coordinates	Alien Coordinates
18	(10, 124)	(236, 72)
19	(17, 123)	(236, 86)

continues

Table 5.3   (continued)

Frame	Robot Coordinates	Alien Coordinates
20	(24, 122)	(236, 100)
21	(31, 121)	(236, 114)
22	(38, 120)	(236, 114)
23	(45, 119)	(236, 114)
24	(52, 118)	(236, 114)
25	(59, 117)	(236, 114)
26	(66, 116)	(236, 114)
27	(73, 115)	(236, 114)
28	(80, 114)	(236, 114)
29	(87, 113)	(236, 114)
30	(94, 112)	(236, 114)
31	(101, 111)	(236, 114)
32	(108, 110)	(236, 114)
33	(115, 109)	(236, 114)

Set the frame delay of Frame 33 to 56 instead of 6. This adds an extra half-second delay to the current $^6/_{100}$ second delay before the animation loops back to the first frame. Test the playback by clicking the Play button at the bottom of the document window.

Fading In and Out

It would be nice to do something with that text. It just hangs there for 16 frames and then disappears mysteriously when the animation loops.

I have two suggestions: First, make the text move off the top of the canvas. Second, make the text fade out slowly as it goes.

Both adjustments are straightforward. To make the text move off the canvas, simply supply negative values for the X or Y fields in the Properties panel. Since the text should move off the top of the canvas, you want to make the Y value progressively smaller.

To make the text gradually fade away, adjust its *opacity* value. Here's how. Select the nineteenth frame of the sequence, click the text object in this frame, and go to the Properties panel. Above the effects buttons is a checker-box icon next to a field and a slider (see Figure 5.8). The checker box is the symbol for transparency in Fireworks. The current value in the field is 100%, meaning that the selected object is 100% opaque. Adjust the value to 83% by dragging the slider or typing **83%** directly into the field. The text object begins to fade. To be precise, it's now 83% opaque, which means that it's 17% transparent.

Shop Talk

Opacity and **transparency** are two sides of the same coin. Opacity is the degree to which an image is solid. Transparency is the degree to which an image is clear.

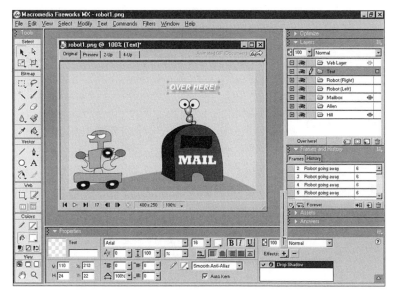

Figure 5.8

Change the transparency of the selected graphic by adjusting the Property panel's opacity slider.

As you reduce the Y value of the text object in the subsequent frames, you'll also reduce its opacity. Table 5.4 gives the appropriate values for each.

Table 5.4   Properties of the Text Object in *The Robot Is Frustrated* (Frames 17–33)

Frame	Coordinates	Opacity
17	(212, 22)	100%
18	(212, 22)	84%
19	(212, 14)	68%
20	(212, 6)	52%

continues

Table 5.4 (continued)

Frame	Coordinates	Opacity
21	(212, –2)	36%
22	(212, –10)	20%
23	(212, –18)	4%
24	(212, –26)	0%
25	(212, –26)	0%
26	(212, –26)	0%
27	(212, –26)	0%
28	(212, –26)	0%
29	(212, –26)	0%
30	(212, –26)	0%
31	(212, –26)	0%
32	(212, –26)	0%
33	(212, –26)	0%

When you finish, test the animation by clicking the Play button. Make adjustments to the playback as necessary. Then, choose File → Save from the menu, and supply a file name like *robot1.png*. This saves the work file. Now, to create the live animated GIF, set the Optimize panel to Animated GIF as you did in Chapter 4 and then choose File → Export. Choose a file name, and click the Save button.

Your handcrafted robot animation is ready to roll. Post it on the web with pride.

The Least You Need to Know

- ◆ A layer is a transparent drawing surface on the canvas.
- ◆ When you animate multiple objects, put each object on its own layer.
- ◆ Poke a layer's eye icon to hide the contents of the layer.
- ◆ Share the layers of static images across frames.
- ◆ Use the plus and minus buttons on the Properties panel to add and remove special effects.
- ◆ Adjust the opacity of an object with the Property panel's transparency slider.

Chapter 6

Using Symbols

In This Chapter

◆ Creating symbols and instances

◆ Tweening instances

◆ Comparing graphic symbols and animation symbols

◆ Repositioning instances for faster editing

Remember that shortcut I mentioned in Chapter 4? I alluded to the fact that Fireworks gives you a better, faster way to create animated GIFs than manipulating every single frame by hand, but I wanted you to build a few animations the long way first.

You've built a few animations the long way. It's time for the shortcut. This chapter explains how to speed up production by using symbols and instances.

About Symbols and Instances

Believe it or not, a good way to explain the concept of the symbol is to go back to the teachings of the philosopher Plato.

Plato believed that every object in the world—a cup, a paperclip, a mouse pad—refers to a definitive version of that object called a form. The form of a mouse pad, then, is the definitive version of a mouse pad. It's perfect in every way. The form of a paper clip is the definitive version of a paper clip. You get the gist.

Plato also believed that these forms don't exist in the physical world—they're intangible ideas or concepts. The actual mouse pads that you find in the world are nothing more than examples of the idea of the mouse pad. No matter how perfect a real mouse pad might seem, it doesn't quite achieve the same level of perfection as its underlying concept. The form and its examples are connected, therefore, but they aren't the same thing. The examples are just imperfect copies of the original. Conceivably, if you could change the characteristics of the form, all the worldly examples of that form would also change. If you ever wake up one morning to find that all the world's mouse pads look different, you'll know that some reader somewhere has managed to change the form of the mouse pad.

In Fireworks and Flash, a *symbol* is a graphic that works much like a Platonic form. It's the definitive version of the graphic. You place copies, or *instances*, of the symbol on the canvas. (Unlike in Plato's philosophy, these instances look exactly like the original.) The instances refer directly to the symbol that spawned them. If you change the characteristics or appearance of the symbol, all the instances in your canvas automatically change, too.

Shop Talk

A **symbol** is a definitive version of a graphic. An instance is the copy of a symbol. The **instance** appears on the canvas, while the symbol resides in the Fireworks library.

The Big Picture

The Greek philosopher Plato lived from roughly 428 to 347 B.C.E. He studied under Socrates in the city of Athens and founded the Academy after Socrates' death. The philosopher Aristotle was Plato's most famous pupil.

That's one advantage to using symbols. Another advantage is that Fireworks can animate them instantly. If you put one instance of a symbol in the top left corner of the canvas and another instance of the same symbol in the bottom right corner, Fireworks can fill in all the steps in between, creating frames automatically for you as it goes.

If all this Platonism and theoretical talk reminds you why you skipped your philosophy seminar in college, fear not. Using symbols will soon be like second nature to you. To prove it, you'll reconstruct *The Robot Is Frustrated* using symbols and instances.

Setting Up the Canvas

Choose File → Open, and load the work file you saved in Chapter 5. This is the one called *robot1.png* or something to that effect.

The first step is to set up the canvas. You'll delete all but the first frame, since Fireworks adds its own frames automatically when you animate with symbols and instances. Now, the first frame contains all the graphics for the animation except the alien life form's line of dialog. This text object doesn't pop up until Frame 17. Since you're going to delete Frames 2 through 33, you'll end up deleting the text object in the process. To save yourself the hassle of recreating it, copy it from Frame 17 and paste it into Frame 1 before you do anything else.

Open the Frames panel, and click Frame 17. This is the frame where the alien life form's line of dialog first appears. Click the text object, and choose Edit → Copy. Now select the first frame in the sequence, go to the Layers panel, select the empty Text Layer, and choose Edit → Paste. Fireworks places the line of dialog into the first frame.

Now you can delete the remaining frames with confidence. Select Frames 2 through 33, and click the trashcan icon at the bottom of the Frames panel. You should now have a single frame in the Frames panel. Choose File → Save As, and specify the file name *robot2.png*. You don't want to risk saving over the original animation that you painstakingly constructed by hand.

Creating Symbols

When you animate with symbols and instances, you create a symbol for every moving image in the animation. Therefore, *The Robot Is Frustrated* will have four symbols: the left-facing robot, the right-facing robot, the alien life form, and the line of dialog.

To create a symbol from a graphic, select the graphic on the canvas. Then, choose Modify → Symbol → Convert To Symbol from the menu. Fireworks moves the image to the symbol library and replaces the graphic on the canvas with an instance of the symbol you just created. I'll step you through the process.

Click the left-facing robot with the Pointer tool. Then, choose Modify → Symbol → Convert To Symbol. The Symbol Properties dialog box appears, as in Figure 6.1.

The first order of business is to supply a name for the symbol. Type **Robot_left** in the field. Then, decide what kind of symbol you want to create. You may be tempted to specify the Animation type, but choose Graphic for now. I'll explain the difference toward the end of this chapter.

Click OK to convert the graphic into a symbol. If you look at the canvas, not much has changed. The left-facing robot appears in its original position, although it has a new, dotted outline and an arrow icon in the lower left corner. This signifies that the left-facing robot is an instance of a symbol. To see the symbol itself, open the Assets panel group, and click the Library tab for the Library panel. There, at the top of the list of library items, is the symbol called Robot_left, the symbol you just created.

Figure 6.1

Use the Symbol Properties dialog box to convert a graphic into a symbol.

Try it again. Select the bitmap image of the right-facing robot in the Layers panel. The right-facing robot is currently hidden, but selecting it in the Layers panel causes it to appear automatically. Choose Modify → Symbol → Convert to Symbol again, and the Symbol Properties dialog box reappears. Type **Robot_right** in the Name field. Specify the Graphic type, and click OK. Fireworks adds the right-facing robot to the symbol library and replaces the bitmap image with an instance of the new symbol.

Animation Advice

If you don't see the Assets panel group or the Library panel on the screen, choose Window → Library.

Now select the image of the alien from the Layers panel. Open the Symbol Properties dialog box, and specify a new graphic symbol called Alien. Finally, click the text object and create a new graphic symbol called Text. After you finish, hide the instances of the text object and the right-facing robot by poking the eyes of the corresponding layers. Your canvas should look like the one in Figure 6.2.

Figure 6.2

After you change the moving graphics into symbols, hide the text object and the right-facing robot by poking the eyes of the corresponding layers.

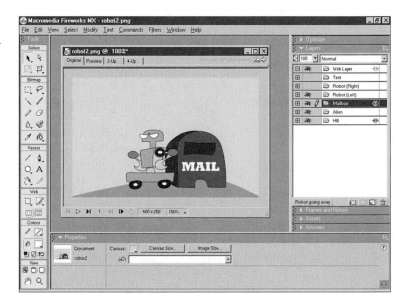

Tweening Instances of Symbols

Animating with symbols and instances involves a process called *tweening*, whereby the computer fills in the steps between a starting position and an ending position. Essentially, what happens is this: You place two instances of a symbol on the canvas. You select them both, and you choose Modify → Symbol → Tween Instances. Fireworks asks you how many in-between steps you would like. You reply with a value. Then Fireworks adds enough frames to your canvas to accommodate the number of steps you specify, generates one new instance of the symbol for each step, and positions these instances so that they fall at regular intervals, creating a nice, smooth, precise line of motion.

To tween instances, then, all you need are two instances. Fireworks does the rest of the work for you.

Shop Talk _____

In Fireworks, **tweening** is the process whereby the computer fills in the intermediary steps between a starting instance and an ending instance.

Consider the left-facing robot. You have one instance of this image on your canvas already. You need another. First, make sure that you select the left-facing robot's layer in the Layers panel. Then go to the Library panel, click the symbol called Robot_left, hold down the mouse button, and drag this symbol onto the canvas. When you release, a carbon copy of the left-facing robot appears.

You'll recall from Chapter 5 that the ending coordinates of the left-facing robot are (10, 124). Select the new instance of the robot, go to the Properties panel, and type **10** in the X field and **124** in the Y field.

Now, simply tween the instances. Select the first instance, hold down the Shift key, and select the second instance, so that both instances have their dotted-line highlights around them. Then choose Modify → Symbol → Tween Instances. The Tween Instances dialog box appears, as in Figure 6.3.

Specify the number of steps in the Steps field. This value equals the number of frames you want minus two for the two instances on the canvas already. Since you want 16 frames total, type **14** in the Steps field (16 − 2 = 14). Make sure also that you check the option for distributing to frames. If you don't check this option, Fireworks adds all the instances to the same frame, in which case you see them all simultaneously. Click OK to proceed.

Cut! _____

Don't forget to subtract two from the number of frames when you fill in the value for the Steps field on the Tween Instances dialog box. If you don't subtract two, Fireworks creates two more frames than you need.

Check the Frames panel. You have 16 frames, all right. And you have nice, smooth robot animation. To prove it, click the Play button at the bottom of the document window. Surely you can appreciate now how animating with symbols and instances saves you time and headaches.

Now try animating the alien. Go back to the first frame, select the existing alien instance, and choose Edit → Cut, since you don't need the alien until Frame 9. Now select Frame 9, click the Alien Layer, which is currently empty, and choose Edit → Paste. You remember from Chapter 5 that the position of the alien life form in Frame 9 is (236, 107), so type **236** in the X field of the Properties panel and **107** in the Y field.

Without changing the frame, go to the Library panel, and drag a new instance of the Alien symbol into the canvas. Set the coordinates of this instance to (236, 58). You should see both aliens on the screen simultaneously. The one is in its starting position, and the other is in its ending position. Select both instances, and choose Modify → Symbol → Tween Instances. This animation takes place over 8 frames, so type **6** in the Steps field (8 – 2 = 6). Make sure that you distribute the instances to frames by checking the option for this, and click OK.

Fireworks doesn't create any new frames this time. It doesn't have to. It simply uses the frames that already exist. Nevertheless, Fireworks tweens like a charm. Hit the Play button to see for yourself.

Frame 17 is the frame where the alien life form's line of dialog appears. You'll recall that this frame has a delay of 50 instead of 6 to create a half-second pause. Create this frame the old-fashioned way: Highlight Frame 16, and drag it to the New/Duplicate Frame button. Change the frame delay manually to 50. Now, switch back to the first frame, and cut the invisible text object using Edit → Cut. Switch to Frame 17, highlight the empty Text Layer, and choose Edit → Paste. Type **212** in the X field of Properties panel and **22** in the Y field. The line of dialog appears where you want it, when you want it.

> **The Big Picture**
>
> The instance that you added to the canvas first is the one that Fireworks uses as the starting point of the motion tween.

Now, set up the canvas for the last half of the animation. Select Frame 17, and drag it to the New/Duplicate Frame button. Change the frame delay back to 6. Delete the instance of the left-facing robot in the new frame, Frame 18, since you don't need it any more. Click the instance, and choose Edit → Clear. Now, cut the instance of the right-facing robot from the first frame and paste it into its layer in Frame 18.

All you have to do now is the tweening. Drag an instance of the Robot_right symbol onto the canvas, and position it at (115, 109). Select both instances, choose Modify → Symbol → Tween Instances, and type **14** in the Steps field, since you want 16 frames total for this last leg of the journey. Click OK.

Select Frame 18 again. This time, drag an instance of the Alien symbol onto the canvas. Position it at (236, 114). Select both instances, open the Tween Instances dialog box, and type **2** in the Steps field (four frames total). Click OK.

Go back to Frame 18 one last time. Drag a new instance of the Text symbol onto the canvas, and position it at (212, –26). Also set the opacity of the new instance to 0%, since you want the dialog to fade out as it moves off the top of the canvas. Select both instances, choose Modify → Symbol → Tween Instances, and type **6** in the Steps field. Click OK.

Animation Advice

Fireworks can tween more than just the level of opacity, including the size of the image and the degree of rotation.

Test the animation by hitting the Play button. Notice that Fireworks tweened the level of opacity as well as the position of the line of dialog.

The only thing left to do is to set the delay of Frame 33 to 56 instead of 6. Test the animation again, and you see that it plays virtually identically to the animation that you crafted by hand, frame by frame, but it took you much less time and effort.

Save your work as *robot2.png*, and get ready to leverage even more symbol power.

Modifying Symbol Properties

Assume now that, after reviewing your new version of *The Robot Is Frustrated*, you decide that the animation would look better if it took place at night, so that you could showcase the alien life form's bioluminescent properties. This amounts to adding a glow effect to the alien graphic.

Adding effects is easy enough. You added a drop shadow to the line of dialog in Chapter 5 in a few simple steps. However, you added the drop shadow to the text object before you started animating. When you duplicated the frames that contained the text object, the drop shadow was already in place. You duplicated the effect every time you duplicated the text object, in other words. Now you want to change the characteristics of a graphic after you've created the animation.

To add a glow effect to the alien in the first version of *The Robot Is Frustrated*, you need to add the glow manually to every frame that shows the alien above the mailbox. If this sounds like a pain to you, you're right. You can do it, but the process is tedious. However, because you animated the second version using symbols and instances, the task becomes almost ridiculously easy. Remember that all the instances of a symbol refer to that symbol, just like all the worldly examples of a mouse pad refer to the Platonic idea of a mouse pad. Change the symbol, and you instantly change all the instances of that symbol. Therefore, as Plato would say, to add a glow effect to all the instances of the alien simultaneously, simply edit the symbol.

> **Cut!**
>
> Make sure you modify the symbol instead of an instance of the symbol. When you modify an instance, only that instance reflects your modifications. When you modify a symbol, all instances of that symbol reflect your modifications.

First, change the background color of the canvas from blue to black, signifying a night sky instead of a sunny day. Choose Modify → Canvas → Canvas Color, click the color square next to the Custom option, and pick black (#000000) from the swatches that come up. Click OK to change the canvas color to black.

Now, edit the Alien symbol. Go to the Library panel, and double-click the symbol called Alien. Fireworks opens a new document window with the symbol inside it.

Select the graphic with the Pointer tool. The Properties panel shows the effects buttons. Click the Plus button, and choose Shadow And Glow → Glow from the context menu. Click the color square in the Effect options to set the color of the glow. I chose a shade of magenta, #FF66FF, but you can choose whatever color you like.

That's all there is to it. Close the symbol's document window, and test the animation. Sure enough, the scene takes place at night and every frame that contains an instance of the alien also features a magenta-colored glow, as in Figure 6.4.

> **Animation Advice**
>
> To break the relationship between an instance and its symbol, select an instance and choose Modify → Symbol → Break Apart. The image remains in the canvas, but it changes into a regular graphic. Now, whenever you edit the symbol, your changes don't affect the disinherited graphic at all. This technique comes in handy when you're modifying an existing animation with many different instances of the same symbol. If you decide that you need to edit the symbol definition for most but not all of the instances, break apart the instances that you don't want to edit. If you prefer, you can create a new symbol for the broken-apart images.

Figure 6.4

By adding a glow effect to the symbol of the alien, every instance of the alien in the animation acquires the glow effect.

Now that the canvas is black, you no longer need the drop shadow on the text. You can get rid of this effect as easily as you added the glow. Double-click the Text symbol in the Library panel. In the document window that opens, select the text object, highlight the drop-shadow effect on the Properties panel, and click the Minus button to remove the effect. The symbol loses its drop shadow, and, by necessity, so do all the instances of the symbol in the animation.

By adding a few new instances of the alien and tweening them, you can compound the robot's frustration threefold, as Figure 6.5 shows.

Figure 6.5

To include more aliens in the animation, simply drag new instances of the Alien symbol to the canvas and tween them.

Maybe the robot needs some help. Add some new robot instances and tween them to give the robot a friend, as in Figure 6.6.

Figure 6.6

By adding new instances of the Robot symbols and tweening them, you can frustrate as many robots as you like.

After you finish playing around with tweening instances, save your work as *robot3.png*.

Creating Animation Symbols

Fireworks gives you another way to animate with symbols and instances other than tweening. You can use *animation symbols*, or symbols whose instances have animation built into them. When you work with animation symbols, you don't need to drag two instances into the canvas and then tween them. Simply drag one instance into the canvas and then specify how Fireworks should animate it by way of the Animate dialog box.

Shop Talk

An **animation symbol** is a symbol whose instances have built-in animation. Therefore, you don't have to tween instances of animation symbols.

Here's an example. Pop the CD-ROM from this book into your computer, and choose File → Open from the Fireworks menu. Navigate to the Chapter 6 folder on the CD-ROM, and load the image *saucer.png*. This is a very small flying saucer graphic that you may also recognize from my earlier book, *The Complete Idiot's Guide to Computer Illustration* (Alpha Books, 2002).

Choose the first frame in the main animation canvas. Then select the Text Layer, and click the New/Duplicate Layer button. Call this layer Saucer. Copy the saucer graphic from *saucer.png*, and paste in into the new layer. Position the saucer in the top left of the canvas (see Figure 6.7).

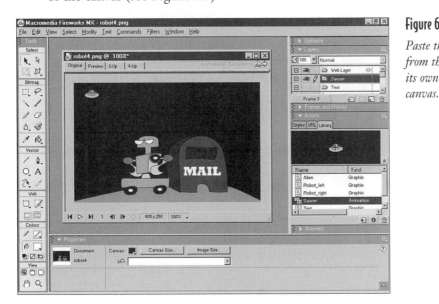

Figure 6.7

Paste the saucer graphic from the CD-ROM into its own layer in the main canvas.

Now, convert the saucer image into an animation symbol. Select the saucer, and choose Modify → Symbol → Convert to Symbol, just like you did earlier. Call the symbol Saucer. Set the type to Animation instead of Graphic, and click OK. The Animate dialog box appears, as in Figure 6.8.

Use the Animate dialog box to explain to Fireworks how you want this instance of the animation symbol to behave. Assume that you want the saucer to fly off the right side of the canvas over the course of 16 frames.

In the Frames field, specify how many frames of the canvas the animation should occupy. Since you want the saucer animation to last 16 frames, type **16** in the Frames field.

> ### The Big Picture
>
> Fifty percent of Americans believe that UFOs are spaceships from alien worlds. Seventy-one percent of Americans believe that the United States government hasn't revealed all it knows about the phenomenon.

Figure 6.8

Use the Animate dialog box to build animation into a symbol.

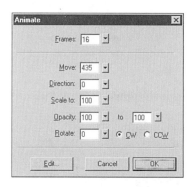

The canvas is 400 pixels wide, while the saucer itself is 30 pixels wide. Since you want the saucer to move off the right side of the canvas, type **430** in the Move field—that's 400 pixels for the width of the canvas plus 30 pixels for the width of the saucer. This way, the saucer disappears off the edge of the canvas instead of mysteriously vanishing.

Now click the button to the right of the Direction field. A dial control pops up. Use the dial to determine the direction of the motion. Since you want the saucer to move from left to right, the current direction value, 0, is correct. If you wanted to move the saucer from right to left, you'd turn the dial so that the indentation faces the right. The corresponding value is 180. But leave 0 in the Direction field for left-to-right motion.

Notice also that you can scale the image, change the opacity of the image, and rotate it either clockwise or counter-clockwise. You don't want to do anything of the sort with the saucer, but keep these options in mind for future animations.

Click OK, and Fireworks animates the instance of the symbol as you specified. Press the Play button at the bottom of the document window to see for yourself. You didn't have to tween two instances of the symbol. Instead, you built the animation into the instance itself.

Animation Advice

You can change a normal graphic into an animation symbol by clicking the graphic and choosing Modify → Animation → Animate Selection.

All of this is fine, but notice that the saucer seems to mysteriously appear on the left side of the canvas when the animation loops. It would be better if the saucer started outside the boundaries of the canvas. This way, your audience won't see the saucer resetting itself when the animation loops. Since you used an animation symbol to create this motion, editing the starting position of the saucer is easy.

Go to the first frame of the animation, and select the saucer instance. A motion line appears, showing the direction and location of the saucer in each frame (see Figure 6.9). The start point shows in green, and the end point shows in red. To change the starting position, drag the green point off the left side of the canvas. Notice how the motion line redistributes the positions of the saucers so that they fall evenly along it. You can change the end position, too, by dragging the red point.

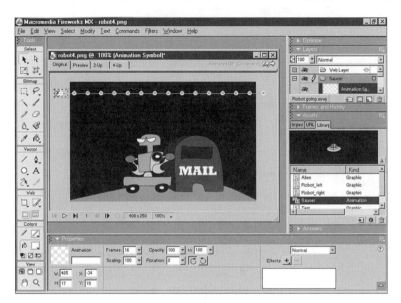

Figure 6.9

When you select an instance of an animation symbol, Fireworks shows you the direction and location of the instance in each frame of the animation.

If you want to change the number of frames in the saucer animation or tweak the behavior, look no further than the Properties panel. Just for fun, type **130** into the Rotation field, and click the Rotate Counter-Clockwise button, which is the button on the right next to the Rotation field. Now, when you play back the animation, it looks as if the gyroscope on the saucer is out of whack (see Figure 6.10).

Assume now that you want to add another flying saucer to the canvas, this one first appearing in Frame 4. Select Frame 4, click the empty Saucer Layer, and drag a new instance of the Saucer animation symbol onto the canvas. Position the instance wherever you like. Then, to build animation into it, select it, and go to the Properties panel. Choose the number of frames for the animation, and define the behavior of the instance as you prefer. Set the starting position and ending position of the motion

> **The Big Picture**
>
> An American newspaper reporter coined the term flying saucer in 1947. The term comes from the eyewitness description of Idaho businessman Kenneth Arnold, who saw something in the sky that looked like pie plates skipping over water.

by dragging the green and red points of the motion line. Test your animation by clicking the Play button.

Figure 6.10

Add some rotation to the saucer, and it appears to spin out of control as it shoots across the canvas.

As you can see, the two instances of the Saucer symbol don't need to have the same behaviors. Each instance can have its own particular flight path and special effects.

Choose File → Save, and save this version of *The Robot Is Frustrated* as *robot4.png*.

The Least You Need to Know

◆ Change a graphic into a symbol by selecting the graphic and choosing Modify → Symbol → Convert To Symbol.

◆ To create an instance of a symbol, drag the symbol from the Library panel to the canvas.

◆ When you tween two instances of a symbol, Fireworks fills in the in-between steps automatically.

◆ Fireworks can tween certain properties of instances, like transparency and degree of rotation.

◆ Use animation symbols instead of graphic symbols to create animation without tweening.

◆ Every instance of an animation symbol can have its own set of animation instructions.

Chapter 7

Exporting the Animation

In This Chapter

- ◆ Optimizing the GIF file
- ◆ Editing the palette
- ◆ Exporting embedded animations
- ◆ Exporting Flash animation from Fireworks

When you're working on web animation, you should never underestimate the importance of achieving the smallest possible file size. A smaller file takes less time to download, which is always a bonus for your time-critical, speed-obsessed viewing audience.

This chapter shows you how to optimize your animated GIF file for the smallest possible size and publish your animation in various forms.

Optimizing the Animation

You know from exporting *Bouncing Red Ball* that, when you're ready to create an animated GIF file, your first stop is the Optimize panel (see Figure 7.1). You'll recall from Chapter 4 that I told you to choose the Animated GIF setting in the Export File Format list, which is the dropdown list to the left of the Matte color square on this panel. Afterwards, you chose File → Export from the menu, and redball.gif came into being.

Figure 7.1

Use the Optimize panel to streamline the file size of your animation.

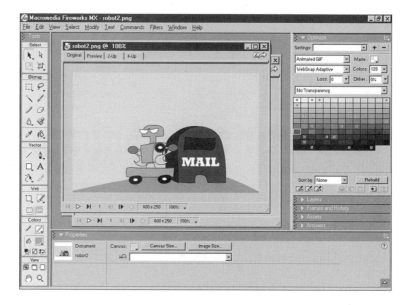

If you suspect that there's more to the Optimize panel than I let on earlier, you're absolutely correct. At the time, I didn't want to bog you down with the details. But now that you have a number of animated GIFs to your credit, a closer look at the Optimize panel is in order. In a nutshell, the Optimize panel allows you to change the characteristics of the file that you export, which helps you to achieve the best possible image quality with the smallest possible file size.

To test out the Optimize panel, choose File → Open from the menu, and load the three versions of *The Robot Is Frustrated* that you created in Chapter 6. These are *robot2.png*, *robot3.png*, and *robot4.png*. Start with *robot2.png*. Maximize the document window for this file so that your screen looks like Figure 7.2.

Animation Advice

In 2-Up and 4-Up view, you can set any of the panes to show the original view by choosing Original from the dropdown list directly under the canvas.

If you look at the top of the document window, you find four tabs: Original, Preview, 2-Up, and 4-Up. These tabs control the view of the canvas. So far, you've used Original view. This is the view for adding art to the canvas and building the animation. The Preview view shows what the animation looks like given the optimization settings you pick from the Optimize panel. The 2-Up and 4-Up views allow you to compare multiple optimization settings side by side.

Figure 7.2

Maximize the document window for robot2.png.

Click the Preview tab. Fireworks takes a moment to generate the preview of the animated GIF. When the image returns to the canvas, you see what the exported file will look like. Chances are, you don't see much difference between the Original and Preview versions of the canvas.

Preview view also tells you in the upper right corner of the document window the file size of the exported animated GIF. As you can see in Figure 7.3, my *robot2.png* weighs in at about 112K. Yours is probably close if not exactly the same. According to Fireworks, this file will take 17 seconds to download over a 56K modem connection. Seventeen seconds is a bit long to ask your audience to wait, especially for such a goofy animation. By adjusting the options in the Optimize panel, though, you can reduce the file size of the animated GIF and therefore also cut down on the download time.

Before you start pulling values from drop-down lists, I should mention a few things about the GIF file format. It's a raster format, as you already know, which means that it's made up of pixels. A GIF file also has a built-in palette of colors. Every pixel in the GIF uses a color from this palette. The more colors in the *palette*, the larger the overall file size of the GIF. The Optimize palette shows you the palette for the current file, as you can see in Figure 7.4.

Shop Talk

A **palette** is the built-in set of colors in certain graphics file formats, including GIFs. The computer uses these colors when displaying the image. The maximum number of colors in a GIF's palette is 256. Not all graphics formats have their own palettes. The JPEG format, for instance, doesn't use one.

Figure 7.3

Click the Preview tab in the document window to see what the exported animated GIF will look like.

Figure 7.4

The palette in the Optimize panel shows you the set of colors that your animated GIF uses.

The maximum number of colors in the palette is 256. You can usually get away with fewer colors. As it stands right now, *robot2.png* uses 128 colors. You can tell because the value in the Colors list on the Optimize panel is 128. Switch the number of colors in the palette to 64 by pulling this value from the Colors list. Fireworks optimizes your animation according to this setting, and, in a moment, the document window in Preview mode displays the new end product.

The image looks very much the same. Press the Play button, and watch the sequence a few times. It's hard to tell much of a difference at all. But note that the overall file size is smaller. Mine dropped from approximately 112K to about 99K—a 13K difference. That's not bad for no perceptible loss of image quality. Still, it could be better. My download time has dropped to only 15 seconds from the previous 17 seconds. You are probably experiencing similar results.

Try reducing the number of colors from 64 to 32. My animated GIF drops another 13K to 86K or so, with a download time of 13 seconds. The robot and the mailbox still look the same, although when you preview the part with the alien, you notice that it isn't quite as colorful as it is in Original view. To refresh your memory, click the Original tab. Better yet, click the 2-Up tab to see Original view and Preview view on the same screen, as in Figure 7.5.

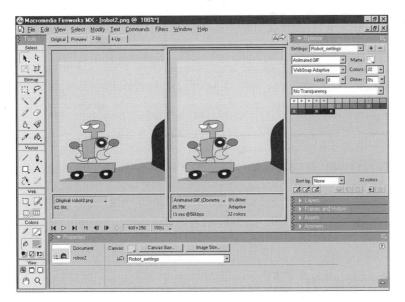

Figure 7.5

Use 2-Up view to compare the original robot2.png *with a 32-color animated GIF.*

Click the right half of the document window to select the preview side. Now, reduce the number of colors from 32 to 16. The image size drops to 73K with an 11-second download time, but the alien is really beginning to take a visual beating. The robot is also beginning to show signs of wear. This particular animation can't survive with a palette of only 16 colors. Remember, your viewers demand small file sizes, but they also demand image quality. They would rather wait 13 seconds to watch a clear animation than wait 11 seconds to watch a grainy, over-optimized one. Wouldn't you?

Thirty-two colors is the winner. Set the Color list back to 32 to confirm your choice. Your final file size is in the neighborhood of 86K with a 13-second download time over a 56K modem. I'll admit this could be better. I come from a web design background, so give me a file size over 40 or 50K and I start to flinch. But when you figure in that this animated GIF requires 33 frames, 86K isn't a bad number at all. That's only about 2.5K per frame. Plus, Fireworks saved a total of 26K and shaved 4 seconds off the download time without appreciably affecting the end result. I can live with the trade-off.

Just for a kick, try reducing the number of colors to four or two.

Exporting a Standalone Graphic

When you finish horsing around with the palette, set the Colors list to 32, and export the animated GIF file. You've done this part at least once already. Choose File → Export, navigate to a convenient spot on your hard drive, and set the Save As Type list to Images Only. Click the Save button, and Fireworks exports the animated GIF file to the specified location.

Call this procedure exporting a standalone graphic. Why standalone? Because the only thing that Fireworks creates is the animated GIF file. Granted, the animated GIF file is all you need. This is the file that you can post on the web or attach to the signature of your e-mails. As you'll see in the next section, by picking a different option from the Save As Type list, you can export the animation with a ready-made web-page file for playback in a browser.

Embedding the Animated GIF

An animated GIF is *embedded* when it appears in a web-page file. You open the web page in a browser, and the embedded animated GIF appears on the page. Fireworks can export the animated GIF along with its own web page.

If you already have a web page, you don't need to use this feature. You'll probably want to embed your animated GIF into the page manually with a tool like Macromedia Dreamweaver, Adobe GoLive, or Microsoft FrontPage. However, if you don't already have a web page, you can take Fireworks up on its generous offer to create one for you.

The page that Fireworks creates isn't spectacular. It's completely blank, except for the animated GIF, which appears in the upper left corner. The color of the page is the same as the canvas color of your animation. Even if the page won't win any best-of-web awards for its design, the page functions as it should. Embedding the animated GIF allows you to view the animation in your favorite graphics-enabled browser instead of Fireworks.

Try creating an embedded file for one of your robot animations. Close the document window for *robot2.png*, and maximize the one for *robot3.png*.

The first order of business is to click the Preview tab and go to the Optimize panel for some color reduction. Thirty-two colors seemed to be the best choice for the previous version of *The Robot Is Frustrated*, so that makes a logical place to start for the current version. Adjust the Color list to 32, and wait a few seconds for Fireworks to optimize the file.

The results aren't bad, as I'm sure you'll agree. My file went from 102K in 128-color mode to about 77K in 32-color mode and dropped from 16 seconds download time to 12 seconds. Notice, though, that the glow around the alien is just starting to *band*, or appear in discrete areas of color. A glow uses a number of very similar colors to produce its effect. Because there are so many colors in such close proximity, your eye can't pick out the individual shades. It stands to reason that, when you reduce the number of colors in the palette, Fireworks has fewer colors to create the effect, and the result is as you see—discrete, discernable bands of color.

Still, the banding at the 32-color level in this animation is acceptable. Take the palette down to 16 colors, and you can really start to see a difference, as Figure 7.6 shows. Even if the discolored alien doesn't bother you, the banding on the glow ruins the effect. You'd be better off with no glow at all.

> ## The Big Picture
>
> If you know basic HTML, you can write your own web page to embed the animated GIF. You don't have to use the page that Fireworks generates.

> ## Shop Talk
>
> **Banding** happens when color effects like shadows or glows become too colorcompressed, and distinct layers of color appear in the image. Use **dithering** to reduce banding. Dithering is a technique that increases the number of virtual colors in the GIF.

Figure 7.6

Watch out for banding if you over-optimize an animation with a color effect like a glow.

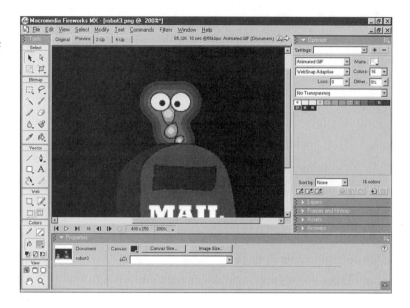

While you have the GIF at 16 colors, let me show you a trick to soften some of the banding. This trick is called *dithering*. Dithering takes advantage of the small size of the average pixel. Because pixels are so tiny, your eye has difficulty seeing them individually. Put a red pixel next to a blue pixel, and your eye tends to see a single spot of purple instead of separate red and blue components. This, in essence, is dithering. By dithering your image, you can achieve dozens of virtual, phony colors from a small palette of actual ones.

To see what I mean, drag the slider next to the Dither field all the way to 100. Wait a few moments as Fireworks processes the image. When it finishes, note that the banding softens, as in Figure 7.7. The glow becomes more like light again, at the expense of some download time, since dithering increases the size of the file, sometimes drastically so. My version of *robot3.png* jumped from 65K at 0% dithering to 72K at 100% dithering—not what I would call a drastic change, but a significant one nonetheless. I picked up an extra second of download time.

Switch the Color list back to 32 while the dithering is still at 100%. Then, drag the dithering value back to 0. I don't notice much of a difference between the two extremes, so I'll keep my setting at 0. If you prefer the dithered look, then, by all means, specify a dithering value.

Thirty-two colors must be the magic number for *The Robot Is Frustrated*. Since it appears that you'll be using this setting frequently, you can save it as a preset. Go to the top of the Optimize panel, and click the Plus button next to the Settings list. The Preset Name dialog box comes up, as in Figure 7.8. Type Robot settings or something to that effect in the Name field, and click OK. Fireworks creates a new setting and adds it to the current list of defaults. When you want to apply this setting, which includes a 32-color palette and perhaps a dithering value depending on your tastes, all you have to do is pull the preset from the Settings list. No more dragging sliders around. To remove a setting, select it from the list and click the Minus button.

Figure 7.7

When you have color effects like glows, dithering helps to improve the image quality at the expense of some download time.

Figure 7.8

Save frequently used optimization settings as a preset with the Preset Name dialog box.

Now that you have optimized the image, you can export it. Choose File → Export, and the Export dialog box appears as it always does. This time, instead of Images Only, choose HTML and Images from the Save As Type list. *HTML* stands for hypertext markup language. It's a computer language that contains instructions for presenting a web page. You don't see this code per se when you view a web page in your favorite browser, but you see the code's results. Web browsers translate the HTML code into visual pages.

Animation Advice

Create presets for frequently used optimization settings.

For some reason, whenever I mention the words "computer language" to designers and graphics people, I wind up clearing the room in a hurry. Hopefully you haven't just closed this book or skipped ahead to the next chapter. Most right-brained creative types find little enjoyment in the left-brained pleasures of writing computer code. Fortunately, the good people at Macromedia understand this, and Fireworks actually writes the HTML code for you when you choose the HTML And Images option from the Save As Type list.

Shop Talk

HTML (hypertext markup language) is computer code for displaying web pages.

Navigate to a convenient spot on your hard drive as before, and click the Save button. Fireworks creates two files this time: an animated GIF called *robot3.gif* and a web-page file called *robot3.htm*. This *robot3.gif* is the same as a standalone file of the same name. If you had selected Images Only from the Save As Type list, the *robot3.gif* that Fireworks would have created would be the same as this one. There's no advantage to creating an embedded file, at least as far as the file itself is concerned.

The advantage to you is more a practical one. You now have the pleasure of viewing your animation in a live setting, as it were. Minimize Fireworks for a moment, and use your computer's operating system to navigate to the place that you exported the embedded file. Double-click the *robot3.htm* file, the one with the web-page icon, not the graphics-file icon. Your system's default web browser opens, and your animation appears against a black background (see Figure 7.9). Why black? Because that's the canvas color of the image.

Figure 7.9

Double-click the HTML file to view the embedded animation in your default web browser.

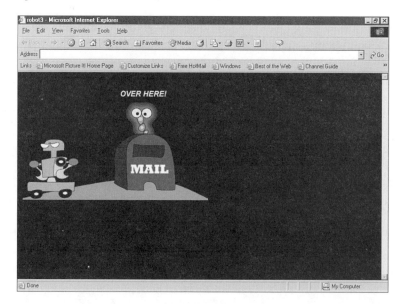

Go to your browser's menu and choose View → Source (Internet Explorer) or View → Page Source (Netscape). This calls up the HTML code that Fireworks created. As you can see, the code is very short and to the point. The embedded animation comes in on the second-to-last line:

```
<img name="robot3" src="robot3.gif" width="400" height="250" border="0" alt="">
```

Essentially, this tells the browser to place an image file called *robot3.gif* on the page; *robot3.gif*, of course, is the animated GIF that Fireworks exported with the HTML file. The width of the image is 400 pixels, and the height is 250 pixels. You should recognize these numbers. They're the same ones that you typed in Chapter 5 when you created the canvas for the very first version of *The Robot Is Frustrated*. The image tag is only one of many in the rich vocabulary of HTML. To see a number of different tags in action, point your browser to just about any web page and view the source. Try to associate the image tags in the code listing with the graphics that appear in the browser window.

If you want to include your animation in your e-mail signature, don't bother with the HTML file. The standalone *robot3.gif* works just fine. Use the HTML file for your personal viewing pleasure. If you want to post your animation on the web, use the embedded version. Be sure to upload both the animated GIF and the HTML file to the same folder on your website for the HTML file to work properly.

> **The Big Picture**
>
> HTML elements that appear inside angle brackets (<, >) are called tags. A tag's attributes determine the characteristics of the HTML element, such as width="400" and height="250."

Exporting a Flash Animation

Fireworks doesn't just export animated GIFs. It can also export SWF files. Try exporting *robot4.png* in Flash format instead of as an animated GIF.

First, close the document window for *robot3.png*, and maximize the window for *robot4.png*. Pull the preset optimization scheme from the Settings list on the Optimize panel. This animation has a few more colors than the previous version, thanks to the addition of the flying saucer in the first half. Those few extra colors seem to make the banding more prevalent around the alien's glow effect. I recommend dithering here to help soften up the edges. Drag the Dithering slider to 100 if your preset Robot scheme doesn't already have this value.

The image is optimized. Choose File → Export from the menu, and pull Macromedia Flash SWF from the Save As Type menu. Before you click Save, click the Options button. This calls up the Macromedia Flash SWF Export Options dialog box, as in Figure 7.10.

Figure 7.10

Choose your preferences for the Flash file in the Macromedia Flash SWF Export Options dialog box.

Once again, it comes down to appearance versus file size. Choose the Maintain Paths and Maintain Editability options if you want a smaller file that tends to lose some image quality. (This type of file is also easier to edit in Macromedia Flash MX.) Choose the Maintain Appearance and Convert To Paths options for a larger, better-looking, more unwieldy file. For demonstration purposes, choose the second set of options.

Animation Advice

It usually makes more sense to export a SWF file from Macromedia Flash MX instead of Macromedia Fireworks MX, since the Fireworks version is usually larger in terms of file size.

Under Frames, select whether you want Fireworks to turn all the frames into a Flash file or just a range of consecutive frames. Choose the All option for now.

In the Frame Rate dialog box, set the playback to 12 frames per second. This is slower than the 16 frames per second that you used for animated GIFs, but 12 frames per second is the Flash default playback speed. Flash also tends to keep better time, so 16 frames per second in Flash seems to move much faster than 16 frames per second in an animated GIF.

Click OK to close the dialog box. Navigate to a convenient spot on your hard drive, and click Save to export the SWF using the options you specified.

The deed is done. Minimize Fireworks, navigate to the place that you just saved the SWF file, and double-click the file. The movie opens in a Flash Player window. It looks fine, but get a load of that file size—mine is 378K! That's far too large for such a ridiculous movie.

Go back to Fireworks now, and choose File → Export again. Pull Macromedia Flash SWF from the Save As Type list. Click the Options button as before. This time, choose Maintain Paths and Maintain Editability to create a smaller file, and click OK. Type **robot5.swf** in the File Name field so that you don't overwrite the existing *robot4.swf*, and click Save.

Ouch! The file size is still tremendous. I get 371K. Compared to the original 378K, that's not much of a difference. Play *robot5.swf*, and the image quality seems comparable to *robot4.swf*. At least you lucked out in that regard.

The point of this exercise is, while you can use Fireworks to create SWF files, and while it's undeniably cool that Fireworks gives you this feature, it may not always be smart to create Flash animation this way. I promise that you can—and will—improve dramatically on that 378K file size by constructing the animation from scratch in Flash MX. In fact, your Flash-compiled SWF file will improve on the 70–80K size of the animated GIFs. All this and more happens in Part 3.

Cut!

Chances are, you have the Flash Player Plug-In installed on your system. But if you don't, go to www.macromedia.com and download the plug-in before you attempt to play the SWF file. Otherwise, you won't see the animation.

The Least You Need to Know

◆ Use the Optimize panel to set the properties of your animated GIF.

◆ Click the Preview tab at the top of the document window to see what the exported GIF will look like.

◆ Reduce the number of colors in the palette to decrease the GIF's file size.

◆ Use dithering to increase the number of virtual colors in your animated GIF's palette.

◆ When you export an embedded animation, Fireworks creates a standalone graphic plus an HTML file.

◆ You can export a Flash file from Fireworks, although this file is generally too large for practical use on the web.

Part 3

Creating Flash Movies

Animated GIFs are fine for what they are, but there's only so much you can do with them. It's time now to see where web animation can take you. This part shows you how to use Macromedia Flash MX to create the kinds of movies that you want to see.

Introducing Flash

In This Chapter

◆ Examining the interface of Flash MX

◆ Creating a stage

◆ Using the drawing and editing tools

◆ Grouping Flash graphics

So far, you've looked at one form of web animation: the animated GIF. While Fireworks allows you to do more with animated GIFs than you may have been expecting, the file sizes of those last few *The Robot Is Frustrated* examples tended to be pretty large. Perhaps a different kind of web animation—perhaps Flash—can improve on file size.

Before you get down to business, though, it's a good idea to take the software for a test drive. This chapter helps to get you comfortable with the Flash environment and invites you to test out Flash's drawing and editing capabilities.

Exploring the Interface

Install the trial version of Macromedia Flash MX from the CD-ROM that comes with this book. It includes the Flash MX development environment, which is where you build your SWF animation, and an assortment of Flash Player 6 plug-ins for the web browsers on your system. The Flash Player is the software you use to play back your work. Remember, you don't develop anything with the Flash Player. When I talk about Flash from this point on, you can assume that I'm speaking about the development environment, Flash MX.

Run the software after you install it. After a brief title card, the Flash MX workspace appears, as in Figure 8.1.

Figure 8.1

Does the Flash MX work-space remind you of Fireworks MX? The MX line of software from Macromedia shares a common interface design.

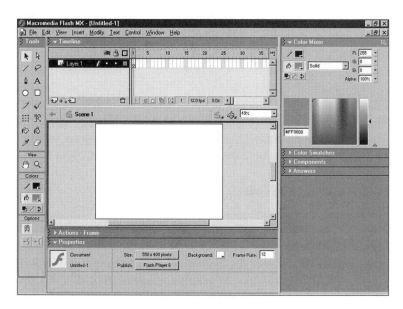

You've seen a similar interface in Fireworks MX. The screen is divided into panels, like before, which are expandable and collapsible. Click the triangle icon to expand or collapse a panel.

Like before, there's a Tools panel on the left side of the screen with icons that represent common drawing and editing commands. The Flash Tools panel doesn't have any hidden toolsets like the Fireworks Tools panel has. Hence, none of the tool icons on the Flash Tools panel have black triangles in the lower right corner. Notice also that there are comparatively fewer tools in Flash than there are in Fireworks.

Like before, there's a Properties panel across the bottom of the screen. The Properties panel in Flash allows you to edit the characteristics of the currently selected item. It's a good idea to keep the Properties panel expanded at all times.

The *stage* takes up a good chunk of real estate in the center of the screen. The stage in Flash equates to the canvas in Fireworks. It's where you draw art and create animation.

Directly above the stage is the *Timeline panel*, the heart of Flash. The numbers across the top of the Timeline panel represent the frames of the movie. Like Fireworks, Flash breaks down your animation into a series of frames. The sequence plays back at a certain number of frames per second, 12 by default. However, each frame in a Flash movie isn't necessarily a separate image file like each frame of an animated GIF. The Flash format is more streamlined than an animated GIF. The total number of frames in a Flash movie isn't as important to the overall size of the SWF file, unlike in Fireworks, where the total number of frames is directly proportional to the final file size of the animated GIF.

Shop Talk

The **stage** is the area on which you build your Flash movie. It's the equivalent of the canvas in Fireworks. The **Timeline panel,** or the timeline for short, keeps track of the order of events in your movie. The numbered columns of the Timeline panel represent frames.

Setting Up the Stage

Even though Flash is a vector-based environment, Flash measures the size of the stage in pixels. Computer graphics people tend to visualize distances in pixels better than inches or centimeters. Keep in mind that there aren't really any pixels in the stage itself. If there were, though, Flash's default stage would be 550 pixels wide by 400 pixels high.

Before you begin a Flash project, it's smart to set the size of the stage to match the aspect ratio of the final animation. The aspect ratio is the width of the movie divided by the height. For instance, assume that you want to create a Flash movie that sits in a 300-by-200 area of your home page. This movie has an aspect ratio of 1.5, since $300 \div 200 = 1.5$. To maintain this aspect ratio, you could set the size of the stage to 300 pixels by 200 pixels, the exact dimensions of the finished movie. You could also set the size of the stage to 600 pixels by 400 pixels, 150 pixels by 100 pixels, or 1,200 pixels by 800 pixels and still maintain the aspect ratio of 1.5.

How can you get away with flexible sizing like this? The answer lies in the vector nature of Flash. You'll recall from Chapter 1 that vector graphics scale, or change size, without loss of image quality. The stage and the movie that plays on it have the same size-changing properties. If you prefer to work on a large stage and export the movie in a smaller format, you can do so easily. Just maintain the same aspect ratio.

To set the size of the stage, choose the Arrow tool from the Tools panel. The Arrow tool is the tool in the upper left corner. It looks just like the Pointer tool from Fireworks. Its icon is the black arrow. (Don't click the Subselection tool, the white arrow, by mistake. This is a different tool with a different function.) Move the mouse pointer onto a blank area of the stage, and click. The Properties panel at the bottom of the screen shows the current properties of the stage, as in Figure 8.2.

Figure 8.2

Click a blank area of the stage with the Arrow tool, and the Properties panel shows options for modifying the stage.

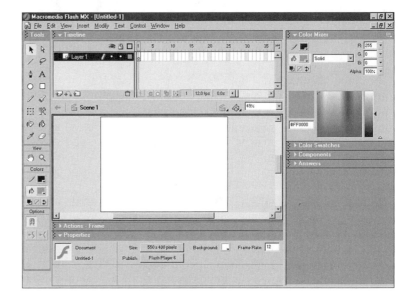

Click the Size button on the Properties panel to call up the Document Properties dialog box (shown in Figure 8.3). Type values in the Width and Height fields to change the dimensions of the stage. To change the dimensions to match the size of a printed page, click the Printer button. To crop the stage to fit the art on it, click the Contents button. Clicking the Contents button does nothing right now, since you don't have any content on the stage. To return the stage to its default setting of 550 pixels by 400 pixels, click the Default button. Click OK to register the changes, and the Document Properties dialog box closes.

Figure 8.3

Change the size of the stage and other movie properties with the Document Properties dialog box.

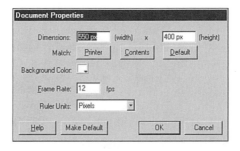

The Properties panel has a color square for the background color of the stage. White is the default background color. To change the color, click the color square, and a window of color swatches pops up, just like in Fireworks. Click the swatch of the color that you want, and the stage changes accordingly.

You can also set the frame rate for the movie from the Properties panel. The default frame rate is 12 frames per second. You probably remember this number from Chapter 7 when you created a SWF file from Fireworks. I recommend that you use the default frame rate for most purposes. Twelve frames per second gives you decent playback over the web.

Animation Advice

To adjust your view of the stage, use the Zoom tool on the Tools panel. The Zoom tool's icon looks like a magnifying glass. Look under the Options section of the Tools panel to set the action of the Zoom tool. Click the first icon, the one with the plus, to zoom in. Click the second icon, the one with the minus, to zoom out. Then, position the Zoom tool on the stage, and click.

Using the Drawing Tools

Flash's drawing tools work much like the drawing tools in Fireworks. Grab the Oval tool from the Tools panel, move the mouse pointer onto the stage, hold down the mouse button, and drag the shape. If you press Shift while you draw, you constrain the shape to a perfect circle. Otherwise, you can draw ellipses of various sizes. Release the mouse button to finish. The Oval tool, by the way, is the tool whose icon looks like a white circle.

You just added a vector shape to the stage. Remember, Flash's drawing tools are vector based. As in Fireworks, the shape has a stroke and a fill. The stroke is the outline or contour of the shape, and the fill is the interior region. However, unlike in Fireworks, the stroke and the fill are entirely separate elements. To see what I mean, grab the Arrow tool—the black arrow, not the white—and click inside of the shape you just drew. Hold down the mouse button, and drag the fill outside the stroke. Release the mouse button, and you find that you now have two shapes: one that's a bare stroke without a fill, and another that's a bare fill without a stroke, as in Figure 8.4.

Animation Advice

Use the Subselection tool—the white arrow—to move the stroke and the fill of a shape simultaneously. Click anywhere along the stroke of a shape with the Subselection tool to select the shape. Then, hold down the mouse button, and drag the stroke and fill together to a new location on the stage. Release the mouse button to finish.

Figure 8.4

In Flash, the fill and the stroke of a shape are separate elements. Therefore, you can drag the fill away from the stroke with the Arrow tool.

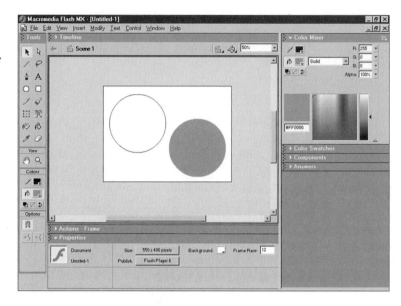

Here's another important difference. Drag the fill so that it partially superimposes its old stroke, as in Figure 8.5. Click on a blank area of the stage to deselect the fill. Now, select the fill again, and drag it away. Notice that the fill has erased the region of the stroke where the two shapes overlapped, as in Figure 8.6.

Figure 8.5

Drag the fill so that it partially superimposes the stroke, and deselect the fill by clicking on an empty area of the stage.

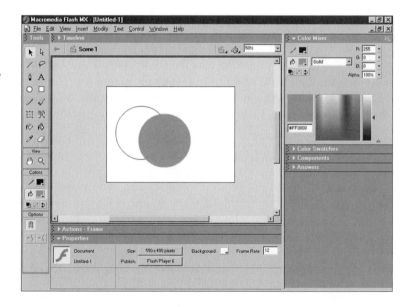

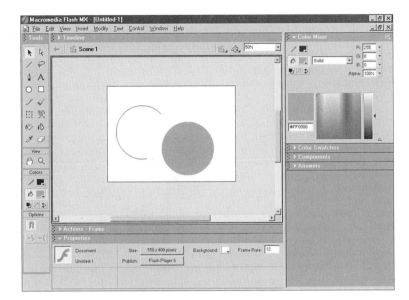

Figure 8.6

When you move the fill away again, you find that it has erased the segment of the stroke that it covered up.

For most graphics people, this takes a bit of getting used to. The shapes in Flash don't behave like they do in other drawing programs. To circumvent the potential problems that separate fills and strokes create, change the fill-and-stroke combination into a *group*, or combined element.

First, clear the stage. Take the Arrow tool, and, starting in the upper left corner of the stage, drag a rectangular marquee or selection region around the stroke fragment and the fill. Release the mouse button. Everything on the stage should now be selected. Press the Delete key or choose Edit → Clear from the menu to erase the selected items.

Now, grab a drawing tool. You used the Oval tool already, so now give the Rectangle tool a try. The Rectangle tool is the one with the white square icon. It sits to the right of the Oval tool. Click the Rectangle tool in the Tools panel, come onto the stage with the mouse pointer, and drag the shape. Release the mouse button to finish. You have a shape with a separate stroke and fill, just like before. Now, take the Arrow tool again, and drag a marquee around the entire shape to select both the stroke and fill. Go to the menu, and choose Modify → Group. Flash combines the stroke and fill into a single package, if you will. You can move the group around the stage without inadvertently separating the stroke and the fill.

Shop Talk

A **group** in Flash is a collection of vector graphics that behaves like a single unit. You must group the stroke of a graphic to its fill to manipulate the two as a single object.

Animation Advice _____

Here's a rule of thumb for you. If you want the shapes in Flash to behave like shapes in other drawing programs, always group the stroke and fill before doing anything else. If you want the shapes to behave like Flash shapes, with removable fills and overlapping erasures, don't group the stroke and fill.

Moreover, you can superimpose the group over another group without erasing the overlapping area. Give it a try. Grab the Oval tool again, and draw a new shape. Drag a marquee around the stroke and fill of the new shape, and choose Modify → Group. Superimpose the new shape over the old, deselect by clicking a blank area of the stage, and then select the new shape again and move it away. The rectangle group remains intact.

Choosing Stroke and Fill Colors

Because Flash shapes behave unusually, it's a good idea to set the stroke and fill colors of the shape before you draw. Choose the Rectangle tool again, and, before you drag the shape, go to the Properties panel. As Figure 8.7 shows, you find two color squares: one with a pencil icon and another with a paint-bucket icon. The color square next to the pencil icon represents the stroke color. Click this square to set the color of the stroke. You can also change the *weight* or thickness of the stroke by typing a value in the field to the right of the stroke's color square or clicking the arrow button and dragging the slider that pops up. Set the style of the stroke with the dropdown list on the right. Flash gives you options for solid, dashed, dotted, and rough strokes, among others.

Shop Talk _____
The **weight** of a stroke is its thickness.

The color square next to the paint-bucket icon represents the fill color. Click this color square to set the fill.

Some drawing tools like the Rectangle tool have additional options. Find icons for these at the bottom of the Tools panel, as in Figure 8.8. In the case of the Rectangle, there's one new icon in the Options section of the Tools panel. Click this icon to open the Rectangle Settings dialog box (see Figure 8.9), with which you can set the roundness of the rectangle's corners.

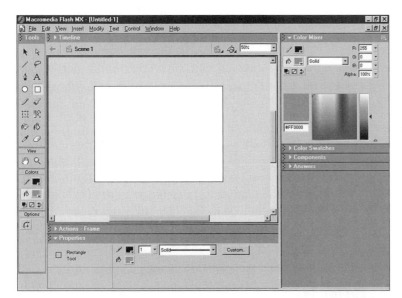

Figure 8.7

When you choose a drawing tool from the Tools panel, the Properties panel allows you to set the appearance of the stroke and fill. Set these properties before you draw the shape.

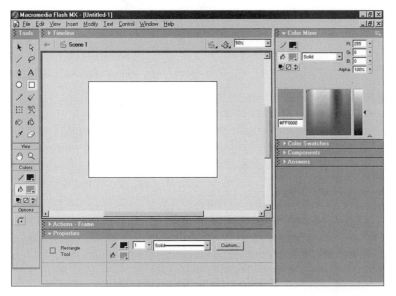

Figure 8.8

Some drawing tools like the Rectangle have additional options that appear at the bottom of the Tools panel.

Figure 8.9

Set the roundness of a rectangle's corners with the Rectangle Settings dialog box.

When the properties of the stroke and fill meet with your approval, drag the shape.

You can change the stroke and fill after the fact by clicking the appropriate area with the Arrow tool and picking a new set of appearance attributes from the Properties panel. However, since the stroke and fill are separate elements, you have to change them separately. Moreover, the four straight lines that make up the rectangle's stroke are actually four separate elements! If you want to change a solid stroke into a dotted one, for instance, you would have to select all four sides of the stroke. Hold down the Shift key while you click with the Arrow tool to select multiple elements. Then, go to the Properties panel and make the appropriate changes. This is far too much of a bother for most animators, so save yourself some hassle and set the stroke and fill before you draw.

Animation Advice

Hold down the Shift key to select multiple elements with the Arrow tool.

Adding Strokes and Fills Separately

The Pencil tool and the Brush tool allow you to draw individual strokes and fills, respectively. The Pencil tool sits below the Oval tool on the Tools panel, and the Brush tool sits below the Rectangle tool.

Choose the Pencil tool from the Tools panel, and set the stroke color, weight, and style on the Properties panel. Look under the Options area of the Tools panel for a special icon. Click this icon to reveal a menu of three Pencil modes: Straighten, Smooth, and Ink. Straighten mode improves the corners of your Pencil lines. Use this mode when you want to draw a stroke with hard corners like right angles. Smooth mode helps to make your Pencil lines more fluid. Use Smooth mode when you're drawing curves or round shapes. Ink mode is the what-you-draw-is-what-you-get mode. This mode doesn't process your Pencil lines for tighter corners or smoother curves. Use Ink mode when you want precise or detailed Pencil strokes.

Cut!

When you set the Brush mode, Flash remembers your choice for all subsequent uses of the Brush tool. In other words, the tool doesn't revert to its default mode of Paint Normal. Before you paint with the Brush, make sure the Tools panel shows the right painting mode. (By the way, you can further customize Flash's factory presets under Edit → Preferences.)

When you click the Brush tool, the Properties panel allows you to set the fill color for the Brush. However, the more interesting options appear under the Options heading of the Tools panel, as Figure 8.10 shows. Set the size and shape of the brush with the dropdown lists at the bottom of the panel. Click the icon above the lists to set the Brush mode. There are five modes: Paint Normal, Paint Fills, Paint Behind, Paint Selection, and Paint Inside.

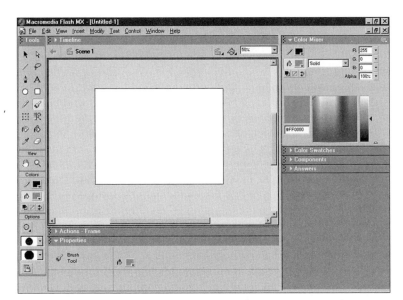

Figure 8.10

The options for the Brush tool include Brush Mode (top), Brush Size (middle), and Brush Shape (bottom).

Paint Normal causes the Brush to paint on top of existing art. If the underlying art isn't in a group, the paint from the Brush erases it. Paint Fills causes the Brush to paint on top of fills only, ignoring strokes. When you drag the Brush initially, it appears that its fill covers everything, stroke and fill alike. But when you release the mouse button, only the paint that falls on top of fills remains. Paint Behind causes the Brush to paint behind existing art instead of in front of it.

Use Paint Selection in conjunction with the Arrow tool. Select an element on the stage with the Arrow, and then set the Brush tool to Paint Selection mode. The Brush fills over only the current selection.

Paint Inside keeps the Brush within the lines, so to speak. When you start painting with the Brush in this mode, the stroke of the surrounding element serves as the borders. Flash removes any paint that falls outside the borders when you release the mouse button.

Adjusting the Stacking Order

When you create a group from a stroke and fill combination, the group takes its place in the stacking order of the stage. The *stacking order* determines which elements sit on top of which other elements.

By default, Flash puts the most recently drawn shape at the top of the stacking order, so that it superimposes everything else on the stage. You can change the position of a

Shop Talk

The **stacking order** in Flash is the order in which objects like groups appear on top of one another on the stage.

group in the stack by selecting it with the Arrow tool and choosing from the submenu under Modify → Arrange. The Bring To Front command brings the selected group to the top of the stacking order. The Send To Back command sends the group to the bottom of the stack. Bring Forward brings the group one step forward in the stack, while Send Backward sends the group one step back.

The stacking order applies only to objects in Flash, or special elements that Flash treats different from regular graphics. Groups are objects, which is why they behave less schizophrenically than garden-variety shapes. Instances of symbols are also objects. (As in Fireworks, you animate in Flash with symbols and instances. I'll spend the beginning part of Chapter 9 talking about it. But I digress.) Strokes and fills that you haven't grouped together aren't objects. These nonobjects sit beneath even the lowest object in the stacking order. Therefore, if you take the Brush tool and attempt to paint over an existing group object, you find that you can't. No matter what you do, the paint always falls behind the group, because the paint by itself is beneath the stacking order. However, if you select the splash of color that you painted and choose Modify → Group, thereby turning the color into an object, you can manipulate the color object in relation to the other objects on the stage by tweaking the stacking order.

Inserting Text

Use the Flash Text tool much like the Fireworks version. (The Text tool is above the Rectangle tool in the Tools panel.) Grab the Text tool, and click anywhere on the stage to create a variable-width text object. Just as in Fireworks, a variable-width text object has no set right border. The more text you type, the longer the text object becomes. It even grows beyond the boundaries of the stage. You have to press Enter or Return to insert a manual line break. However, if you drag the Text tool across the stage, you create a fixed-width text object, which has a set right border, just as in Fireworks.

Animation Advice

Use variable-width text objects for short pieces of text like captions or legends. Use fixed-width text objects for longer pieces of text like paragraphs.

When the flashing cursor inside the text object reaches the right border, the text automatically wraps to the next line.

You can tell by the box around a text object what kind of text object it is. On a variable-width text object, the handle in the upper right corner of the box is round, while the handle is square on a fixed-width text object, as Figure 8.11 shows.

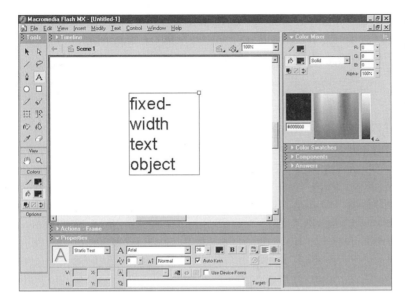

Figure 8.11

A round handle denotes a variable-width text object, while a square handle denotes a fixed-width text object.

Set the properties for the text, including the font, the size, the color, and the style, with the Properties panel (see Figure 8.12). To edit the properties of an existing text object, click it once with the Arrow tool, and change the fields in the Properties panel accordingly. To edit the content of a text object, double-click it with the Arrow tool.

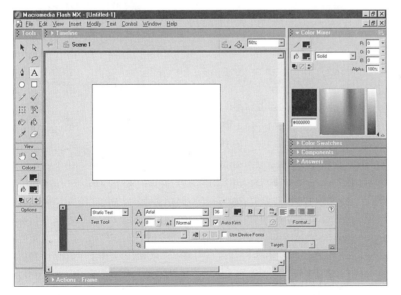

Figure 8.12

When you work with the Text tool, the Properties panel allows you to change the font, size, color, and style of the text.

You can also change a variable-width text object into a fixed-width text object by dragging the round handle in the upper right corner. It doesn't take much. Just a slight nudge changes the round handle into a square handle, signifying that Flash has converted the text object to fixed width.

A text object is an object in Flash, obviously, just like a group. Therefore, the text is subject to the stacking order. Bring it forward or send it backward as you require.

Modifying Your Art

Because Flash art is vector based, you can bend it and twist it with great ease and even greater confidence that you won't sacrifice image quality in the process.

Perhaps Flash art is too malleable. You saw already how you can separate the fill from a stroke in a shape like an ellipse, and I explained that the stroke around a rectangle is actually four separate lines, each of which you can modify to suit your needs.

Flash provides more methodical ways to modify what you've drawn, such as erasing, bending the stroke, and manipulating anchor points.

Using the Eraser

Grab the Eraser tool to erase a portion of a graphic. The Eraser tool is the one with the yellowish eraser icon. The Options section of the Tools panel allows you to set the mode of the Eraser as well as change its shape. The Eraser tool has five modes corresponding to the five modes of the Brush tool: Erase Normal, Erase Fills, Erase Lines, Erase Selected Fills, and Erase Inside.

The Eraser also has a faucet option, which automatically erases an element on the stage. Click the faucet icon at the bottom of the Tools panel to turn on this option. The mouse pointer changes from the shape of the Eraser tool to a faucet. Position the drip of the faucet over the item you want to erase, and click. To change the Eraser tool back to normal, click the faucet icon again.

The Eraser doesn't work on groups, at least not directly. To erase a portion of a group, double-click the group with the Arrow tool. Flash enters Group-Editing mode. You can now take the Eraser to the individual elements in the group, but be careful! Flash treats the stroke and fill as distinct elements in Group-Editing mode, so the elements get back some of their weird behavior. When you finish erasing, click the left-arrow icon in the bar above the stage (see Figure 8.13). The group behaves like a group again.

> **The Big Picture**
>
> Recall that the Fireworks Eraser tool doesn't work on vector graphics. You need the Knife tool in Fireworks to cut away segments of a vector. The Flash Eraser tool, though, works on vectors splendidly.

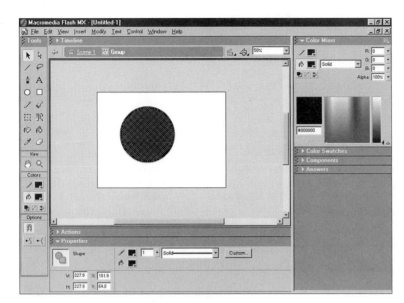

Figure 8.13

Double-click a group with the Arrow tool to enter Group-Editing mode. To return to Normal mode, click the left-arrow icon in the bar above the stage.

Bending the Stroke

The Arrow tool lets you change the shape of a nongrouped graphic by bending its stroke. Grab the Arrow tool, and position the mouse pointer on a stroke. A curved line appears under the mouse pointer. Hold down the mouse button and drag, bending the stroke as you go. If the stroke is part of a closed shape like a rectangle or ellipse, the fill automatically reconfigures itself to the new shape of the stroke, as Figure 8.14 shows.

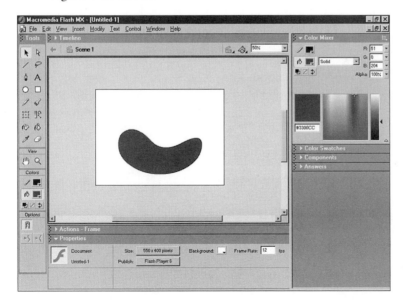

Figure 8.14

Bend the stroke of a closed shape, and the fill automatically adjusts itself to the new contours. This used to be an ellipse.

You can't bend a stroke if that stroke is part of a group. Double-click the group with the Arrow tool to enter Group-Editing mode, though, and you can bend away. Afterwards, click the left-arrow icon to return to Normal mode.

Manipulating Anchor Points

As you may remember from Fireworks, anchor points are the mathematical coordinates that control the shape of a vector graphic. By dragging the anchor points of a graphic in Flash, you can change the shape of the graphic.

Use the Subselection tool, the white arrow, for the job. Grab the Subselection tool, and click the stroke of a nongrouped graphic. A series of small square handles appears along the stroke. These handles are the anchor points. Drag the anchor point, and, when you release the mouse button, the shape of the graphic changes. Like with bending strokes, the fill adjusts to the new contours of the graphic.

To delete an anchor point, click the anchor with the Subselection tool and press the Delete key or choose Edit → Clear from the menu.

The Subselection tool doesn't work on grouped graphics until you switch to Group-Editing mode.

Saving Your Work

Remember from Fireworks that you created two versions of your animation files. The first version was a PNG, the work version. The second version, the live version, was an animated GIF. The same principle holds true in Flash. You save a work version of your file in FLA format, and you export a playable movie file in SWF format. The FLA format doesn't play in a web browser. It's for editing purposes only.

To save the FLA version of your work, choose File → Save or File → Save As. The Save command saves the current stage using the existing file name. If you haven't saved the stage before, Flash treats the Save command as Save As, which allows you to specify a new file name or location by way of the Save As dialog box, as shown in Figure 8.15.

Choose a location on your hard drive for the FLA file, and type a name for the file in the File Name field. In the Save As list, choose whether you want to save the file in Flash MX or Flash 5 format. In most cases, go with Flash MX format. If you want to share your FLA file with another animator who hasn't upgraded to Flash MX yet, use Flash 5 format.

Figure 8.15

Use the Save As dialog box to save your work in FLA format.

Click the Save button to create the FLA file. Remember, the FLA is for editing only. Don't post this version of the file on the web. I'll talk about exporting the playable SWF version of the movie in Chapter 9.

The Least You Need to Know

- The stage is the area in which you create your Flash movie.

- The stroke and the fill of a Flash shape behave independently unless you group them together.

- Only objects like groups participate in the stacking order of the stage.

- The Eraser tool and other editing tools don't work directly on objects like groups.

- Double-click a group with the Arrow tool to enter Group-Editing mode; in this mode the elements of the group behave like independent graphics.

- Use File → Save to save an FLA version of your movie.

Building a Flash Movie

In This Chapter

◆ Using layers

◆ Defining symbols and instances

◆ Creating motion tweens

◆ Previewing the movie

The goal of this chapter is to recreate the classic version of *The Robot Is Frustrated* using Flash instead of Fireworks. When you exported the animation as an SWF in Fireworks, you'll recall that Fireworks gave you a file in the neighborhood of 380K. But by building the animation in Flash, you'll see by the end of this chapter that you get a much more manageable SWF file and a better animation to boot.

In some respects, building a Flash movie is easier than creating an animated GIF. In some respects, it's harder, because it's less intuitive. Getting the hang of the process is the trick. I have every confidence in your abilities. So, take this chapter at your own pace, and repeat the exercises as often as you need to feel comfortable.

Preparing the Stage

Launch Flash, and you get a blank stage. The first step in Fireworks was to set up the canvas. Likewise, set up the stage in Flash before you get down to business.

Go to the Properties panel. You see the default stage size of 550 pixels by 400 pixels. This is fine for *The Robot Is Frustrated*, so keep the default size. Also keep the default frame rate of 12 frames per second. I mentioned in Chapter 8 that 12 frames per second is a good frame rate for most Flash animations. The only thing you should change is the background color of the stage. Click the color square, and choose a shade of blue to represent the sunny afternoon sky. I'm going with #CCCCFF again.

Importing Existing Artwork

Next, bring in the alien life form, the robots, the mailbox, and the hill, all of which you can find on the CD-ROM that comes with this book.

Pop the CD-ROM into your computer, and choose File → Import. The Import dialog box appears, as in Figure 9.1. Navigate to the Chapter 9 folder on the CD-ROM to find five vector images in SWF format: *alien.swf, hill.swf, mailbox.swf, robot_left.swf,* and *robot_right.swf*. Hold down Ctrl (Windows) or Command (Mac), and click each of the files to select them all. Click Open to bring them onto the stage.

Figure 9.1

Use the Import dialog box to bring in artwork from an external source, like the CD-ROM that comes with this book.

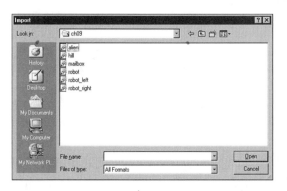

Your screen should look something like Figure 9.2. All the artwork appears bunched up in the middle of the stage. Look above the stage to the Timeline panel, and note that Flash has imported each piece of art into its own layer. Layers in Flash are very much like layers in Fireworks. They're separate, transparent drawing surfaces, and they stack from the bottom of the Timeline panel to the top. Notice also the thin gray rectangle with a black dot next to each layer in the 1 column of the Timeline. This symbol represents a *keyframe*, or a frame in which something happens in the

movie. Flash inserts a keyframe in the timeline whenever a piece of art debuts on the
stage for the first time. Keyframes have other
uses, too, as you'll soon see. (You may recall
from Chapter 1 that keyframes represent the
starting and ending positions of a motion-
tweened image. This is one of those other
uses.)

Shop Talk _____

A **keyframe** is a frame
in the Flash timeline in which
something happens, such as the
starting or ending position of a
motion-tweened graphic.

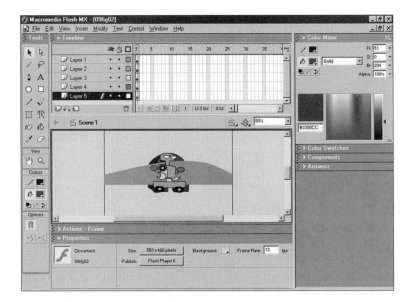

Figure 9.2

_Flash imports each piece of
art into its own layer._

Shuffling the Layers

For now, grab the Arrow tool, and drag the various graphics to their respective places
on the stage. Chances are, the layers aren't in the right order. If so, you can remedy
the situation easily by dragging the layers in the Timeline panel. Layers stack from
bottom to top, so select the hill with the Arrow tool to see which layer contains it.
Then, drag this layer to the very bottom of the Timeline panel. While you're at it,
double-click the name of the layer, and type Hill or something of a more descriptive
nature. Press Enter or Return to register the new name.

Click the alien to determine its layer, and drag this layer to the second-to-bottom
spot. Change the layer's name to **Alien.** Continue with the mailbox, the left-facing
robot, and the right-facing robot, supplying names for the layers like **Mailbox,
Robot (Left),** and **Robot (Right).** When you finish, your screen should look something like Figure 9.3.

Animation Advice _____

Setting the exact position of the hill can be trying by eyes alone. Select the hill with the Arrow tool, and use the X and Y fields on the Properties panel. The hill is 550 pixels wide, wide enough to fit exactly on the 550-pixel-wide stage, so type **0** in the X field and press Enter or Return. The hill is 100 pixels high. You want to position it at the bottom of the 400-pixel-high stage. Doing some quick subtraction, you get 400 − 100 = 300. Type **300** in the Y field and press Enter or Return.

Figure 9.3

Places, everyone! Drag the layers of the various graphics to their proper positions in the Timeline panel.

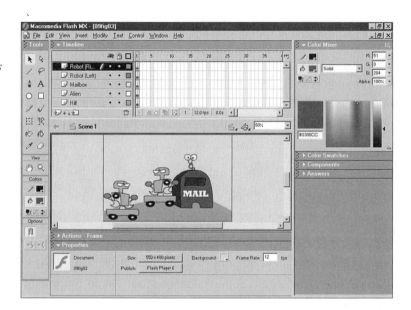

Adding a New Layer

There's only one object missing: the alien life form's line of dialog. You can create this object easily enough, but first add a new layer to the top of the stage.

Select the uppermost layer in the Timeline panel, which should be Robot (Right). Then, click the Insert Layer icon at the bottom of the Timeline panel. This is the first icon on the left, the one that looks like a sideways sheet of paper. Flash adds a new layer to the Timeline panel. Double-click its name, type **Text,** and press Enter or Return. Now, grab the Text tool, move onto the stage, and click to create a variable-width text object. Choose a font, size, color, and style for the text from the Properties panel. I went with Arial, size 21, color black, and style bold and italic, but use the settings that you like best.

Notice that I didn't make the text white this time. In Fireworks, I used a drop shadow to improve the contrast between the white text and the blue background. In Flash, unfortunately, you don't get visual effects like drop shadows or glows, so I opted for plain black text, which stands out well enough. See for yourself in Figure 9.4. Notice also that, after you create the text object, Flash inserts a new keyframe for the object in the 1 column of the Timeline panel.

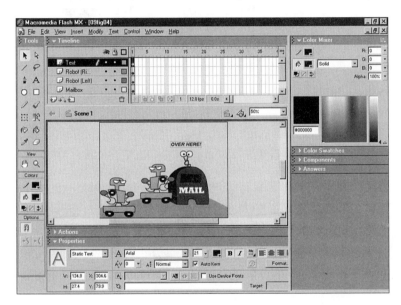

Figure 9.4

Add a new layer to the top of the Timeline panel, and insert a text object for the alien life form's line of dialog.

In case you ever want to remove a layer entirely, select the layer and click the trash-can icon at the bottom of the Timeline panel.

Creating Symbols

The layers are in the proper order. The cast is in place. It's time to do some animating.

I mentioned earlier in this chapter that you animate in Flash with symbols and instances much like you did in Fireworks. A symbol, as you recall, is the definitive version of a graphic. It resides in the library, not on the canvas, or, in this case, the stage. An instance is a copy of a symbol. This object appears on the stage, and it's the object you animate.

Symbols and instances have the same relationship in Flash. If you edit the appearance or characteristics of a symbol, all the instances of that symbol automatically change. However, you can alter the characteristics of a particular instance without affecting the characteristics of the symbol, the definitive version.

> ### The Big Picture
>
> A **motion tween** in Flash is a set of instructions to move a particular object from one location on the stage to another.

You needed symbols and instances to create tweens in Fireworks, and you need symbols and instances to create motion tweens in Flash. *Motion tweens* are instructions to move a particular instance from one position on the stage to another. You place one instance of the symbol in one location and another instance of the same symbol in another location, and Flash fills in all the intermediate steps.

But now I'm getting ahead of myself again. Before you can create a motion tween, you need instances, and before you have instances, you need a symbol. More specifically, you should create a symbol for every moving graphic in the movie.

The Robot Is Frustrated has four moving graphics: the left-facing robot, the right-facing robot, the alien life form, and the alien's line of dialog. Therefore, you need four symbols. Start with the left-facing robot. Select this graphic with the Arrow tool, and choose Insert → Convert To Symbol. This calls up the Convert To Symbol dialog box, as in Figure 9.5.

Figure 9.5

Change a graphic into a symbol with the Convert To Symbol dialog box.

Supply a name for the symbol in the Name field. Why mess with success? Type **Robot (Left)** in the field. Set the behavior of the symbol to Graphic. This behavior is for essentially static images. I'll discuss Movie Clip and Button behaviors in Chapter 10 and Chapter 13, respectively.

Click OK to convert the graphic into a symbol. Flash replaces the image on the stage into an instance of the symbol called Robot (Left). To view the symbol itself, choose Window → Library to call up the Library panel, as in Figure 9.6. Select the entry for the left-facing robot to see a thumbnail of the symbol.

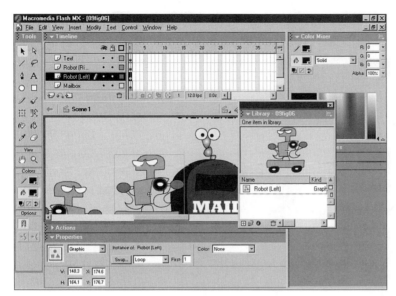

Figure 9.6

Keep track of your movie's symbols with the Library panel.

Now click the right-facing robot on the stage, choose Insert → Convert To Symbol, and create another graphical symbol called Robot (Right). Select the alien life form, and convert it into the graphical symbol Alien. Finally, select the text object, and convert it into the graphical symbol Text.

You're just about ready to go. In the Timeline panel, select the Robot (Right) layer and click the dot in the eye column to the right of the layer name. This is the equivalent of poking out the eye icon in Fireworks. A red X appears in the eye column, and the right-facing robot disappears. You haven't deleted the instance. Note that the keyframe is still sitting in the 1 column. If the keyframe is still there, the instance is still there. It's just hiding. You can click the red X to restore the robot to full visibility, but keep this image hidden for now. Do the same to the layer called Text. When you finish, your stage should look something like Figure 9.7.

Animation Advice

If your Library panel comes up as a floating window, you can (and probably should) drag it into the permanent interface. Move the mouse pointer to the dot pattern at the top of the Library panel, hold down the mouse button, and drag the panel to the right of the screen. Release the mouse button when the panel docks with the others on the interface.

Figure 9.7

Click the dots in the eye column of the Timeline panel to hide temporarily the contents of the corresponding layers.

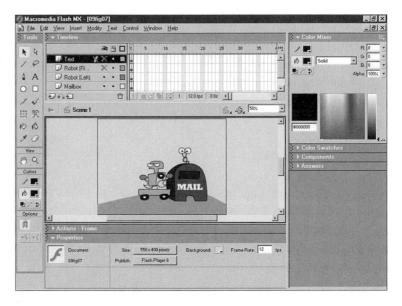

Setting Up the Motion

You have the symbols. The next step is to create the motion tweens.

A motion tween happens between two instances of the same symbol. Start with the left-facing robot. You have one instance of this symbol in the Robot (Left) layer of the Timeline panel, represented by the keyframe in the 1 column. Adding a new keyframe to a different column in this layer inserts a second instance of the Robot (Left) symbol.

CAUTION

Cut! _____

To insert a keyframe with another instance of the most recent symbol, choose Insert → Keyframe, not Insert → Blank Keyframe. This command creates a blank keyframe, or a keyframe awaiting some art. You should insert a blank keyframe only when you want to add a new piece of art to the layer.

Adding a Keyframe

Assume that you want to give the robot one second to go down the hill, as in the animated GIF. For a one-second motion tween, you should add the second keyframe to the 13 column of the Timeline panel. Why 13? Remember that the movie plays back at a rate of 12 frames per second, and the motion starts in the first frame. Frame 1 plus 12 more frames equals Frame 13. This frame marks off the first second of the movie.

Click the space at position 13 in the Robot (Left) layer. (The number 13 isn't marked, so count over three from the 10 column.) The rectangular space turns blue, meaning that it's selected. Choose Insert → Keyframe from the menu, and Flash adds a second keyframe to the layer at Frame 12. As you can see in Figure 9.8, this keyframe contains the second instance of the Robot (Left) symbol, although all the other images have disappeared. Why? Read on and see!

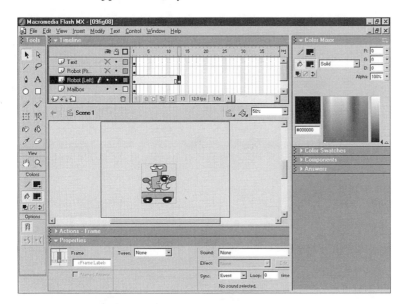

Figure 9.8

Select the thirteenth frame in the Robot (Left) layer and choose Insert → Keyframe to create a new keyframe containing a new instance of the symbol.

Adding Frames

Notice the salmon-colored playback head at the top of the Timeline panel. This pointer shows the current position of the movie. Right now, the pointer is on Frame 13. The only defined frame at Frame 13 is the one containing the second instance of the left-facing robot. This is why all the other graphics have disappeared. They don't exist in the movie at Frame 13. As a matter of fact, they don't exist in the movie past the first frame.

To solve this problem, inform Flash that the hill and mailbox graphics should appear from Frame 1 through Frame 13. Don't worry about the alien or the right-facing robot for now. Concentrate on the static images.

> ### The Big Picture
>
> Remember, the numbers in the columns of the Timeline panel represent the frames of the movie.

Click Frame 13 in the Hill layer, and choose Insert → Frame. Don't choose Insert → Keyframe, because you don't need a keyframe. Remember, you need a keyframe only

Animation Advice

If graphics seem to disappear without warning in your movie, go to the Timeline panel, and make sure that your graphics exist in the later frames. Nine times out of 10, they don't. This is an easy step to miss when you're building a Flash movie.

when something happens in the movie. Since the hill and the mailbox don't do anything more exciting than exist in this movie, a regular, garden-variety frame works nicely.

So, choose Insert → Frame. Flash adds a thirteenth frame to the layer with the hill. The hill now extends from Frame 1, the initial keyframe, through Frame 13, and the graphic reappears on the stage.

Now for the mailbox. Click Frame 13 in the Mailbox layer, and choose Insert → Frame from the menu. The mailbox reappears also, as you can see in Figure 9.9.

Figure 9.9

Add frames to the Hill and Mailbox layers to extend the static images in these layers beyond the first frame.

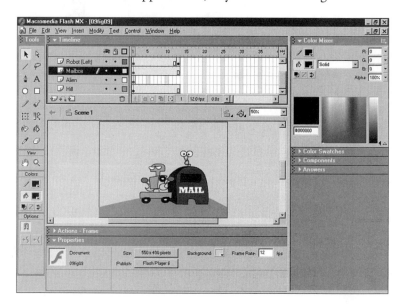

Positioning the Second Instance

Now, to create the motion tween, set the position of the second instance.

Select the second keyframe in the Robot (Left) layer. This automatically selects the second instance of the left-facing robot. Take the Arrow tool, and position this instance in the lower left corner of the stage, as in Figure 9.10.

Now, go back to the Timeline panel, and click the first keyframe in the Robot (Left) layer. Notice that the Properties panel gives you options for modifying the frame, including a Tween dropdown list. Pull the Motion option from this list, and Flash creates a motion tween between the two instances of this symbol. You can tell because the Timeline panel shows an arrow in a blue field pointing from the first keyframe in Frame 1 to the second keyframe in Frame 13, as in Figure 9.11.

Drag the playback head back and forth to see the motion tween in action.

Figure 9.10

Using the Arrow tool, drag the second instance of the Robot (Left) symbol to the lower left corner of the screen.

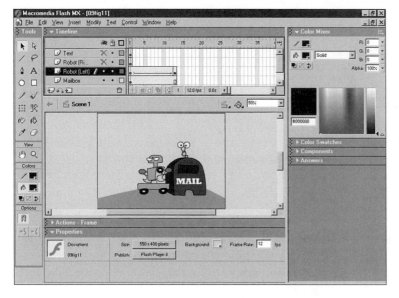

Figure 9.11

Set the Tween list on the Properties panel to Motion, and Flash creates a motion tween between the two keyframes, as indicated by the arrow in the Timeline panel.

Moving Keyframes

Now create a motion tween for the alien life form. Have the alien emerge from the mailbox at Frame 7 and finish in Frame 13 to coincide with the ending position of the left-facing robot.

If you want the motion tween to begin at Frame 7, the first keyframe needs to be in the 7 column of the Timeline panel. Currently, the keyframe is in the 1 column. To move the keyframe, click it, and release the mouse button. Then, click the keyframe again, and this time hold down the mouse button and drag the keyframe from Frame 1 to Frame 7. The alien life form now appears in the movie for the first time in Frame 7. To prove it, drag the playback head to Frame 1. The alien life form is nowhere in sight. Drag the pointer back to Frame 7, and the alien appears.

> **CAUTION**
>
> **Cut!**
>
> To move a keyframe, make sure that you click it once, release the mouse button, and then click it again, holding down the mouse button this time and dragging. If you drag after the first click instead of the second, you end up selecting multiple frames.

The first instance of the Alien symbol should sit behind the mailbox. Make sure that you select the keyframe for this instance in the Timeline panel, and then drag the alien behind the mailbox.

A motion tween requires a second instance of the same symbol. Click the thirteenth frame in the Alien layer of the Timeline panel, since you want the alien to stop moving by Frame 13. Choose Insert → Keyframe from the menu. Flash adds a new instance of the Alien symbol to Frame 13 of the movie, only you can't see it right now, because it's hiding behind the mailbox.

Make sure that the second alien keyframe is selected in the Timeline panel, and tap the up-arrow key until the alien emerges from the mailbox. (Hold down Shift while you tap the arrow key to increase the amount of nudge.) Then, grab the instance with the Arrow tool, and move the instance to its final position.

Finally, click the first keyframe in the Alien layer, and go to the Properties panel. Pull the Motion option from the Tween dropdown list, and Flash creates a motion tween for the alien. An arrow appears in the Timeline panel between the two keyframes, as in Figure 9.12.

The alien's line of dialog should appear at Frame 13 also. Go to the Text layer in the Timeline panel, click the red X in the eye column to restore visibility, and drag the keyframe from Frame 1 to Frame 13. Remember to click once on the keyframe, release, and then click again and drag. When you finish, Frame 13 of the movie should look something like Figure 9.13.

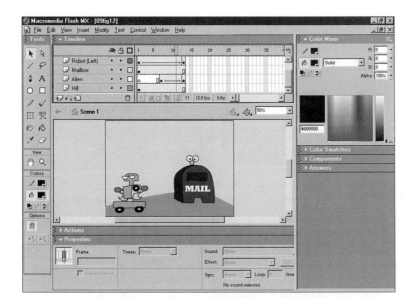

Figure 9.12

Create a motion tween for the alien life form.

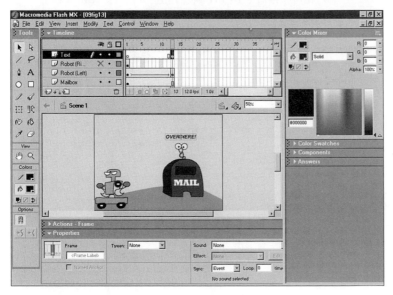

Figure 9.13

Move the keyframe for the alien life form's line of dialog to Frame 13. The text now appears as soon as the alien completes its motion tween.

Inserting a Pause

You're doing great so far!

At this point of the movie, you want a one-second pause so that the audience has a chance to read the line of dialog. To insert a pause in Fireworks, you simply increased the frame delay of the appropriate frame. The process is slightly different here. In Flash, the frame delay is constant. You can't alter the speed of one frame without altering the speed of every frame in the movie.

This is nothing that some quick math can't solve. You know that your movie plays at a constant rate of 12 frames per second. Therefore, to insert a one-second pause, simply add 12 frames to each visible layer. You have five visible layers at this point: Text, Robot (Left), Mailbox, Alien, and Hill. Add 12 frames to each of these. The last frame in the movie is Frame 13, so adding 12 frames brings you to Frame 25 by the end of the pause.

Click Frame 25 in the Text layer, and choose Insert → Frame. The line of dialog extends from Frame 13 to Frame 25, as the Timeline panel shows.

The Big Picture

In Flash, unlike in Fireworks, the frame rate of a movie is a constant value. In other words, you can't alter the frame rate for a particular frame in the animation.

Proceed to the Robot (Left) layer. Click Frame 25, and choose Insert → Frame. Now the left-facing robot stands in place at the bottom left of the stage for a full second.

Repeat this procedure in the Mailbox, Alien, and Hill layers. Each time, click Frame 25, and each time, choose Insert → Frame. Check your work when you finish against Figure 9.14.

Figure 9.14

Insert a one-second pause in the movie by adding 12 frames to each visible layer. The last frame in the movie is now Frame 25.

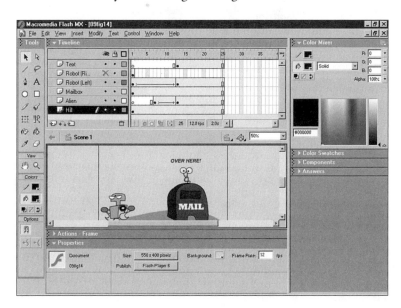

Adding More Motion Tweens

Click the red X in the eye column of the Robot (Right) layer, and drag the keyframe in this layer to Frame 26. The right-facing robot appears now for the first time in

Frame 26. All the rest of the graphics disappear, though, because they don't currently exist in Frame 26.

Fix this by adding frames to the layers of the static graphics. Since you want the right-facing robot to take one second to climb the hill, and since 12 frames equal 1 second, you want to insert new frames at Frame 37 (25 + 12 = 37) of the Mailbox and Hill layers. Click Frame 37 in the Mailbox layer, and choose Insert → Frame. Then click Frame 37 in the Hill layer, and invoke the same command.

Go back to the Robot (Right) layer and insert a keyframe at Frame 37 for the second instance of the symbol. Position this second instance at the top of the hill. Then, click the first keyframe in this layer, go to the Properties panel, and create the motion tween. The robot travels up the hill when you drag the playback head.

Create the motion tween for the alien ducking back down behind the mailbox. Click Frame 26 in the Alien layer, and choose Insert → Keyframe. This creates a third instance of the Alien symbol, or the first keyframe for the second motion tween. Go to Frame 28, and create another keyframe. Drag this new instance of the Alien symbol behind the mailbox. Then, select the keyframe in Frame 26, go to the Properties panel, and create the motion tween. The alien life form makes a hasty exit.

There's one last motion tween to create, the one where the line of dialog disappears off the top of the stage. Go to the Text layer, and create a new keyframe at Frame 26. This is the first keyframe for the motion tween. Create a second new keyframe at Frame 31. Drag this instance of the symbol off the top of the stage.

While the instance of the Text symbol is still selected, look at the Properties panel, as in Figure 9.15. Find the Color dropdown box on the right side of the panel. Choose Alpha from this list, and set the value of the field that appears to 0% by typing **0** or dragging the slider beside it. The instance of the Text symbol seems to disappear. In Flash, the alpha value controls the opacity of the instance. Therefore, an instance with 0% alpha is the same as an instance with 0% opacity, which is the same as 100% transparency.

Click the keyframe in Frame 26 of the Text layer, go to the Properties panel, and create the motion tween. As you drag the playback head across the Timeline panel, notice that the line of dialog gradually fades away as it moves toward the top of the stage. Flash tweened the alpha value of the instance as well as its horizontal position.

Figure 9.15

When you select an instance of a symbol with the Arrow tool, the Properties panel allows you to adjust the instance's characteristics.

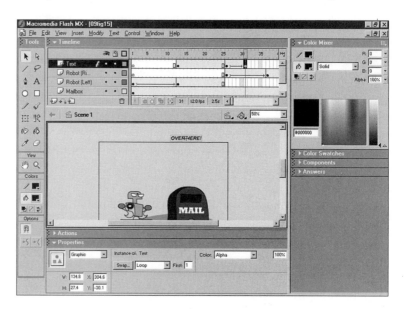

You're just about done. The last task is to add another one-second pause to the end of the layers with visible art: Robot (Right), Mailbox, and Hill. It's time for some more quick math. The last frame in the movie is currently Frame 37. A 1-second, 12-frame pause brings the movie to Frame 49, since 37 + 12 = 49.

Animation Advice

Always preview your movie in a Flash Player window at least once before you export the SWF file and post to the web.

Click Frame 49 in the Robot (Right) layer, and choose Insert → Frame. Do the same thing to the Mailbox and Hill layers, and your movie is finished. Your Timeline panel should look like the one in Figure 9.16.

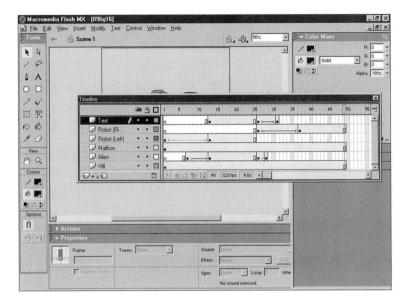

Figure 9.16

When you finish The Robot Is Frustrated, *your Timeline panel should look like this. Check your timeline carefully against this one.*

Previewing the Movie

To test the movie in the Flash Player, choose Control → Test Movie from the menu. Flash compiles a temporary SWF file of the movie and displays it in a new window, as in Figure 9.17. Click the Close icon at the top of the Flash Player window to return to Flash. Be careful that you don't click the uppermost Close icon! This one belongs to Flash MX, not the Flash Player. Closing this window causes Flash MX to quit.

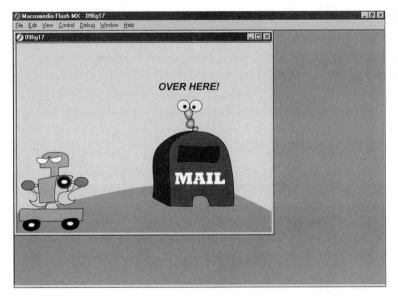

Figure 9.17

Choose Control → Test Movie to preview your movie in a Flash Player window.

Exporting the Movie

If you like what you see, you're ready to export the final SWF file.

Well, you're almost ready. First, save the FLA version of the file for your archives. Choose File → Save, navigate to the location on your hard drive where you want to store the file, and type **robot.fla** in the File Name field. Click Save to save the file.

Now, create the playable SWF file. Choose File → Export Movie from the menu this time. The Export Movie dialog box appears, as in Figure 9.18. Type **robot.swf** in the File Name field, and click Save. This calls up the Export Flash Player dialog box. I'll talk more about the settings on this dialog box in Chapter 14. For now, keep the defaults. Click OK to create the SWF file.

Figure 9.18

Create a playable SWF movie with the Export Movie dialog box.

Now comes the moment of truth. I boasted in Chapter 7 that Flash's SWF of *The Robot Is Frustrated* would be much smaller than the SWF you got from Fireworks. I also claimed that the Flash-generated SWF file would be much smaller than the animated GIFs of *The Robot Is Frustrated*. At the time, you may have blown me off as a know-it-all loud mouth, for which I can't blame you. But if you close out of Flash MX for the time being and find the SWF file you just exported, you'll find that the Flash-generated SWF version of *The Robot Is Frustrated* weighs in at a slender 4K! That's the size of two or three single frames in the animated GIFs, and it's just a fraction of the massive 380K of the Fireworks-generated version.

Double-click the SWF file to open it in the Flash Player. The graphics are sharp, and the animation is smooth. The Flash version looks better than the animated GIFs, and it's only 4K. Now this is what web animation is all about.

The Least You Need to Know

♦ Getting the hang of the process is the trick to building Flash movies.

♦ A keyframe is a frame in the Timeline panel that indicates when something happens in the movie, such as the starting or ending position of a motion-tweened image.

♦ Put each moving graphic in its own layer of the Timeline panel.

♦ Create motion tweens between two instances of the same symbol.

♦ Insert frames to extend the appearance of a particular static graphic in the movie.

♦ Preview your movie in a Flash Player window using Control → Test Movie.

Chapter 10

Animating Symbols

In This Chapter

- ◆ Building animation into a movie-clip symbol
- ◆ Using the frame-by-frame technique for complex motion
- ◆ Combining movie-clip instances with motion tweens
- ◆ Troubleshooting movie clips

In Chapter 9 you created symbols with the Graphic behavior. In this chapter, you'll create a symbol with the Movie Clip behavior.

What's the difference? I'm glad you asked. A movie-clip symbol has built-in animation. When you combine movie clips with motion tweens, you can achieve some sophisticated effects, as you'll see shortly.

Preparing the Stage

This chapter's animation is called *Astro Ape's Moon Walk*. It features Astro Ape, the space-suit-wearing simian who first appeared in my book, *The Complete Idiot's Guide to Computer Illustration* (Alpha Books, 2002). I mentioned in Chapter 1 that any computer graphic is an animation waiting to happen. This chapter's exercise serves as proof of concept. Readers of the previous *Idiot's Guide* spent several chapters creating a static image of the monkey, and now the monkey comes to life by way of Flash.

The plot of *Astro Ape's Moon Walk* is not exactly highbrow. In this movie, Astro Ape is on the moon. He walks from one side of the stage to the other while the planet Earth rises majestically behind him. The end.

What *Astro Ape's Moon Walk* lacks in plot, it makes up for in sophistication. The symbol of Astro Ape that you'll create has built-in animation, causing the monkey's arms and legs to move as the instance of the symbol traverses the stage.

To begin, launch Flash MX. Set the background color of the stage to a dark blue, simulating the blackness of space. Don't choose actual black, though. I used black in the monkey's design, and you don't want the black areas to disappear completely against a black background. I'm opting for #003366, a murky shade of blue, as the background color. Keep the default width and height for the stage, namely 550 pixels by 400 pixels, and also keep the default frame rate, namely 12 frames per second.

The Big Picture

Those six-digit codes like #003366 that crop up whenever I talk about color deserve some explanation. These are hexadecimal color codes, the preferred method for representing color in HTML. Hexadecimal is a base-16 number system, which means that it uses 16 digits instead of the usual 10: 0 through 9 and A through F. (A through F are numbers, not letters or variable names, in the hexadecimal world.) Every computer color has a unique hexadecimal identifier. The first two digits represent the color's red component, the middle two digits represent the green component, and the last two digits represent the blue component. Color #000000 is black: no red, green, or blue. Color #FFFFFF is white: full red, green, and blue.

Open the CD-ROM tray of your computer, and insert the CD-ROM that comes with this book. Choose File → Import from the Flash menu. Navigate to the Chapter 10 folder on the CD-ROM, and select the file called *moon.swf.* Flash imports a moonscape graphic for the background into Frame 1 of Layer 1. Move this graphic to the bottom of the stage with the Arrow tool, and change the name of Layer 1 to Moon. (To do this, double-click the name of the layer in the Timeline panel.)

Choose File → Import again, and bring in the file called *earth.swf.* Flash creates Layer 2 in the Timeline and inserts a graphic of the planet Earth in Frame 1 of this layer. Position this graphic just below the horizon of the moon on the left side of the stage, and rename its layer Earth. By now, your stage should look like Figure 10.1.

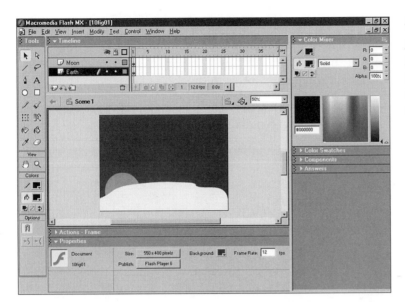

Figure 10.1

Import the moonscape and Earth graphics from the CD-ROM that comes with this book, and position them on a dark blue stage.

Reviewing Motion Tweening

To practice your motion tweening, go ahead and create the Earthrise.

As soon as you think motion tween, your very next thought should be symbol. Remember, you need instances of symbols to create motion tweens. Before you do anything else, convert the Earth graphic into a symbol. Select this graphic with the Arrow tool, and choose Insert → Convert To Symbol from the menu for the Convert To Symbol dialog box. Type **Earth** in the Name field, and set the behavior to Graphic, like you did for all the symbols in *The Robot Is Frustrated*. Click OK to create the symbol. Flash moves the graphic to the Library panel and replaces the image in Frame 1 with an instance of the new symbol Earth.

You may now proceed with the tween in good conscience. *Astro Ape's Moon Walk* lasts for five seconds from start to finish, and the Earthrise happens over the duration of the movie, which means that you need a five-second motion tween. At 12 frames per second, 5 seconds equals 60 frames (12 × 5). The first keyframe occupies Frame 1. Therefore, Frame 61 marks the 5-second mark in the movie (60 + 1). Click Frame 61 in the Earth layer, and choose Insert → Keyframe. As you know from experience, Flash creates a new keyframe at Frame 61, inserting a new instance of the symbol at this point in the movie.

The Big Picture

The most common element on the moon is oxygen, believe·it or not—oxygen in the form of oxides. There is no green cheese.

As you also know from experience, the moonscape disappears, since it doesn't currently exist in Frame 61, nor does it exist beyond the first frame. You know how to fix the situation. Click Frame 61 in the Moon layer, and choose Insert → Frame. The moonscape occupies Frames 1 through 61 consecutively.

Now, position the second instance of the Earth symbol. Select it with the Arrow tool, and drag it to about the middle of the screen, like in Figure 10.2.

Figure 10.2

Move the second instance of the Earth symbol to the middle of the screen, more or less.

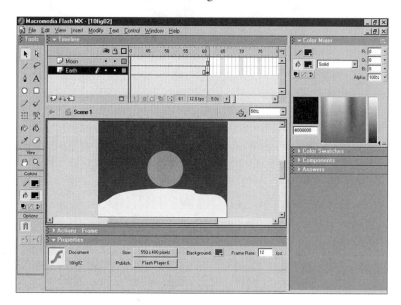

Finally, create the motion tween. Click the first keyframe in the Earth layer. Set the Tween list on the Properties panel to Motion, and the Earth rises over the horizon when you drag the salmon-colored playback head on the Timeline panel. Good job!

Creating a New Symbol

You have the Earthrise. Next comes Astro Ape.

The symbol for Astro Ape is different from the other symbols you've created so far for two reasons. First, it's going to have the Movie Clip behavior instead of the Graphic behavior. Second, it's going to use a technique called *frame-by-frame animation* instead of motion tweening. I'll explain the second reason first.

Working with Frame-by-Frame Animation

Frame-by-frame animation is very much like the kind you created in Fireworks for animated GIFs. You'll recall that every frame of an animated GIF was a separate graphics file. Likewise, in frame-by-frame animation, each frame contains a different piece of art, which means that each frame has its own keyframe in the Timeline panel. Frame-by-frame animation is especially helpful for complex motions like a space monkey walking or a flower blooming. If you think about it, there's no good way to create a motion tween to express this type of movement. By adding a series of keyframes to your movie, each with a different pose of the walking monkey or a different stage of the blooming flower, you create the illusion of motion the old-fashioned way.

Shop Talk

In **frame-by-frame animation,** each frame in a sequence contains a keyframe with slightly different art.

The upshot of this is that the symbol for Astro Ape won't just be a single, static image. It'll be a sequence of several related images, which is why you'll specify the Movie Clip behavior instead of the Graphic behavior. A movie-clip symbol is like a separate Flash animation that sits inside the main animation. This type of symbol has its own, independent timeline that plays simultaneously with the main timeline. It's like you're watching two movies at once, only the second movie is actually part of the first movie.

How to Create a Movie Clip Symbol

Since the symbol for Astro Ape is going to be a movie clip, it'll be easier to create the symbol first and then import the art from the CD-ROM directly into the movie clip's timeline. To do this, click on a blank area of the stage with the Arrow tool so that nothing is selected. Then, choose Insert → New Symbol from the menu. The Create New Symbol dialog box appears, as in Figure 10.3.

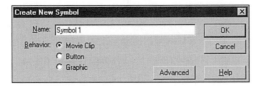

Figure 10.3

Build a new symbol from scratch with the Create New Symbol dialog box.

As you can see, the Create New Symbol dialog box looks almost exactly like the Convert To Symbol dialog box. Both dialog boxes work very much the same, too. Type the name of the symbol, **Astro Ape**, into the Name field, and specify the Movie Clip behavior. Click OK to create the symbol.

Flash enters Symbol-Editing mode. The graphics on the stage disappear temporarily, as do the layers in the Timeline panel. In Symbol-Editing mode, the stage shows the content of the symbol you're editing, which is why you get a blank screen. The symbol you just created doesn't have any content yet. Similarly, Layer 1 in the Timeline panel is the first layer of the movie-clip symbol, not the first layer of the main animation.

> **The Big Picture**
>
> A symbol's timeline can have multiple layers, just like the main timeline.

Now, import art from the CD-ROM directly into the new symbol. Choose File → Import, and double-click the file *ape1.swf*. Flash inserts the first frame of the walking sequence into the first frame of Layer 1. Using the Arrow tool, drag the graphic so that it's roughly centered on the plus icon in the middle of the stage, as in Figure 10.4.

Figure 10.4

Import the first frame of the walking sequence directly into the new symbol, and center the graphic on the plus icon in the middle of the stage.

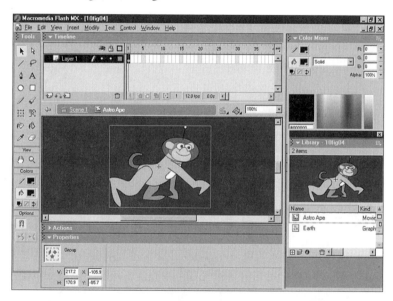

Now, import the second frame of the sequence. Choose File → Import again, and double-click *ape2.swf*. Flash creates a new Layer 2 in the symbol and inserts the graphic in Frame 1 of the new layer. Center this graphic on the plus icon also. Continue importing ape images through *ape7.swf*, but don't import *ape.swf*, *ape_bl.swf*, *ape_s.swf*, or *ape_sbl.swf*. Just import the ape images that have numbers in their file names. When you finish, your symbol should have seven layers.

Creating Keyframes for Frame-by-Frame Animation

To create frame-by-frame animation, all the keyframes need to be on the same layer. This is easy enough to achieve. Click the keyframe in Frame 1 of Layer 2, the second graphic in the walking sequence. Release the mouse button and click again, this time dragging the keyframe to Frame 2 of Layer 1. Select the empty Layer 2, and click the trashcan icon at the bottom of the Timeline panel to delete the layer. Drag the keyframe in Layer 3 to Frame 3 of Layer 1, and then delete the empty Layer 3. Keep going in order until all seven keyframes are in Layer 1 and Layer 1 is the last remaining layer in the symbol, as in Figure 10.5. Drag the playback head to test the frame-by-frame animation thus far.

Animation Advice

To create frame-by-frame animation, all the keyframes need to be on the same layer.

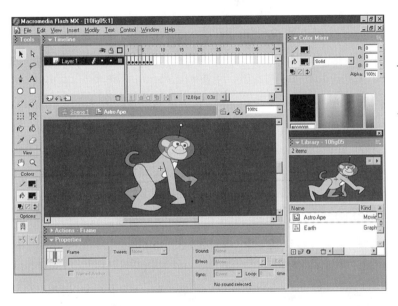

Figure 10.5

To set up the frame-by-frame animation, move all seven keyframes to Layer 1, deleting the extra layers as you go.

Now, repeat this sequence two times. Select the keyframe in Frame 1, hold down Shift, and select the keyframe in Frame 7. This selects all seven keyframes. Choose Edit → Copy Frames from the menu. Make sure you select Edit → Copy Frames! Don't select Edit → Copy. This is a different command.

Click Frame 8 in the Timeline panel, and choose Edit → Paste Frames. Again, make sure that you choose Edit → Paste Frames instead of Edit → Paste. Flash pastes a copy of the sequence starting at Frame 8 and ending at Frame 14. Click Frame 15, and choose Edit → Paste again for the second repetition of the sequence.

When you add an instance of a movie-clip symbol to the main animation, the movie clip loops. When it reaches the last frame in its internal sequence, it starts again at the first frame. Given this information, you may wonder why you just created two repetitions of the walking sequence. Since the movie clip loops already, you shouldn't need any repetitions.

The Big Picture

Movie-clip instances loop automatically in the main animation.

True enough. However, it would be nice if Astro Ape blinked his eyes at some point in the sequence for an added touch. Cartoon characters blink their eyes all the time in the movies and on TV. Why not also on the web?

The main walking sequence is seven frames long. From start to finish, it's little more than a half second. If one of these seven frames shows Astro Ape blinking, then, when the movie clip loops, the character ends up blinking almost twice a second, which is too often. But now that the symbol has three identical sets of the seven-frame sequence, you can substitute a blinking pose for 1 of the 21 frames, and the character seems to blink once every second and a half or so.

The file *ape_bl.swf* on the CD-ROM looks just like *ape7.swf*, only the monkey's eyes are closed. Substitute this graphic for the one in the twenty-first frame of the symbol. Choose File → Import, and double-click *ape_bl.swf*. Flash imports this graphic into a new layer. Use the Arrow tool to center the graphic on the plus icon as you did before.

Now, replace the last keyframe in Layer 1 with the keyframe in the new layer. Click Frame 21 in Layer 1, and choose Edit → Clear Frames. This command erases the currently selected frame. Drag the keyframe from the new layer to the newly cleared Frame 21 of Layer 1, and delete the empty layer. The walking sequence is complete! Check it out by dragging the pointer in the Timeline panel back and forth. Your timeline should match the one in Figure 10.6.

Figure 10.6

The walking sequence has 21 frames total, and the very last one shows Astro Ape blinking.

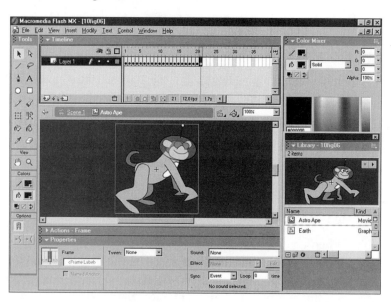

Motion Tweening the Movie Clip

Click the blue left-arrow icon above the stage to exit Symbol-Editing mode. The moonscape and the Earth reappear, but Astro Ape is nowhere to be found. That's because you haven't yet inserted an instance of the movie-clip symbol you just created.

Select the Moon layer in the Timeline panel, and create a new layer by clicking the piece-of-paper icon. Flash inserts a new layer above the current one. Rename this layer Astro Ape. To insert an instance of this symbol, open the Library panel under Window → Library. Make sure that the new Astro Ape layer is selected on the Timeline, and drag the Astro Ape symbol onto the stage. Flash adds an instance of this symbol to the layer.

Cut!

When you create a symbol from scratch, don't forget to place an instance of the symbol in the main timeline. If you don't, the symbol doesn't appear in your movie.

Drag the playback head at the top of the Timeline panel, and it looks as if you have problems. The Earth graphic rises nicely, but the ape graphic doesn't appear to walk. Not to worry—Flash's editing environment doesn't display the built-in animation of a movie-clip instance. The best way to see the total effect is to preview the movie under Control → Test Movie.

When you do, you notice that the walking sequence seems to work in and of itself, only Astro Ape appears to be walking in place, as in Figure 10.7. The movie-clip instance may have built-in animation, but the instance isn't moving across the stage in the main animation.

Moving instances across the stage? That sounds suspiciously like motion tweening. If you're wondering whether you can combine the built-in animation of a movie clip with motion tweening in the main timeline, the answer is a resounding yes.

Click Frame 61 of the Astro Ape layer, and choose Insert → Keyframe. Flash inserts a second instance of the movie-clip symbol. Drag this instance off the right side of the stage. Now, click Frame 1 of the Astro Ape layer, and drag its instance off the left side of the stage. While this keyframe is still selected, go to the Properties panel, and set the Tween list to Motion.

The Big Picture

Windows users can invoke the Insert Keyframe command by right-clicking the desired position in the Timeline panel.

Figure 10.7

When you test the movie in a Flash Player window, Astro Ape appears to walk in place. To fix this, create a motion tween from two instances of the movie clip.

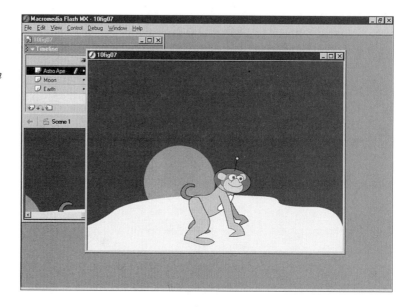

Now, when you drag the pointer at the top of the Timeline panel, Astro Ape appears to slide across the lunar surface. The legs and arms don't appear to move. Again, this is just a function of the Flash MX editing environment. I guarantee that the internal animation of the symbol is still intact. To prove it, choose Control → Test Movie. The monkey ambles across the lunar surface, as Figure 10.8 shows.

Figure 10.8

After you create the motion tween, Astro Ape seems to walk across the moon.

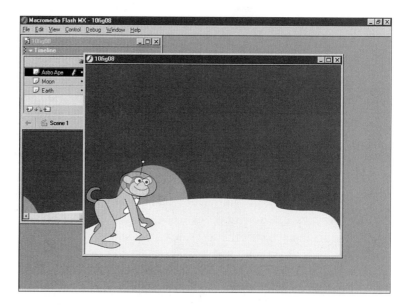

Stopping the Motion

The only problem with movie-clip symbols is that they don't stop playing in the main animation. Assume that you want Astro Ape to stop in the middle of the stage for one second before continuing off the right side. To do this, you need two separate motion tweens: one from stage left to center stage, and one from center stage to stage right, with a one-second pause in between. However, during the one-second pause, the built-in animation of the instance continues to play. The result is that the monkey appears to walk in place for a second before finding his traction again and moving to the right.

To circumvent this problem, you need a new symbol, one without moving arms and legs. During the one-second pause, you remove the walking symbol and show the standing symbol instead. After the pause, you remove the standing symbol and place the walking symbol back on the stage.

Create a Standing Pose Symbol

I'll step you through the process. First, create the standing version of the symbol. Choose Insert → New Symbol from the Create New Symbol dialog box. Type **Astro Ape (Standing)** in the Name field, and set the behavior to Movie Clip—even though the arms and legs don't move in the standing version, the eyes blink. Click OK to create the symbol.

Now, import the art for the symbol. Choose File → Import, and double-click the file *ape_s.swf*. Flash adds a standing image of Astro Ape to Layer 1 of the new symbol. Center this image on the plus icon in the middle of the stage with the Arrow tool.

Choose File → Import again to import *ape_sbl.swf*, the blinking version of the standing pose. Flash creates a new layer for this image.

Use the Arrow tool to select the keyframe in Layer 1. Then, click the graphic on the stage. Note the X and Y values in the Properties panel. Now, click the keyframe in Layer 2, and click the graphic on the stage. Go to the Properties panel, and type the same X and Y values in the X and Y fields. This positions the blinking pose in the same place as the nonblinking pose.

Animation Advice

You could create a new layer for Astro Ape's standing pose, but since the standing pose and the walking pose don't appear on the stage at the same time, you can get away with using the same layer for both symbols.

Using the Arrow tool again, drag the keyframe in Layer 2 to the twelfth frame of Layer 1. This gives you some frame-by-frame animation in the first layer. Astro Ape stands motionless for 11 frames, and he blinks in the twelfth. You no longer need the second layer, so select it and click the trashcan icon to remove it from the Timeline panel. Check your new symbol's timeline against the one in Figure 10.9.

Figure 10.9

The timeline of your Astro Ape (Standing) symbol should have 12 frames, the twelfth being the one that blinks.

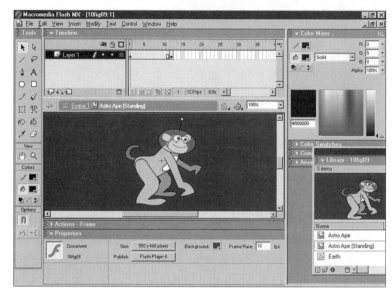

Rearranging the Timeline

You have a symbol for the standing pose. Next, rearrange the timeline. Go to the Astro Ape layer, and click the last keyframe in the layer, the one in Frame 61. Release the mouse button, and then click the keyframe again, dragging the keyframe to Frame 25. Reposition the art in this keyframe to the middle of the stage, as in Figure 10.10. Click the graphic on the stage, and jot down the X and Y values from the Properties panel on a piece of scratch paper.

Click Frame 26 in the Astro Ape layer, and choose Insert → Blank Keyframe from the menu. Flash changes Frame 26 into a blank keyframe, or a keyframe awaiting some art. Keep Frame 26 selected, and open the Library panel under Window → Library. Drag the Astro Ape (Standing) symbol onto the stage. Type the X and Y values you jotted down in the X and Y fields of the Properties panel to place the standing version of Astro Ape in the most recent location of the walking version.

Figure 10.10

Drag the second keyframe in the Astro Ape layer to Frame 25, and reposition the art in this keyframe to the middle of the stage.

You want a one-second pause, so the standing symbol should remain on the stage from Frame 26 to Frame 37. Click Frame 38 of the Astro Ape layer, and choose Insert → Blank Keyframe again. Drag a new instance of the original Astro Ape symbol onto the stage, and type the same X and Y values into the fields on the Properties panel.

Now, you need the last motion tween, the one that takes Astro Ape off the right side of the stage. Click Frame 61 of the Astro Ape layer. Choose Insert → Keyframe to insert a keyframe with another instance of the Astro Ape symbol. Drag this instance off the right side of the screen. Click the keyframe at Frame 38, go to the Properties panel, and create the motion tween. Your timeline should look like the one in Figure 10.11.

That should do the trick. Choose Control → Test Movie to see. Astro Ape wanders onto center stage, pauses, blinks at the audience, and resumes his journey off stage right. You achieved this feat by switching movie-clip symbols in the middle of the action.

Animation Advice

If the transition between the walking pose and the standing pose seems too abrupt or jerky, try adjusting the position of the standing pose toward the right side of the stage. Use the X and Y values as a guide, but don't adhere to them slavishly if doing so creates a less convincing animation.

Figure 10.11

Add an instance of the new symbol to the main timeline and create the second motion tween with two more instances of the original symbol.

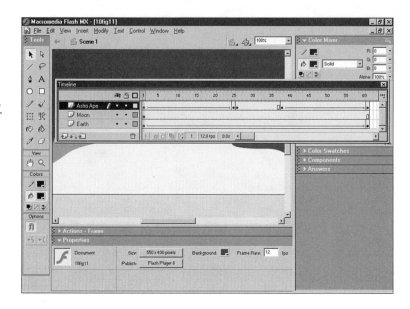

Saving the Movie

And there you have it: *Astro Ape's Moon Walk*. Choose File → Save, and save this movie as *ape.fla*. Then, export a playable SWF version. Choose File → Export Movie, and supply the file name *ape.swf*. Keep the default settings in the Export Flash Player dialog box. Your final, web-ready SWF file is only 7K. That's small enough for anyone to download, even someone with a slow modem connection.

The Least You Need to Know

- Use frame-by-frame animation to achieve complex motion sequences.
- Movie-clip symbols can have built-in animation.
- Create a symbol from scratch using Insert → New Symbol.
- A symbol's timeline can have multiple layers.
- Double-click an instance of a symbol on the stage to enter Symbol-Editing mode.
- Instances of movie-clip symbols loop automatically in your movie.

Applying Special Effects

In This Chapter

♦ Easing motion tweens in and out

♦ Using motion guides

♦ Using masks

♦ Transforming properties of instances

Whether you use graphic symbols or movie-clip symbols, you get a lot of mileage out of garden-variety motion tweens. But Flash doesn't stop there. You can create even more interesting effects by tweaking the behavior of the motion tween, by adding motion guide layers and mask layers to the stage, and by modifying the properties of the instances.

This chapter shows you how to combine special animation effects with motion tweens.

Opening the Animation

In this chapter, you modify a Flash movie called *Alien's Joy Ride*. To save you some time, you can find the movie on the CD-ROM that comes with this book.

Launch Flash MX, and load the CD-ROM into your computer. Choose File → Open for the Open dialog box. Navigate to the Chapter 11 folder, and double-click the file called *joyride.fla*. Flash loads the FLA file, as Figure 11.1 shows.

Figure 11.1

Open the file called joyride.fla *from the CD-ROM that comes with this book.*

The first thing you'll notice about this movie is that it uses a photographic background instead of cartoon art. The photo itself is a raster file called *bg.jpg*, which you can also find on the CD-ROM.

Flash may be a vector-based format, but you can bring in raster graphics for use in your movies. To do so, choose File → Import, the same command you used to import vector graphics. Navigate to the raster graphic that you want to use, and double-click it. Flash brings in the raster graphic as a symbol. Choose Window → Library to prove it. In the Library panel, you find an entry for *bg.jpg*, which makes the photo on the stage an instance of this symbol.

Instances of raster symbols are very much like instances of vector symbols. You can even create motion tweens with them, although *Alien's Joy Ride* doesn't. The background image remains stationary, as the Timeline panel for the Background layer shows. There are no arrows in this layer to indicate motion tweens.

> **The Big Picture**
>
> When you import a raster graphic into Flash, the software creates a symbol in the Library panel to hold the raster object.

Judging by the arrows, motion tweens happen in the Saucer layer. There are two motion tweens, to be precise. The first one brings the alien life form's flying saucer from the top left of the stage to the bottom center. The second one sends the saucer to the top right of the stage. Drag the playback head at the top of the Timeline panel to give you an idea of the motion.

Notice that the two motion tweens share a keyframe. That is, the last keyframe in the first motion tween is the same as the first keyframe in the second motion tween. You can use this trick whenever two motion tweens with the same symbol sit side by side in the Timeline panel.

Look in the Library panel again, and you see a second symbol, one called Saucer. This is the Flying-Saucer symbol, of course. It's a movie-clip symbol, and it uses the frame-by-frame animation technique to create a spinning effect. The alien also blinks its eyes at the end of the sequence.

To examine the makeup of the Saucer symbol, double-click it in the Library. Flash enters Symbol-Editing mode, as in Figure 11.2. You find that the symbol has 1 layer and 21 frames. Preview the built-in animation by dragging the pointer at the top of the Timeline panel. Exit Symbol-Editing mode by clicking the blue left-arrow icon above the stage.

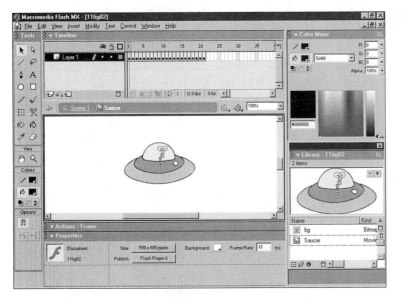

Figure 11.2

The symbol called Saucer uses frame-by-frame anima- tion to create a spinning effect.

Before you begin modifying the movie, preview the original under Control → Test Movie. This will help you to compare the original with the changes you make in this chapter.

Easing Motion Tweens

The first modification to make to *Alien's Joy Ride* is to ease the motion tweens in the Saucer layer. *Easing* motion tweens causes the tweened object to move at a different rate in different frames of the tween. By default, the object moves at a constant speed. But by easing the motion tween, you can force the object to start out slow and then speed up (easing in) or start out fast and then slow down (easing out). When you ease a motion tween, the total distance from keyframe to keyframe is the same. The positions of the instances don't change. What changes is the object's rate of speed as it goes along.

Shop Talk

When you ease a motion tween, you vary the rate of speed at which the object completes the tween. Easing in causes the object to start out slow and then speed up. Easing out causes the object to start out fast and then slow down.

Try this exercise as an example. Select the first keyframe in the Saucer layer, and find the Ease field on the Properties panel. Assume that you want the saucer to slow down during this motion tween. Starting out fast and slowing down is easing out in Flash terminology. Type a positive value between 1 and 100 into the Ease field to ease the motion tween out. The higher the number, the more drastic the effect. For now, I recommend that you make no attempt at subtlety. Type **100** into the field. You can also click the triangle icon beside the field and drag the slider all the way to the top.

Now, since you eased out the first motion tween, ease in the second one, so that the saucer starts out slowly at the bottom of the stage but then picks up speed as it zooms toward the upper right. Click the keyframe at the start of the second motion tween, and type **–100** into the Ease field, or drag the slider all the way to the bottom. Easing in requires a negative value between –1 and –100. The lower the value, the more drastic the effect.

To see the effects of easing in and easing out on *Alien's Joy Ride*, choose Control → Test Movie. The saucer almost seems to hover at the bottom of the stage. Notice also that easing in and easing out doesn't change the speed at which the saucer's internal animation plays. The Ease value affects only the motion tweens in the main timeline.

To turn off easing for a motion tween, select the first keyframe in the motion tween, and type **0** in the Ease field on the Properties panel.

Save this version of the movie as *joyride1.fla* under File → Save As, and export *joyride1.swf* under File → Export Movie.

Defining Motion Guide Layers

In Flash, a motion guide layer is a layer containing a path for a motion-tweened object to follow. You've probably noticed so far that all the motion tweens have followed a straight line: the rising planet Earth in *Astro Ape's Moon Walk*, the robot's back and forth behavior in *The Robot Is Frustrated*, the saucer's diving down in *Alien's Joy Ride*, and so on. With a motion guide layer, the object can follow almost any path that you can draw. It can zigzag, swoop, and even turn loops.

Go to the Timeline panel, and select the Saucer layer. Then, click the icon between the sideways-paper icon and the folder icon. This is the Add Motion Guide icon. Clicking it causes Flash to add a motion guide layer to the currently selected layer, which in this case is Saucer, as Figure 11.3 shows.

> ### The Big Picture
>
> Every layer in the Timeline panel can have its own motion guide layer, but each single layer can't have more than one motion guide layer.

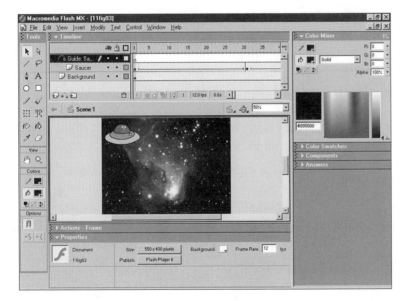

Figure 11.3

Click the icon between the sideways paper and the folder to create a motion guide layer.

Creating a motion guide is simple. Keep the motion guide layer selected, and grab the Pencil tool from the Tools panel. Set the stroke color of the Pencil to something that will stand out well against the background. Then, bring the Pencil onto the stage, hold down the mouse button, and draw the path that you want the saucer to follow. Be creative! The motion path I drew (see Figure 11.4) has a loop-the-loop. This ought to make the alien's flight pattern appropriately erratic.

Figure 11.4

In the motion guide layer, use the Pencil tool to draw the path that you want the object to follow.

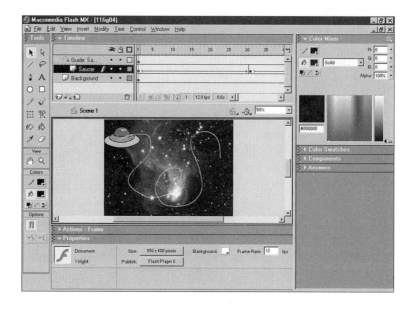

Now, attach each instance of the symbol to the motion guide. Select the first keyframe in the Saucer layer. Drag the plus icon in the middle of the instance to a position on the motion guide. You'll know you have the right spot when the instance snaps to the motion guide. Then, release the mouse button. You can position the instance anywhere along the guide to start. You don't have to choose the upper left extremity, although this makes the most sense, since the current instance marks the beginning of the first motion tween.

Select the second keyframe in the Saucer layer, and position this instance at another point along the motion guide. Finally, select the last keyframe, and do the same thing. Test the animation by dragging the pointer at the top of the Timeline panel. If the object doesn't appear to follow the motion path, make sure that you attached the plus icons of all three instances of the object to the motion path. If you're certain that you did this, then unfortunately your motion path is too complex! Delete the current Motion Path layer, create a new one, and start again.

View the results under Control → Test Movie, and the alien's saucer goes through the paces. The motion guide is completely invisible in the Flash

> **Cut!**
>
> Be creative with your motion path, but don't be too complex, or Flash can get confused. When Flash doesn't understand your motion path, Flash ignores it.

> **Animation Advice**
>
> If easing in and easing out doesn't look right when you add a motion path, type 0 in the Ease field for the starting keyframes of the motion tweens.

Player, although its effects are very much present. Save this version of the movie as *joyride2.fla*, and export *joyride2.swf*.

Notice as the movie plays that the orientation of the object remains the same. That is, the saucer starts out perfectly horizontal and remains perfectly horizontal for the entire animation.

Close the Flash Player window, and click the first keyframe in the Saucer layer again. Go to the Properties panel, and check the option for Orient To Path. This causes Flash to orient the object according to the direction of the motion guide. Click the second keyframe in the Saucer layer, and check the same option. Now when you drag the pointer at the top of the Timeline panel, the saucer spins and turns at the whim of the motion guide (see Figure 11.5). Choose Control → Test Movie for a better representation of the effect. Then, save this version of the movie as *joyride3.fla*, and export *joyride3.swf*.

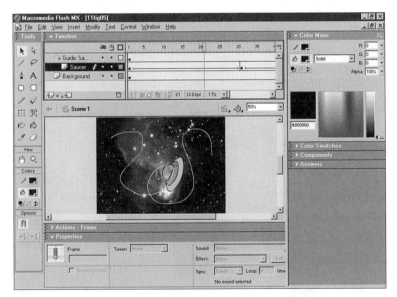

Figure 11.5

When you choose the Orient To Path option on the Properties panel, Flash orients the object according to the direction of the motion guide.

Masking

A *mask layer* in Flash is a layer whose artwork acts like a window on the layers underneath. The filled areas of the mask layer become transparent, allowing you to see the underlying artwork. The rest of the mask layer becomes completely opaque. Nothing from the underlying layers shows through the opaque regions.

Use masking to create unusual borders for the stage. Here's how.

First, select the motion guide layer, and click the trashcan icon at the bottom of the Timeline panel. Motion guide and mask layers don't mix. Then, select the Saucer layer, and click the sideways-paper icon to create a new layer above it. Double-click the name of this layer, and type **Mask** in the field.

To convert this layer into a mask layer, right-click it (Windows) or click while holding down the Command button (Mac). Choose Mask from the context menu that appears. Flash changes the new layer into a mask layer and applies the layer automatically to Saucer. The Saucer layer sits inside the mask layer, while the Background layer sits outside. Since you want the mask to apply to both layers, not just Saucer, click the name of the Background layer, hold down the mouse button, and drag the layer until it just touches the bottom of the Saucer layer. When you release the mouse button, you find that you moved the Background layer under the mask layer as well, as Figure 11.6 shows.

Shop Talk

A **mask layer** is a layer whose artwork acts like a window on the layers underneath. The filled areas of the mask layer are transparent. The unfilled areas are opaque.

Figure 11.6

When you convert a layer into a mask layer, Flash automatically includes the layer immediately under the mask with the masking group. Drag the Background layer into the masking group as well.

Flash may also automatically lock the mask layer and the layers under it. A layer is locked when it has a lock icon in the lock column of the Timeline panel. You can't add art to locked layers. Unlock all the locked layers at this point by clicking the lock icons.

Now, with the mask layer selected, grab the drawing tools, and draw shapes on the layer to represent visible areas. It doesn't matter what stroke or fill colors you use. Flash interprets any color on the mask layer as transparent. I decided to create an oval-shaped border, so my mask layer looks like Figure 11.7. Don't be boring like me, though. Make the border interesting by adding various shapes or alternating filled and unfilled regions.

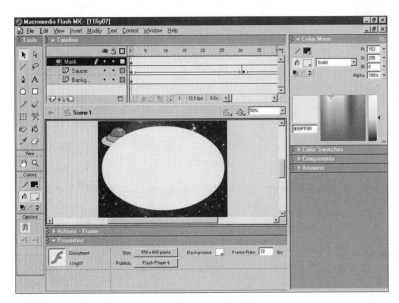

Figure 11.7

Draw shapes in the mask layer to create the mask. All filled areas become transparent. All clear areas become opaque. This mask will create an oval-shaped window on the stage.

To preview the effects of the mask layer, click the dot in the lock column of the mask layer and all the layers under it, thereby locking these layers down. The fill in the mask layer becomes transparent, and you see the contents of the underlying layers through it, as in Figure 11.8.

To edit the shape of the mask, unlock the mask layer, and modify the graphic with any of the usual editing tools like the Eraser, the Subselection tool, and the Arrow.

By dragging the Saucer layer outside the mask layer, as in Figure 11.9, the mask no longer affects its contents. Notice that the background is still masked, but the saucer appears normally.

Set up the layers the way you prefer, and save this version of the movie as *joyride4.fla*. Export *joyride4.swf*.

> **The Big Picture**
>
> To preview the effects of the mask in Flash, you must lock the mask layer as well as the layers that it masks.

Figure 11.8

To preview the effects of the mask, lock the mask layer and all the layers under it.

Figure 11.9

Drag a layer outside the mask layer to remove its contents from the mask.

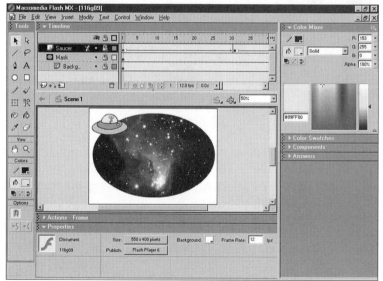

Applying Transformations

Flash can tween other properties of an object besides its X and Y locations. By applying a *transformation* like rotation or scaling to one or both of the instances in a motion tween, you can achieve some interesting effects.

Flash permits you to use these transformations in conjunction with Motion Path layers and mask layers. For now, though, to make things easier, delete the current mask layer, and unlock the remaining layers.

Rotating Objects

Suppose you want to rotate the saucer so that it pitches on its side at the beginning of the first motion tween and at the end of the second motion tween. This is as simple as selecting the appropriate keyframes in the Timeline panel and using the Free Transform tool. The Free Transform tool sits directly under the Pencil in the Tools panel.

Shop Talk

A **transformation** is any operation that changes the appearance or properties of an object. When you transform the instance of a symbol, the symbol itself doesn't acquire the transformed properties. Remember, the symbol is the definitive version of the graphic.

Select the first keyframe in the Saucer layer, and grab the Free Transform tool. The border around the instance of the Saucer symbol in this keyframe acquires a set of square handles, and a round reference point appears in the middle, as Figure 11.10 shows. The reference point goes by different names in different graphics packages. Sometimes it's the anchor point. Sometimes it's the point of origin. The idea is the same, even if the terminology is different.

Figure 11.10

When you select a keyframe and grab the Free Transform tool, the border around the instance of the symbol acquires square handles, and a round reference point appears in the middle.

In a rotation, the reference point is like a thumbtack. It's the pivot around which the object rotates. Right now, the reference point sits in the middle of the object, which means that, when you rotate the object, you rotate it around its middle. Move the reference point by clicking it, holding down the mouse button, and dragging it to a new location on the stage. This allows you to change the point around which you rotate the object.

The Big Picture

Think of the reference point of a transformation as a thumbtack. It's the point at which you, the designer, hold down the object and the point from which the transformation occurs.

Now, to rotate the object, bring the mouse pointer toward one of the corner handles. Watch for the pointer to change into a curved arrow. When this happens, you're in the rotation zone. Hold down the mouse button, and drag the mouse toward you to rotate the object clockwise. Drag the mouse away from you to rotate the object counterclockwise. Release the mouse button when the saucer pitches on its side, as in Figure 11.11.

Figure 11.11

Rotate the first instance of the saucer so that it looks like this.

Drag the salmon-colored playback head at the top of the Timeline panel to preview the effect. The saucer begins in a vertical position at the top left of the stage and ends in a horizontal position at the bottom middle of the stage. Flash tweens not only the X and Y coordinates of the object but also the degree of rotation.

Now click the last keyframe in the Saucer layer, the one that marks the endpoint of the second motion tween. Use the Free Transform tool to rotate the saucer as in

Figure 11.12. Now when you preview the animation, the saucer seems to lose control again as soon as it leaves the bottom of the stage. Flash tweens the horizontal orientation of the saucer in the second keyframe with the vertical orientation in the third.

Save this version of the movie as *joyride5.fla*, and export *joyride5.swf*.

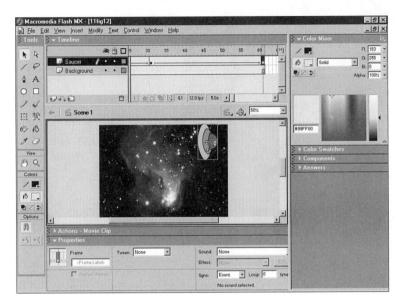

Figure 11.12

Rotate the third instance of the saucer so that it looks like this.

Animation Advice

If you want an object to rotate completely around, select the starting keyframe of the motion tween, and go to the Properties panel. Set the Rotate list to CW for clockwise or CCW for counterclockwise, and, in the Times field, type the number of complete, 360-degree rotations that you want, but be careful! In short tweens, specifying any more than one complete rotation makes the object spin like mad!

Scaling Objects

When you scale an object, you change its size. The handles that appear on the object's border when you grab the Free Transform tool are for scaling. Drag one of the corner borders and hold down the Shift key to scale the object in proportion. Drag one of the side borders to stretch the object.

Assume that you want the saucer to appear in the distance at the beginning of the animation, zoom toward the audience in the middle, and disappear into deep space again at the end. You can achieve these effects easily with scaling.

Select the first keyframe in the Saucer layer, and check the Scaling option on the Properties panel. Now, grab the Free Transform tool. Hold down Shift, and drag one of the corner handles toward the instance. The object shrinks, as in Figure 11.13.

Figure 11.13

Select the first keyframe in the Saucer layer, set the Scaling option on the Properties panel, grab the Free Transform tool, hold down Shift, and drag one of the corner handles toward the instance to shrink it.

Cut!

If you don't check the Scaling option on the Properties panel, Flash doesn't tween the scaling value of the object.

Animation Advice

To achieve more realistic motion, ease in a motion tween when the object starts in the distance and ends close. Ease out a motion tween when the object starts close and ends in the distance. The closer the object in relation to the audience, the faster it should appear to move.

Select the middle keyframe, and check the Scaling option again. Grab the Free Transform tool, hold down Shift, and drag one of the corner handles away from the instance to increase its size, as in Figure 11.14.

Finally, select the last keyframe. You don't have to check the Scaling option on the Properties panel this time, since this keyframe doesn't initiate a new motion tween. In fact, when you select this keyframe, the Properties panel doesn't give you a scaling option to check.

Scale this instance of the Saucer symbol as you did in the first keyframe. When you drag the pointer at the top of the Timeline panel, you see the alien's craft approach during the first motion tween and then depart during the second. Flash tweens the scaling value of the object as well as the object's degree of rotation and X and Y coordinates.

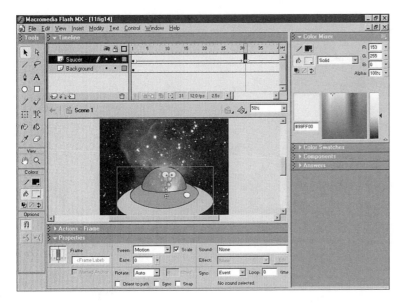

Save this version of the movie as *joyride6.fla*, and export *joyride6.swf*.

Adjusting Color

You can also change the color settings of instances in a motion tween. You already know from Chapter 9 that changing the alpha value causes the object to become transparent. By altering the brightness, you can make the object get brighter or darker as it moves. By altering the tint, you can make the object change shades.

Create a new version of *Alien's Joy Ride* where you darken the instances of the Saucer symbol at the top left and top right of the stage. Click the first keyframe in the Saucer layer, and use the Arrow tool to select the instance of this symbol on the stage. A Color list appears on the Properties panel. Set the list to the Brightness option, and a field appears to the right, as Figure 11.15 shows. Type a positive value between 1 and 100 in the Brightness field to increase the brightness of the object. The higher the value, the brighter the object becomes. Since you want to darken the object, type a negative value between –1 and –100 in the field. To make this instance of the symbol completely black, make the value –100.

Select the last keyframe in the Saucer layer, and click the instance with the Arrow tool. Set the brightness for this instance to –100 also. When you test the movie, the saucer is dark in the distance and fully visible in the foreground. Flash tweens the darkness level with the other properties of the instances.

Figure 11.15

The Brightness field on the Properties panel affects the brightness of the selected object.

Save this version of the movie as *joyride7.fla*, export *joyride7.swf*, and return the brightness values in the first and third instances of the Saucer symbol to 0.

Now, experiment with the tint. Albert Einstein theorized that, when an object travels close to the speed of light, the colors of the object shift toward the blue portion of the spectrum when the object moves toward you, and the colors shift to the red portion of the spectrum when the object moves away from you. You can bring *Alien's Joy Ride* into line with the theory of relativity by altering the tint of the first and third instances of the Saucer symbol.

> **The Big Picture**
>
> Albert Einstein (1879–1955) played the violin and turned down an offer to serve as president of the state of Israel. He was also a famous theoretical physicist.

Select the first keyframe, and click the instance with the Arrow tool. Set the Color list to Tint, and a few additional controls appear on the Properties panel, as Figure 11.16 shows.

Set the color of the tint by clicking the color square to the right of the Color list. This object should be red-shifted, so choose a shade of blue from the swatches that pop up. The field to the right of the color square gives the amount or intensity of the tint. Type a value between 0 and 100 in this field. The higher the value, the more intense the tint becomes. With a value of 100%, the object appears entirely in the tint color. With a value of 0%, the object appears entirely in its original shade. Type **50** in the Tint Amount field for the purposes of this experiment.

Figure 11.16

Use the tint controls on the Properties panel to apply a tint to the selected object.

Now select the third keyframe in the Saucer layer, and click the instance with the Arrow tool. Choose a red tint at 50% for this instance. Preview the animation, and the saucer changes color as it approaches and departs. Flash tweens the degree of tint along with all the other properties.

Save this version of the movie as *joyride8.fla*, and export *joyride8.swf*.

The Least You Need to Know

♦ You can use raster objects like photographs in your Flash movie.

♦ Easing in causes a motion tween to start out slow and then pick up speed; easing out causes a motion tween to start out fast and then slow down.

♦ Create a motion guide layer when you want a moving object to follow a different path from a straight line.

♦ Use mask layers to conceal portions of the stage.

♦ Flash tweens object properties like degree of rotation and size as well as X and Y coordinates.

♦ Tween color settings like transparency (alpha), brightness, and tint with the Properties panel.

Chapter 12

Tweening Shapes and Adding Sound

In This Chapter

◆ Creating and editing shape tweens

◆ Using shape hints

◆ Adding sound to your movie

◆ Compressing sound to reduce file size

For all their many uses, motion tweens in Flash are just the beginning.
Flash enables you to do more with its peculiar graphics than you may realize, and you've yet to explore the format's multimedia capabilities.

If I haven't sold you yet on the possibilities of Flash, maybe this chapter
will do the trick. Here you'll learn two stunts that you won't find in
Fireworks. The first is shape tweening, which is a method for changing
one shape into another. The second is adding sound to your movie.

Tweening Shapes

You already know about motion tweens. By placing one instance of a symbol in one frame of the Timeline panel and another instance of the same

symbol in another frame, Flash automatically calculates the difference in position or appearance between the two instances.

There's another kind of tweening in Flash that may interest you: *shape tweening.* In shape tweening, Flash automatically calculates the difference in shape between one piece of art in one keyframe and another piece of art in another keyframe. If you're thinking that you can use shape tweens to turn circles into squares, space monkeys into ostriches, or Republicans into Democrats, you're absolutely right. Take any two shapes and tween them, and the first shape flows smoothly into the second, violating all known laws of physics and perhaps also good taste.

You'll recall that the crucial first step for creating motion tweens was to convert the moving art into a symbol first. I explained that motion tweens worked only when you set them up between instances of symbols. You can forget this advice in shape tweening. For shape tweens to work, the art in either keyframe can't be any kind of object. The shapes can't be instances of symbols, in other words, and they can't even be text objects or groups. If you have objects in the keyframes, you need to break them apart, as you'll see shortly.

Creating a Shape Tween

Let me show you about shape tweening by way of an example movie. This one is called *Meaning.* It's a 13-second vehicle for the Astro Ape character, in which the monkey makes a pilgrimage to the wise and mysterious monolith from *The Complete Idiot's Guide to Computer Illustration* (Alpha Books, 2002) (see Figure 12.1). Astro Ape asks the meaning of life and receives an answer, as Figure 12.2 shows.

Figure 12.1

Astro Ape poses an important philosophical question to the all-knowing monolith.

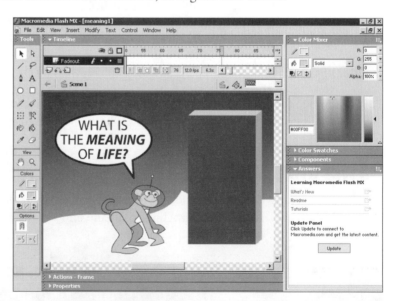

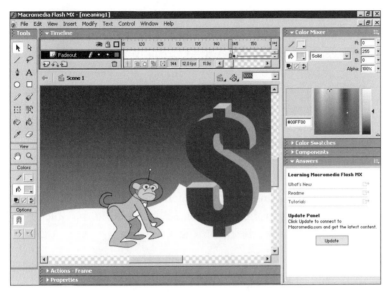

Figure 12.2

The answer is something of a letdown.

The idea here is that the monolith changes into the dollar sign by way of a *shape tween*. All you need is the monolith shape in one keyframe and the dollar-sign shape in another.

You can see what I have so far by loading the CD-ROM that comes with this book. Launch Flash, choose File → Open, and navigate to the Chapter 12 folder on the CD-ROM. You want the file called *meaning1.fla*.

Shop Talk

A **shape tween** in Flash is a gradual transformation from one shape to another.

After the file loads, preview the animation under Control → Test Movie. A motion tween brings the monkey onto the stage from Frame 1 to Frame 25 of the Astro Ape layer. The Dialog 1 and Dialog 2 layers show word balloons for three seconds each. Then, the monolith changes into a dollar sign in the Monolith layer between Frames 121 and 133, but the transformation is abrupt, because there isn't a shape tween yet. Finally, the stage fades to black from Frames 145 to 157. I achieved this effect by creating a black rectangle exactly the same size as the stage, 550 pixels by 400 pixels. I converted this rectangle into a symbol called Fadeout, and I put one instance of the symbol in Frame 145 of the Fadeout layer and another in Frame 157, so that the black rectangle conceals everything in the layers underneath. Then, I set the alpha value of the first instance to 0%, which is the same as 100% transparency. I left the alpha value of the second instance at 100%, which is the same as 100% opacity. A simple motion tween does the rest: The black rectangle gradually fades in over a period of one second, creating the effect of a fade to black.

Creating a shape tween in the Monolith layer is easy, but first you need to make sure that the starting shape and the ending shape are nonobjects. Select the keyframe in Frame 121 of the Monolith layer, and choose Modify → Break Apart. This command converts instances of symbols, text objects, or groups into regular Flash art, essentially revoking whatever object status the art in the keyframe possesses. Look under the Modify menu again, and the Break Apart command should be grayed out. This is how you know that there are no other objects in the keyframe. Occasionally, you may need to use the Break Apart command more than once to get rid of all the objects in the keyframe. Keep breaking the objects apart until the command grays out.

> **⚠ CAUTION**
>
> **Cut!**
>
> If either shape in a shape tween is an object like a symbol instance, a group, or a block of text, the shape tween won't work. Make sure that you break apart both shapes before you create the shape tween.

Now select Frame 133 of the Monolith layer, and break apart the object in this keyframe. Check under the Modify menu again to make sure that the Break Apart command is grayed out.

You now have two nonobject shapes in two different keyframes. You're ready for the shape tween. Select Frame 121 again, and go to the Properties panel. Pull Shape from the Tween list. Flash adds an arrow to the Timelines panel to indicate a tween, but the background color of the frames becomes green instead of blue. This color signifies that you have a shape tween, not a motion tween.

Drag the salmon-colored playback head back and forth between the keyframes to see the shape tween in action, and choose File → Save As to save this version of the movie as *meaning2.fla*.

Modifying the Shape Tween

When you select Shape from the Tween list on the Properties panel, Flash gives you options for easing and blending. Easing in shape tweens is just like easing for motion tweens. Easing in causes the shape tween to start off slowly and then work rapidly toward the end. Easing out causes the shape tween to start off rapidly and then peter off at the end. Drag the Easing slider up to ease the shape tween out, or down to ease the shape tween in.

Blending is a property that applies only to shape tweens. The Blend list on the Properties panel gives you two choices: Distributive and Angular. Distributive blending creates intermediate shapes with rounder, more abstract corners, while angular blending retains sharp edges. By default, Flash uses the Distributive setting, but you can change this by pulling Angular from the Blend list. In general, you should keep distributive blending when the starting and ending shapes have curved or rounded edges, and switch to angular blending when the starting and ending shapes have hard or angled edges.

Changing the blend of the shape tween in the current movie doesn't have much of an effect, because the starting monolith shape has sharp edges, while the ending dollar-sign shape has rounded edges. Angular blending may not be quite as chaotic in this case, but it still produces abstract results. Easing in or easing out works exactly as described, though. Adjust the easing if you prefer, and save your changes to *meaning2.fla*.

Animation Advice

To achieve better control over a complicated shape tween, try drawing one or two of the intermediate shapes manually. Insert these as keyframes between the keyframes of the starting and ending shapes, and then define a series of shape tweens from one keyframe to the next. Often, a sequence of smaller changes looks less abstract than a single leap from one shape to another.

Using Shape Hints

When you create a shape tween, Flash determines the way in which the shape tween plays out. In other words, Flash decides which portions of the first shape turn into which portions of the second shape. By adding shape hints to the art, you reclaim some control over the tweening process.

Shape hints set up correspondences between a point on the art in the first keyframe and a point on the art in the second keyframe. The shape hint itself appears as a small circle with a letter from *a* to *z*. You can have as many as 26 shape hints per tween, one for each letter of the alphabet. You position these hints manually on the art. Then, during the tween, Flash moves the shape hints on the first shape toward the corresponding hints on the second shape. Sounds easy enough, right?

See if you can improve the shape tween in the current movie using shape hints. As of now, some of the intermediate shapes seem to float in the air.

Shop Talk

Shape hints are pairs of corresponding points on the starting and ending shapes of a shape tween. During the shape tween, Flash moves the position of the starting shape hint toward the corresponding position of the ending shape hint. If you open a movie with shape hints but don't see the hints on the shapes, choose View → Show Shape Hints.

Select Frame 121 of the Monolith layer, and choose Modify → Shape → Add Shape Hint. A circle with the letter *a* appears on the stage. Drag this shape hint to the top left corner of the back of the monolith, as in Figure 12.3.

Figure 12.3

Create a shape hint, and position it on the back of the monolith as shown in this figure.

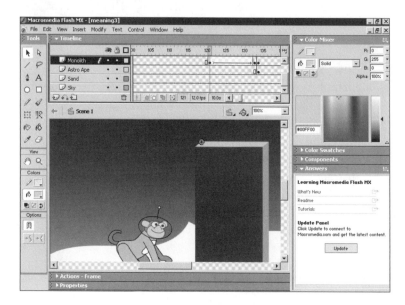

Now select Frame 133, and notice that another shape hint *a* is waiting for you. All you have to do is drag this shape hint to the corresponding location on the new shape, which is the top left corner of the back of the dollar sign, as in Figure 12.4.

Figure 12.4

In Frame 133, drag the corresponding shape hint to the corresponding position on the dollar sign.

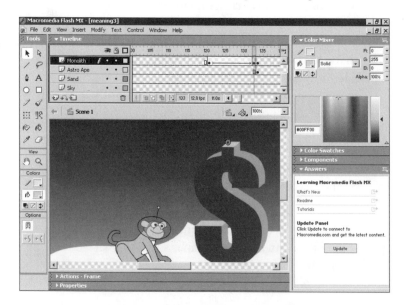

Switch back to Frame 121, and create a new shape hint by choosing Modify → Shape → Add Shape Hint again. Position this one at the bottom right corner of the back of the monolith, as in Figure 12.5.

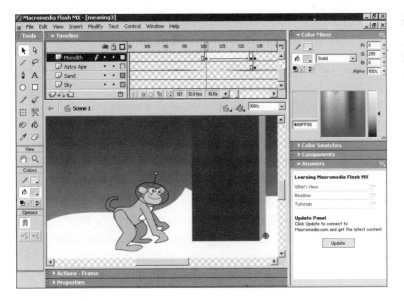

Figure 12.5

Back in Frame 121, create a new shape hint, and position it like this.

Drag the corresponding shape hint in Frame 133 to the bottom right corner of the back of the dollar sign, as in Figure 12.6.

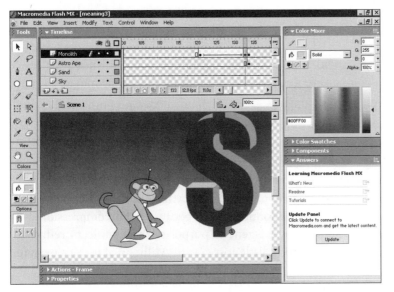

Figure 12.6

Finish by positioning the new shape hint on the corresponding corner of the dollar sign.

You now have two correspondences on the shapes in Frames 121 and 133. When Flash tweens the shapes, it moves the corners with the hints in Frame 121 toward the corners with the hints in Frame 133. Drag the playback head between the two keyframes to see the difference. Notice especially how the top of the monolith seems to shrink into the top of the dollar sign. Plus, the bottom of the monolith seems to stay on the ground, or at least closer to the ground than it did before. Without shape hints, the tween plays out differently, because Flash by itself chooses different correspondences.

Even with shape hints, the tween may not behave exactly as you would like it. Flash simply isn't built for sophisticated morphing, as in 3-D animation for the movies. If you have a very specific transformation sequence in mind, you can always draw each frame manually and then use frame-by-frame techniques to animate it.

> ### The Big Picture
>
> In 1991, the film *Terminator 2* gave audiences their first taste of computer animated morphing, or the process of changing one 3-D model into another. Morphing has become a staple of 3-D animation in Hollywood.

To remove all the shape hints in the current frame, choose Modify → Shape → Remove All Hints. To remove a single shape hint, drag it off the stage, or, if you have a right mouse button, right-click it and choose Remove Hint from the context menu.

When you finish experimenting with shape hints to guide the tweening process, save this version of the movie as *meaning3.fla*.

Adding Sound

The Flash format supports audio. Unlike animated GIFs, you can enhance your Flash movies with sound. All you have to do is import a sound file into your movie.

Sound files, like graphics files, come in a variety of formats. Some of the more common formats are WAV (Microsoft audio format), AIFF (Macintosh audio format), and MP3 (Moving Picture Expert Group Layer 3). WAV and AIFF audio files are similar to BMP graphics files in that they're uncompressed. These files tend to have the best audio quality, and they usually carry a hefty file size for their trouble. MP3 files are similar to JPEG images in that they're compressed. They have smaller file sizes than WAVs or AIFFs at the expense of some sound quality, because MP3 compression tosses out audio information. However, for general purposes, the significant reduction in file size more than makes up for a little lost clarity. Millions of former peer-to-peer music swappers can tell you that.

If you're using Flash MX for Windows, you can import WAV and MP3 files into your movie. If you're using Flash MX for Macintosh, you can import AIFF and MP3 audio. But if you have QuickTime version 4 or better on your system, Windows users can import AIFF sounds in Flash, and Mac users can import WAV sounds. If you don't already have QuickTime, I suggest installing it from the CD-ROM that comes with this book, especially if you're a Mac user, since the sound effects for the examples in this chapter come in WAV format.

Animation Advice

Installing QuickTime version 4 or better on your system allows you to use a greater variety of audio files in Flash.

Importing a Sound File

Speaking of the CD-ROM, pop it into your CD tray, choose File → Import from the Flash menu, and navigate to the Chapter 5 folder. In this folder, you'll find three WAV sound files: *wind.wav*, a 13-second clip of howling wind; *laughs.wav*, a 1.5-second cheesy sitcom-style laugh track; and *cashreg.wav*, a 1.6-second cha-ching sound effect that sounds like an old-time cash register. I told you that WAV files are uncompressed, and I meant it. The 1.5-second laugh track weighs in at 344K, while the 13-second wind effect occupies a bandwidth-clogging 1.09MB. Neither of these sound effects is worth the download time. Only the cash register's cha-ching at 68K or so seems reasonable, but that's just because the other files are so large by comparison. Fortunately, Flash provides built-in audio compression, as you'll see.

Hold down Ctrl (Windows) or Command (Mac), and select all three audio files. Then, click the Open button. The computer pauses for a moment, and then the Import dialog box goes away. It may seem as though nothing has happened, but that's just because Flash imports sounds directly to the Library. To prove it, choose Window → Library from the menu. There, among the symbols for the movie, are three new sound files.

To audition a sound, select it, and click the play button that appears in the view area at the top of the Library panel. The blue wave under the play button, by the way, isn't just eye candy (see Figure 12.7). It's the actual visual representation of the sound file. Notice that the laugh

Shop Talk

A stereo sound has two audio channels, left and right, while a monaural or mono sound has only one audio channel. Although Flash supports stereo sound, mono sounds tend to work better because of their more compact file size.

track, which is in stereo, shows two blue waves. The wave on the top is the left channel, and the wave on the bottom is the right.

Figure 12.1

When you import a sound file into your movie, the Library panel in Flash shows a graphical representation of the actual sound wave. In the case of a stereo sound, you get two waves, one for the left channel, and one for the right.

Attaching Sound to a Keyframe

There are two methods for adding imported sounds to your movie, both of which involve keyframes. The first is to attach a sound to an existing keyframe. This technique works well when you want to associate a sound with a particular event in your movie, like the cha-ching of the cash register with the monolith's shape tween. The second is to create a new layer for the sound, attach the sound to its blank keyframe, and then move the keyframe to the desired location in the movie. Use this technique when you have a sound that doesn't correspond nicely with any existing keyframe in the movie, or if you want to be able to edit the timing of the sound without disrupting the timing of your animation.

Try the first method with the cash-register sound effect. Select Frame 121 in the Monolith layer, which marks the beginning of the shape tween. Find the Sound list in the Properties panel, and set it to cashreg. Flash adds the blue sound wave to the layer, signifying that the sound effect is in place. To test the movie with its new sound effect, position the playback head a few frames to the left of Frame 121, and choose Control → Play from the menu, or simply press Enter or Return. The playback head advances automatically. When it hits Frame 121, the cash register chimes in, exactly on cue. Press Enter or Return to stop the playback head, or choose Control → Stop.

Now for the wind effect. Select Frame 1 of the Sky layer, and pull Wind from the Sound list on the Properties panel. Once again, Flash adds the blue sound wave to the layer. Position the playback head at Frame 1, and press Enter or Return to roll the movie. Notice that the wind effect doesn't drop out when the cash register comes in. In Flash, you can have as many sounds as you like playing simultaneously.

> ### The Big Picture
>
> *The Hank McCune Show* on NBC was the first television program to use a laugh track. The year was 1950.

The laugh track is next. For this sound, try creating a new layer. Select the Fadeout layer, which is currently the uppermost layer in the movie, and click the New Layer button in the Timeline panel. Call this layer Laughs. Select the blank keyframe in Frame 1 of this layer, and pull Laughs from the Sound list on the Properties panel. Flash draws the blue sound wave in this layer, just like before. Drag the keyframe to the vicinity of Frame 130, position the playback head a few frames to the left, and roll the movie. If the laughs come in too soon, simply drag the keyframe to the right. If the laughs come in too late, drag the keyframe to the left. You don't have this kind of flexibility when you attach sounds to keyframes that also control animation. After much fiddling, I'm settling on Frame 132 for the start of the laugh track.

When you're satisfied with the timing of the laughter, reposition the playback head at the beginning of the movie, and roll the animation all the way through. Notice how a few simple sounds can improve the entertainment value of an essentially ridiculous movie. Save this one as *meaning4.fla*.

Synchronizing the Sound

The three sound effects you added to the example movie in this chapter use the Flash default synchronization setting of Event. Select a keyframe to which you attached a sound, and the Sync list on the Properties panel tells you as much.

Event synchronization associates the sound with a particular event in the movie so that, when the movie reaches the keyframe that signifies the event, the corresponding sound plays. Moreover, an event sound plays from start to finish, even if the movie ends before the sound does.

Shop Talk

Event synchronization associates a sound with a particular event in a movie, while **stream synchronization** ties the audio to the animation timeline.

You can change the way that Flash synchronizes a sound in your movie by selecting the keyframe and pulling a different setting from the Sync list. Besides Event, there are three other settings: Start, Stop, and Stream.

Start synchronization works much like Event synchronization, except if the same sound is currently playing in the movie, Flash doesn't produce a new instance of the sound. Try attaching the Wind sound to any keyframe in the Astro Ape layer, and set the Sync list to Start for this sound. Position the playback head in Frame 1, and then press Enter or Return. The wind sound begins in Frame 1 of the Sky layer, as before. When the playback head hits the frame in the Astro Ape layer with the Wind sound, nothing happens. Why? Because the Wind sound is already playing, and you set the synchronization of the second sound to Start. If you change the synchronization to Event, you get two wind effects.

Stop synchronization automatically discontinues playback of all instances of its sound. Select the keyframe in the Astro Ape layer with the Wind sound, and change the Sync list to Stop. Rewind the movie to the beginning, and then roll it forward. The wind effect begins in Frame 1 of the Sky layer, but the sound ceases abruptly as soon as the movie reaches the keyframe with Wind plus stop synchronization. Notice that the keyframes don't need to be in the same layer. As long as the sounds of the keyframes are the same, stop synchronization works as advertised.

> **The Big Picture**
>
> Start and stop synchronization are flavors of event synchronization.

Stream synchronization ties its sound to the animation timeline. If the Flash Player gets backed up, it skips animation frames to maintain tight synchronization with the stream sound. Unlike event sounds, stream sounds last only as long as their graphical representations in the Timelines panel. If another keyframe cuts the sound wave short, the sound stops playing. Likewise, a stream sound ends when the movie ends, regardless of the sound's length. Use Stream synchronization when different segments of a sound file need to correspond closely with different parts of an animation, such as dialog between characters. You can test Stream synchronization with the cashreg sound in the Monolith layer. Set this sound to Stream instead of Event, and roll the movie. Notice that Stream synchronization cuts off the cha-ching at the end, since the sound lasts slightly longer than the portion of its wave that shows in the Timeline panel.

Compressing the Sound

Even small sound files tend to add too much download time to your movie. Luckily, Flash provides built-in audio compression. Better still, the software allows you to set the level of compression for each sound effect individually.

Choose Window → Library to open the Library panel, and double-click the first sound in the list, which happens to be cashreg. This calls up the Sound Properties dialog box, shown in Figure 12.8.

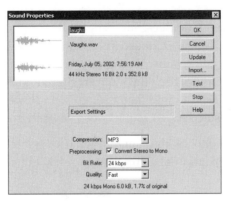

Figure 12.8

Use the Sound Properties dialog box to set the compression level of the sound effects in your movie.

Pull a method of compression from the Compression list. You have five choices: Default, ADPCM, MP3, Raw, and Speech. The Default setting uses the movie's default audio compression—I'll talk more about this in Chapter 14. ADPCM (Adaptive Delta Pulse Code Modulation) works well for short event sounds. MP3 compression is the best all-around compression option, especially with stream sounds, but you can use it with event sounds, too. Raw compression is actually no compression whatsoever. This option increases the file size of your movie significantly, so take care in using it. Speech compression works especially well with spoken-word audio like dialog or narration.

Depending on the compression setting you pick, the Sound Properties dialog box shows different controls and options for compressing the sound. Choose MP3 compression for the cashreg sound effect, and you get Bit Rate and Quality dropdown lists. The value in the Bit Rate list determines the size of the sound: The higher the bit rate, the less compression Flash uses. The value in the Quality list determines the compression speed: The higher the speed, the faster the compression, but the lower the quality of the compressed sound.

Animation Advice

You can easily tell when an audio file has too much compression, because it sounds distorted. Compressing sound means you are literally throwing away audio information which defined that sound—the less information, the more the quality of the sound deteriorates.

Experiment with different settings in the Bit Rate and Quality lists, and click the Test button after each combination to audition the sound. When you find a suitable level of compression, click the OK button. I'm settling for a bit rate of 32 kbps and fast compression speed. When I audition the sound at 24 kbps, the next lowest level, the quality drops too much. It's far better to have no sound at all than to have sound with too much compression.

Back in the Library panel, double-click Laughs, the second sound on the list. This is a stereo sound, as you'll recall. Choose MP3 from the Compression list, and experiment with the bit rate and compression speed. If you select 20 kbps or higher from the Bit Rate list, you can uncheck the Convert Stereo To Mono option, which leaves the sound in stereo. Keep in mind that a stereo sound takes up twice as much memory as a mono sound, since stereo requires two separate sound waves.

I like the sound of a mono 24 kbps laugh track with fast compression speed, but choose whatever combination of settings you prefer, and click OK to close the Sound Properties dialog box.

Finally, double-click the wind sound in the Library panel, set the compression to MP3 once again, and play with the compression levels. A bit rate of 20 kbps and fast compression speed works for me. When you get just the right compression, click OK, and save this version of the movie as *meaning5.fla*.

To preview your movie with compressed sounds in place, choose Control → Test Movie.

The Least You Need to Know

- ◆ Shape tweens work only with nonobjects.
- ◆ Use shape tweens to transform one shape into another; shape hints help you to guide the shape-tweening process.
- ◆ Import sound files into the Library for use in Flash movies.
- ◆ You can attach sounds to existing keyframes or new keyframes in sound-only layers.
- ◆ Associate a sound with a particular event by way of event synchronization.
- ◆ Tie a sound to the animation timeline by way of stream synchronization.
- ◆ Use the Sound Properties dialog box to adjust the compression settings of each sound individually.

Chapter 3

Making Interactive Movies

In This Chapter

♦ Organizing a movie into scenes

♦ Creating buttons

♦ Attaching actions to buttons

♦ Attaching actions to frames

An interactive movie is a movie that relies on audience participation. It doesn't just roll from start to finish. Your viewers have a say in how the movie plays out.

This chapter shows you how to build simple interactivity into your movies for a less passive, more active user experience.

Organizing the Movie

The example movie in this chapter is a variation on *Alien's Joy Ride* from Chapter 11. Insert the CD-ROM that comes with this book. Then, launch Flash, and choose File → Open. Navigate to the Chapter 13 folder on the CD-ROM, and choose the file called *joyride9.fla*.

Have a look at the Timeline panel. Appearances suggest that this movie is only one frame long, as in Figure 13.1. But when you test the movie in the

Flash Player under Control → Test Movie, you find that the movie clearly lasts longer than a single frame. There are a number of motion tweens, in fact. What gives?

Figure 13.1

According to the Timeline panel, this movie is only one frame long—or is it?

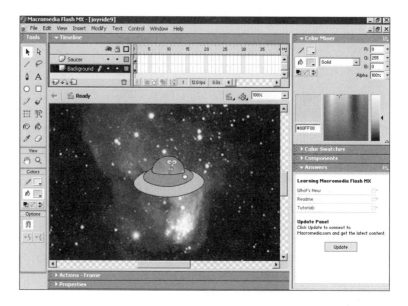

The answer is, I organized this movie into scenes. A *scene* is simply a collection of frames and layers that represents a particular animation sequence. The Timeline panel currently shows a single frame because the first scene of the movie, called Ready, is only one frame long. There are four other scenes in this movie, each with 21 frames. These scenes contain the motion tweens that move the flying saucer.

To examine the additional scenes, choose Window → Scene from the menu. This calls up the Scene panel (see Figure 13.2). Sure enough, you find the scenes Up, Down, Left, and Right. Select a scene to view its timeline in the Timeline panel. Drag the salmon-colored playback head back and forth to see the functions of the motion tweens in the Saucer layer for each scene. Not surprisingly, the Up scene moves the saucer to the top of the stage and back again. The Down scene moves the saucer to the bottom of the stage and back, and so on.

Shop Talk

A **scene** is a collection of frames and layers that represents a particular animation sequence.

To add a new scene to your movie, click the plus button at the bottom of the Scene panel. Flash inserts a new scene with a blank timeline after the currently selected scene. You may build any kind of animation into the new scene that you like, drawing from the existing symbols in the Library panel or adding new symbols as you require.

You can also add as many layers to the new scene as you need. These layers don't have to correspond with the layers in the other scenes. Think of each scene as a movie within a movie.

Figure 13.2

Use the Scene panel to inspect the various scenes of a movie.

To use an existing scene as the basis for a new scene, click the Duplicate Scene button instead. This is the button to the left of the plus button on the Scene panel. Flash copies the timeline of the currently selected scene and inserts them automatically into the new scene. You can modify this timeline freely. It's simply a starting point for the new scene.

To remove a scene from the movie, select it, and click the trashcan icon at the bottom right of the Scene panel.

Normally, the scenes of a movie play back in the order in which they appear in the Scene panel, one after another. You can change the order of a scene by dragging it to a new location in the Scene panel. For instance, dragging the Left scene above the Up scene causes the saucer to move to the left of the stage before it goes to the top of the stage when you play back the movie.

Organizing a movie into scenes is especially useful when you're building an interactive movie, as you'll see in this chapter.

Building Buttons

For an interactive movie to be interactive, you need something in the movie for the audience to click. Enter the button. A button is a type of symbol whose instances respond to mouse clicks. Clicking an instance of a button causes a certain action to happen, which gives the audience control over how the movie plays out.

Adding buttons to a movie is easy. Use the Flash drawing tools to create the shape of the button, and then convert the shape into a symbol that has the Button behavior.

> **The Big Picture**
>
> The three types of symbol behaviors in Flash are Image, Button, and Movie Clip.

Switch to the Ready scene in the Scene panel, which should be the first scene in the list. Now, in the Timeline panel, create a new layer called Buttons. Grab the Oval tool, and set the properties of the oval in the Properties panel. The color of the button should stand out from the background, so I'm picking the saucer's shades of green as the stroke and fill colors. I'm also setting the stroke weight to 4, just to give the button a solid outline. When you're ready, draw a small circle in the lower right of the stage, as shown in Figure 13.3.

Figure 13.3

Create a new layer in the first scene, and draw a button shape.

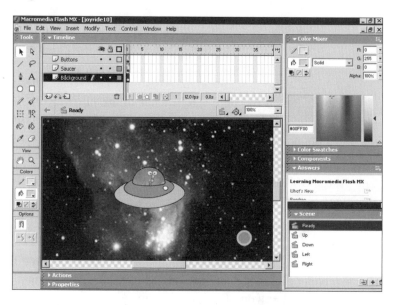

Click the keyframe in the Buttons layer to select the stroke and fill of the button, and choose Insert → Convert To Symbol to open the Convert To Symbol dialog box.

Shop Talk

The **up state** of a button is its default appearance in the movie. The **over state** of a button is its appearance when the viewer hovers over it with the mouse pointer. The **down state** of a button is its appearance when the viewer clicks it. The **hit state** of a button defines its clickable region.

Type **Button** in the Name field, and set the behavior of the symbol to Button. Click OK to convert the circle into a button symbol.

The next step is to open the Library panel under Window → Show Library. Double-click the Button symbol to open its timeline. Notice that a button has a slightly different timeline than other symbols. Instead of numbers, four text labels appear in the Timeline panel: Up, Over, Down, and Hit, as in Figure 13.4.

The Up frame of a button represents the button's *up state*, which is the button's default appearance. As you can see, the Up frame already contains a keyframe—this is the shape that you initially drew for the button.

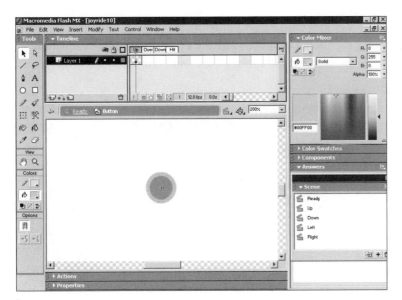

Figure 13.4

A button's timeline has four labeled frames: Up, Over, Down, and Hit.

The Over frame of a button represents the button's *over state*, which is the appearance of the button when the visitor hovers over it with the mouse pointer. Currently, the Over frame has no keyframe, which means that your button doesn't have an over state. That is, hovering over the button with the mouse pointer has no effect on the button's appearance. You can change that easily by selecting the keyframe in the Up frame and choosing Edit → Copy Frames. Click inside the empty Over frame, and choose Edit → Paste Frames. Now, select the keyframe in the Over frame, and edit the appearance of the button's over state. I'm changing the fill color of the button to a brighter shade of green, as Figure 13.5 shows. Now, when the visitor hovers over the button, it changes from drab to bright green.

The Down frame represents the *down state* of the button, which is its appearance when the visitor clicks it. The Down frame is currently undefined, since it has no keyframe. To create a down state quickly and easily, paste another copy of the up state into this frame, and modify away. I'm changing the fill color of the down state to bright green, the same as the over state, and I'm making the stroke color a species of mint green, but you can apply whatever transformation you like.

The Hit frame represents the *hit state* of the button, which is the button's clickable region. If you don't define a hit state for a button, Flash assumes that the entire button is clickable. But by adding a blank keyframe to the Hit frame of the button and drawing a shape into it, the area of the shape becomes the clickable region of the button. That is, the visitor must position the mouse pointer within this area in order to click the button and activate its function. You can make the shape in the Hit frame any color you like, because it doesn't appear in your movie. Flash simply uses its contours to define the button's clickable region. I want the entire button to be clickable in this movie, so I'm not defining a hit state, but you should feel free to create one if you like.

Figure 13.5

Copy the Up frame's keyframe into the Over frame, and edit the button's over state.

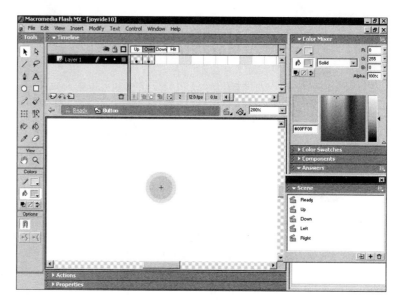

Cut!

Watch out for complex or unintuitive hit states. Since the art in the Hit frame of a button doesn't appear in your movie, your audience might not be able to guess where to click. The purpose of a button is to aid interactivity, not frustrate it. If you define a hit state, make sure that it fits logically or intuitively with the design of your button. By way of example, imagine a button that looks like a light switch in a wall panel. Creating a hit state on the switch itself makes sense—your audience will go for this part of the button by instinct. Creating a hit state on the panel only is a bad idea, because who besides electricians will think to click there?

When you define the over state and down state of a button, you give your audience visual cues, or graphical representations that something has happened. Visual cues help to improve the interactivity of your movie. When the button changes appearance during the over state, the visitor gets the idea that clicking the button will cause something to happen. Then, when the button changes appearance during the down state, the visitor receives visual confirmation that the movie has registered a click. To improve interactivity even more, add sound effects to the over and down states. Sounds give the audience audio cues, which reinforce the visual cues.

Adding sound to the states of a button is just like adding sounds to other elements in your movie. First, import the sounds into the Library. Then, associate the sounds with the keyframes in the various states of the button.

The Chapter 13 folder of the CD-ROM contains two WAV files: *beep.wav* and *click.wav*. My plan is to use Beep for the over state of the button and Click for the down state. Choose File → Import from the Flash menu, and navigate to the Chapter 13 folder. Select both sound files by holding down Ctrl (Windows) or Command (Mac), and click Import to bring the sounds into the Library.

Animation Advice

Audio cues work best when you use them to enhance visual cues. They can be confusing by themselves. If you have to choose between visual cues and audio cues, go with visual.

Now, go to the Library panel, and double-click the Beep sound to open the Sound Properties dialog box. Set the compression to MP3, and fiddle with the bit rate and compression speed to get the right level of compression, just like you did in Chapter 12. I like the sound of 16 kbps at fast compression, although even 8 kbps doesn't sound bad. Pick the level of compression that suits you the best, and click OK.

Double-click the Click sound, set the compression to MP3 again, and adjust the level of compression. I'm gravitating toward 16 kbps at fast compression, just like with the Beep sound, only this time, 8 kbps isn't a passable alternative to these ears.

To attach the Beep sound to the over state, select the keyframe in the Over frame of the button. Go to the Properties panel, and pull Beep from the Sound list. Now, select the keyframe in the Down frame of the button, and pull Click from the Sound list. Event synchronization works fine for both sounds.

You now have a button with an over state and a down state, and both states have sound effects. One instance of this button appears in your movie already. The next step is to create three more instances of this button.

Close the button's timeline by clicking the blue arrow icon above the stage to the left. The timeline of the Ready scene returns. Make sure that the Buttons layer is selected, and drag the Button symbol from the Library panel onto the stage three times. Arrange the four instances of the buttons like the points of a compass, as in Figure 13.6.

Figure 13.6

Add three more instances of the button to the stage, and arrange the instances like this.

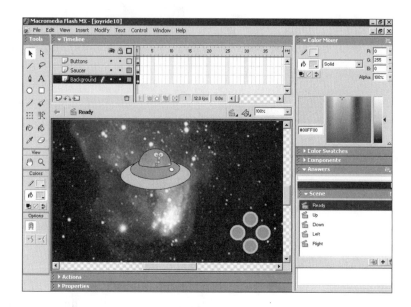

You can probably guess what's coming next. The idea of this movie is for the audience to click a button and choose the direction in which the saucer travels. This kind of interactive movie is called a *branching* or *multipath movie*. Instead of each scene following in linear order, the audience determines when each scene or branch of the movie plays. Clicking the topmost button calls the Up scene, while clicking the bottommost button calls the Down scene, and so on.

Shop Talk

A **branching** or **multipath movie** is an interactive movie that enables the audience to determine the order in which the branches of the movie play.

The buttons are in place. The scenes are ready to go. All you have to do now is program the buttons to perform their intended functions.

Attaching Actions

Programming a button isn't as difficult as it might sound. First, you select the instance of the button that you want to program. Then, you attach an action to the button by way of the Actions panel.

To start, select the uppermost button instance on the stage. This is the button that launches the Up scene. Collapse the Properties panel by clicking its white triangle, and expand the Actions panel by choosing Window → Actions, as in Figure 13.7.

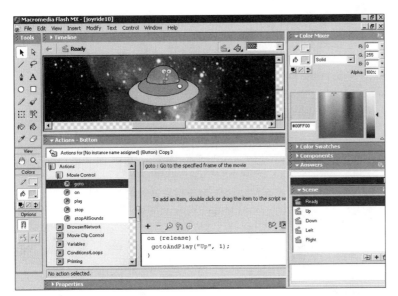

Figure 13.7

Use the Actions panel to add actions to button instances and frames in your movie's timeline.

Click the Actions category on the left of the Action panel, and then click the Movie Control subcategory. Flash presents five actions from which to choose. Since you want this button to launch the Up scene of your movie, double-click the goto action, which jumps to a particular frame or scene.

To the right of the list of actions, Flash gives you several fields for modifying the behavior of the action (see Figure 13.8). You want this button to launch the Up scene, so pull Up from the Scene list. Since you want to go to the first frame in this scene, leave the rest of the fields as they are, with Type set to Frame Number and Frame set to 1.

The narrow window at the bottom of the Actions panel shows the *ActionScript* that controls the button's behavior. ActionScript is the built-in scripting language Flash uses to describe the actions of elements in your movie. You can write your own ActionScripts if you prefer, or you can build them with the keywords in the Actions panel, as you just did. From start to finish, your script looks like this:

```
on (release) {
  gotoAndPlay("Up", 1);
}
```

Animation Advice

If the Actions panel doesn't give you enough room to work, try dragging its title bar. This increases the size of the panel.

Shop Talk

ActionScript is the built-in scripting language Flash uses for interactive movies.

In plain language, this script indicates that when the visitor releases the button, the movie should go to Frame 1 of the scene called Up and play the scene.

Figure 13.8

After you add an action, modify the behavior of the action with the fields on the Actions panel.

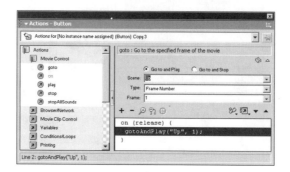

Releasing the mouse button after clicking is an event in ActionScript. There are several others. By changing the event, you change the activating mechanism for the button. To change the event, select the first line of the ActionScript in the Actions panel. The Actions panel, in turn, gives you checkboxes for adding events to the button or removing them, as shown in Figure 13.9.

Figure 13.9

Change the event that triggers the button's action by highlighting the first line of the button's ActionScript.

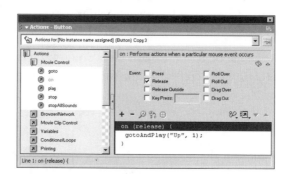

Table 13.1 summarizes the different button events that you can use. Experiment with different events as you like. Notice that you can even assign more than one event to the same action. For example, by checking both the Release and Key Press events, releasing the mouse button or pressing a particular key both cause the movie to jump to the Up scene. For the purposes of this movie, though, just use the Release event.

Table 13.1 Button Events in ActionScript

Event	What Triggers It
Press	Pressing the mouse button on a movie button
Release	Releasing the mouse button after pressing a movie button

Event	What Triggers It
Release Outside	Releasing the mouse button outside the clickable area of a movie button
Key Press	Pressing a particular key on the keyboard
Roll Over	Hovering over a movie button with the mouse pointer
Roll Out	Moving the mouse pointer away from a movie button after hovering over it
Drag Over	Dragging the mouse pointer outside and then over a movie button
Drag Out	Dragging the mouse pointer outside a movie button

One button down, three to go. Go back to the stage, and select the button instance that launches the Left scene. Double-click the goto action in the Actions panel, and set the Scene list to Left. The corresponding ActionScript looks very much like the first. The only difference is the name of the scene in the second line:

```
on (release) {
  gotoAndPlay("Left", 1);
}
```

Select the button instance that launches the Right scene, double-click the goto action, and set the Scene list to Right. Finally, attach the goto action to the button instance for the Down scene, following the same general procedure.

In no time at all, you have programmed all four of the button instances to go to and play their corresponding scenes in the movie, but you're not quite ready to test your movie. You need to add a few frame actions to make sure that the movie behaves as you intend. Frame actions are much like button actions, only you attach them to keyframes in the Timeline panel, not button instances on the stage. When the movie plays a frame that contains an action, the action activates.

Remember I told you that, under normal circumstances, the scenes in a movie play in order. As of now, the current scene lasts only a single frame. It won't take long for this scene to play. When it finishes, Flash automatically jumps to the next scene in the Scene panel, which is Up. You need an action in Frame 1 of the Ready scene that forces Flash to stop playback and wait for the audience to click a button.

The Big Picture

Use button actions when you want the audience to trigger ActionScripts, and use frame actions when you want the animation timeline itself to trigger ActionScripts.

Select any of the three keyframes in Frame 1 of the Ready scene—it doesn't matter which one. Then, go to the Actions panel, and double-click the Stop action. This creates a very simple, one-line ActionScript for a very simple directive: Stop the movie here, please!

```
stop();
```

Notice that the keyframe to which you attached the action shows a small lowercase *a*, as in Figure 13.10. This is the Timeline panel's way of reminding you which keyframe contains the action.

Figure 13.10

When you attach an action to a keyframe in the Timeline panel, the keyframe shows a small lowercase a.

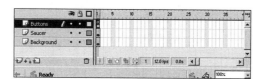

Here's the logic of the movie so far. When the movie begins, the Flash Player loads Frame 1 of the first scene. The action in Frame 1 causes the Flash Player to stop and wait for the audience to click a button. Clicking a button at this point is the only way to advance the movie.

Assume that the audience clicks the button instance for the Up scene. The action on the button sends the movie to Frame 1 of the Up scene, and the scene plays in its entirety. What happens at the end of the Up scene, though? Just as before, Flash continues to play the remaining scenes from start to finish. It looks as if you need another frame behavior at the end of the Up scene to jump back to the Ready scene.

Click the Up scene on the Scene panel, and choose the keyframe in Frame 21 of the Saucer layer. Then, double-click the goto action on the Actions panel, and set the Scene list to Ready. Flash generates the following ActionScript:

```
gotoAndPlay("Ready", 1);
```

Notice that this script doesn't have an on-release event surrounding it like the previous goto scripts do. Why? Because, when you attach an action to a keyframe, there's no button to click, so there are no button events to monitor. The gotoAndPlay statement executes as soon as the playback head hits Frame 21 of the Saucer layer.

In the Down, Left, and Right scenes, add the same action to the same keyframe. Now, no matter which branch of the movie the audience chooses to play, the last frame in that branch automatically sends the movie back to the Ready scene, whose frame action pauses playback until the audience clicks another button.

The logic of your movie seems sound. Save this version as *joyride10.fla*, and then choose Control → Test Movie to try the actions. The buttons appear in the Ready scene and await a response. They beep and light up when you hover over them, as in Figure 13.11, and they make a clicking sound when you click them. Activating a button transfers control of the movie to a different scene, and the buttons disappear, because you added them only to Ready. When the animation finishes, playback reverts to the Ready scene, and the buttons reappear. Amuse yourself for hours by sending the alien life form to the outer reaches of the stage.

Animation Advice

You can test an interactive movie inside Flash by choosing Control → Enable Simple Frame Actions and Control → Enable Simple Buttons. Pressing Enter or Return in the Ready scene starts the movie rolling. Revert to regular editing mode by invoking the same two Control commands.

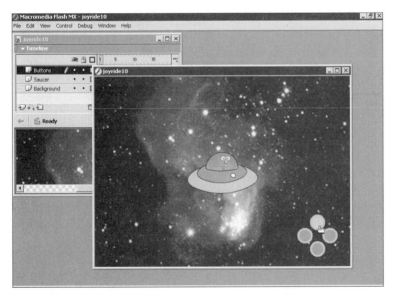

Figure 13.11

Choose Control → Test Movie to try out the interactivity.

The Least You Need to Know

◆ A scene is a collection of frames and layers that represents a particular sequence of animation.

◆ Organizing your movie into scenes is a helpful technique for building interactive movies.

◆ Add buttons to your movie to give your audience a way to interact with it.

- A button in Flash has four states: the up state, the over state, the down state, and the hit state.

- Attach actions to buttons to determine what happens when your audience clicks.

- Flash uses ActionScript to describe movie actions.

- Attach actions to keyframes when you want the animation timeline to trigger ActionScripts.

Chapter 14

Publishing Your Flash Movie

In This Chapter

◆ Exporting a standalone Flash Player

◆ Saving stills from your movie

◆ Creating an embedded movie

◆ Choosing HTML formatting options

You've been exporting SWF files since Chapter 9. Every time the subject came up, though, I recommended that you use the default settings on the Export Flash Player dialog box.

Forget defaults! This chapter explains what those tweakable controls on the Export Flash Player dialog box can do, and it shows you how to publish your work in a variety of formats.

Exporting a Standalone Player

As you know from experience, the Flash Export Movie command compresses the animation, sound effects, and actions of an FLA file into a smaller, playable SWF file. When you double-click this SWF file, the movie opens in a Flash Player window. If you plan to distribute your work by e-mail, CD, or floppy disk, use this publishing option.

Load the movie *robot.fla* from Chapter 9 and choose File → Export Movie from the menu to open the Export Movie dialog box, as shown in Figure 14.1. Choose a location for the SWF file, and type a name in the File Name field. Click Save to proceed.

Figure 14.1

Use the Export Movie command to create a playable SWF file from an FLA file.

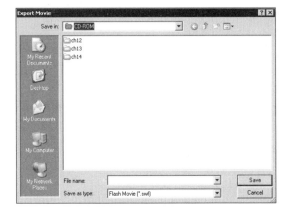

The Export Movie dialog box closes, and the Export Flash Player dialog box takes its place, as in Figure 14.2. Specify the settings of the SWF file from this dialog box. Under Load Order, determine how you want the Flash Player to load the layers of your movie. You have two choices: Bottom Up and Top Down. With Bottom Up, the default setting, the Flash Player loads the bottommost layer first and the topmost layer last. With Top Down, the Flash Player does just the opposite. When you have large pieces of background art in the lower layers of your animation and smaller, moving pieces of art in the upper layers, it's best to use the Bottom Up setting. If the bulkier art appears in the upper layers of your movie, Top Down is the better pick. For *robot.fla*, with its hill and mailbox in the lower layers, go with Bottom Up.

Figure 14.2

Specify the settings of the SWF file in the Export Flash Player dialog box.

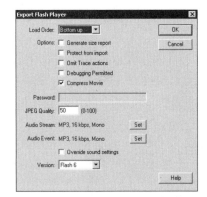

Setting Options

Under Options, check Generate Size Report if you want Flash to draw up a detailed report about the memory requirements for each frame of the movie. Flash saves this report in TXT format in the same location as the exported SWF file. To view the report, simply double-click the TXT file, or open the file in your favorite text editor or word processor.

Check Protect From Import if you want to prohibit viewers who have Flash MX from importing the SWF file into Flash and reverse-engineering the FLA file. For security's sake, it's a good idea to check this option, unless you're sharing your movie with other Flash animators. None of the SWF files on the CD-ROM that comes with this book are import protected.

Check Omit Trace Actions if you want to suppress tracing in the SWF file. I didn't discuss tracing, which is a debugging feature for advanced interactive movies. Interested parties can find out more by referencing the Flash online help. Needless to say, if you didn't use tracing in your FLA file, you have no reason to omit trace actions in your SWF file, so leave this option unchecked.

Animation Advice

Use the Protect From Import option on the Export Flash Player dialog box to prevent other animators from reverse-engineering your work.

Check Debugging Permitted if you want your viewers to be able to debug your movie's ActionScripts. Again, this option is more for movies with complex interactivity. Since *robot.fla* doesn't have any ActionScripts, you can leave this option unchecked also.

Check Compress Movie to make the smallest possible SWF file. Keep this option checked! If your movie has an abundance of text or ActionScript, Flash 6 compression can make a substantial difference in the final size of the SWF file.

If you check the Protect From Import or Debugging Permitted options, supply a password for your movie in the Password field. Animators must enter the correct password to import or debug your movie. If you don't want to protect your movie with a password, leave this field blank.

Type a value in the JPEG Quality field to set the level of compression for raster graphics or bitmap objects in your movie. You know the routine: The higher the value, the less compression Flash uses, giving you better image quality but larger file size. JPEG compression of 50 or 60 is good enough for most movies.

Setting Global Audio Compression

Under Audio Stream and Audio Event, find the Flash default settings for audio compression. Audio Stream applies to sounds with Stream synchronization, while Audio Event applies to sounds with Event, Start, and Stop synchronization. Change the default compression settings for either type of sound by clicking the appropriate Set button. If you already compressed the sound effects in your movie by way of the Sound Properties dialog box, you shouldn't adjust the default settings here, unless you want to override the levels of compression that you already established. In this case, check the Override Sound Settings option. When you do, Flash discards the individual levels of compression for each sound in your movie and recompresses all of them according to the default levels in this dialog box. Since every sound file reacts to compression differently, I don't suggest this course of action! Rely on your individual compression settings, not one-size-fits-all defaults.

For the current movie, all this talk about sound is just an academic discussion. There are no sound effects in *robot.fla*, so leave the default compression settings as they are, and don't check the Override Sound Settings option.

> **Cut!**
>
> Be very careful about overriding individual compression settings for sound effects in your movie. Different sound files react to the same level of compression differently, and it's difficult to find one setting that works equally well with all sounds. It's almost always better in the long run if you compress each sound individually, even if this process takes longer.

Choosing the Version

Finally, from the Version list, choose the version of Flash Player for which you want to create the SWF file. Normally, you should always create an SWF file for the most recent version of Flash Player—version 6—since earlier versions may not support your animation. Furthermore, Flash Player 6 allows the Compress Movie option, while earlier versions do not. Consider creating SWFs for older Flash Players only if your viewers stubbornly refuse to update their software.

Click OK to create the SWF file. Minimize Flash for a moment, and open the folder that contains the SWF. Double-click the file to view your movie in a Flash Player window, as in Figure 14.3. Your SWF plays on any computer with the correct version of the Flash Player.

> **Animation Advice**
>
> Flash Player 6 is the best version of Flash Player for animations that you create in Flash MX.

Figure 14.3

View your movie in a Flash Player window by double-clicking the exported SWF file.

Exporting Stills from the Movie

The Export Image command lets you create a *still*, or a static graphics file, of any frame in your movie's timeline. Position the playback head at the frame you want to capture, and choose File → Export Image. The Export Image dialog box appears, as in Figure 14.4. Choose a name and location for the image file, and pick its format from the Save As Type list. The default format is JPEG. Click Save to proceed.

Shop Talk _____

A **still** is a static graphics file of a frame in your movie's timeline.

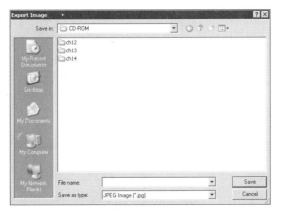

Figure 14.4

Use the Export Image command to create a still of any frame in your movie.

Another dialog box appears with options for the graphics file of the type you specified in the Save As Type list. Figure 14.5 shows the Export JPEG dialog box. If you chose a different file type, you'll have a slightly different set of options.

Figure 14.5

Specify the settings of a JPEG image with the Export JPEG dialog box.

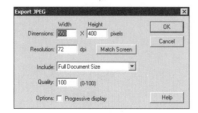

The three Dimensions and Resolution fields affect each other, so that changing one changes the others. The Dimensions fields determine the width and height of the image file, and the Resolution field gives the image's pixels per inch. My advice is to leave these fields alone. Instead, use the Include list to determine the size of the image. Choosing Full Document Size from this list creates a still of the entire stage area. Choosing Minimum Image Area discards the regions of the stage that don't pertain to the frame that you selected.

The rest of the dialog box gives options for the quality or appearance of the image. In the case of JPEG images, you get a Quality field in which to specify the level of compression and a Progressive Display option. Checking this option makes the image appear to load faster in a web browser, although a progressive JPEG is usually larger than a standard JPEG in terms of file size.

Click OK to export the still image. You can open this image in Fireworks or any other graphics program that supports the JPEG format.

Publishing an Embedded Movie

Use the Publish command to create an embedded Flash movie, which is a Flash movie that sits inside a web page and plays in a web browser, not a Flash Player window. If you plan to post your movie on a website, use this publishing option.

The Publish command typically gives you two files: the SWF file for your movie, and the HTML file for the web page that contains the movie. You can create other kinds of files with the Publish command, too, as you'll see shortly.

> **The Big Picture**
>
> An embedded Flash movie plays inside a browser window, not a Flash Player window.

Try creating an embedded movie from *meaning5.fla*, the Astro Ape cartoon with sound effects that you built in Chapter 12. Load this movie, and choose File → Publish. Flash creates an SWF file called *meaning5.swf* and an HTML document called *meaning5.html* in the same location as the existing *meaning5.fla* file. To view the embedded movie, minimize Flash, and open the folder that contains *meaning5.fla*. Double-clicking the *meaning5.html* file opens your default web browser, and the movie plays inside it, as Figure 14.6 shows.

Figure 14.6

An embedded movie plays inside a web browser, not a Flash Player window.

The Publish Settings command lets you edit the types of files that the Publish command creates as well as the options and settings of these files. Choose File → Publish Settings, and the Publish Settings dialog box appears, as in Figure 14.7.

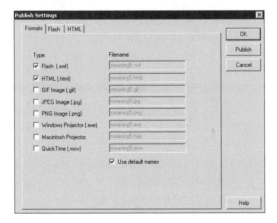

Figure 14.7

Use the Publish Settings dialog box to determine the types of files that the Publish command generates.

Choosing Formats

Under the Formats tab, determine the types of files that the Publish command generates. Check all the files that you want to create, and uncheck all the files that you don't. At the very least, though, check the Flash and HTML options. If you don't check the Flash option, you won't get an SWF file of your movie, and if you don't check the HTML option, you won't get a web page that embeds the movie.

> **CAUTION**
>
> **Cut!**
>
> Different browsers process HTML differently. It's a good idea to test your embedded movie in a variety of browsers like Netscape, Internet Explorer, and Opera, just to make sure that your HTML file works the way you intend.

If you want to specify your own file names for the various files, uncheck the Use Default Names option, and, in the Filename fields, type the names that you want to use.

Every checked file under the Formats tab receives a tab of its own on the Publish Settings dialog box. Click a tab to edit the default settings of the file in question. The options under the Flash tab match the ones on the Export Flash Player dialog box precisely. Remember not to override your individual sound compression settings unless you feel like publishing an inferior animation.

Setting Your HTML Options and Publishing Your Movie

The options under the HTML tab determine the content and structure of the embedded movie's HTML file, as you can see in Figure 14.8. From the Template list, choose the type of HTML file that you want to publish. The default is Flash Only, which supplies just enough HTML code to embed the SWF file. Other options include Detect For Flash 6, which adds a check routine to the HTML page to determine if the viewer's browser has the Flash Player 6 plug-in, and Flash For Pocket PC 2002, which creates an HTML file especially for the Pocket PC with Flash Player 6. To learn more about the selected template, click the Info button.

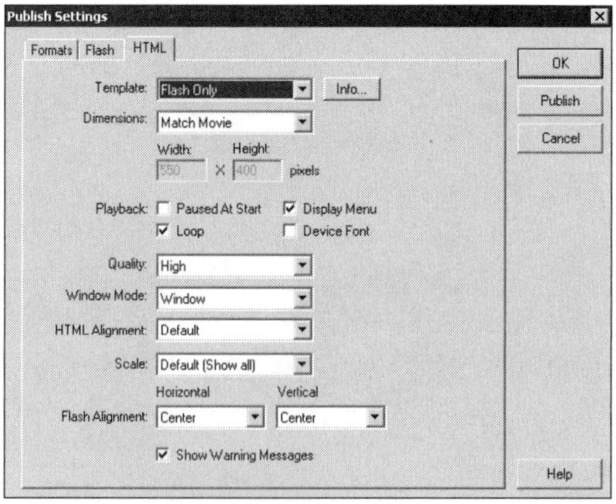

Figure 14.8

Click the HTML tab to determine the content and structure of the HTML file in which you embed your movie.

Under Dimensions, choose Match Movie, Pixels, or Percent. The Match Movie option embeds the movie at precisely the size of the stage. If you choose Pixels or Percent, you can enter values in the Width and Height fields to determine the size of the movie in the browser window. Specifying 50% by 50%, for instance, creates an embedded movie half the original size.

Under Playback, check the Paused at Start option to force the movie to pause as soon as it loads. To begin playback, the viewer must either click a specially programmed button in the first frame of the movie or open the Flash Player plug-in's context menu and choose the Play command.

Check the Loop option to cause the movie to loop automatically when it reaches the final frame. Unchecking this option prevents the movie from looping, unless a frame action in the last frame of the movie explic-itly sends playback to the beginning.

Check the Display Menu option if you want the movie to show its full context menu when the viewer right-clicks the stage (Windows) or holds down Command and clicks the stage (Macintosh). Unchecking this option leaves only a single About Flash command in the con-text menu.

Animation Advice

To guarantee that a movie loops, add a goto action to the last frame of the movie, and direct playback to the first frame of the movie.

Check the Device Font option if you want the movie to substitute Windows system fonts for unusual or less common fonts in your movie when your viewer's system doesn't have these fonts. This option works only on Windows computers. If you don't substitute Windows fonts, small text in your movie may not always be legible.

Under Quality, determine the display quality of the movie. Choosing High or Best gives the viewer the best possible animation but requires more resources and can therefore slow down playback. Choosing Medium or Low uses fewer resources and keeps playback chugging along at the expense of display quality. Choosing Auto Low or Auto High allows the Flash Player plug-in to decide the best setting, given current conditions. Auto Low defaults to speed, while Auto High defaults to display quality.

Under Window Mode, determine how you want to embed the movie. Choosing Window embeds the movie in its own rectangular space on the HTML page. For most movies, this is the best option. Choosing Opaque Windowless prevents the background of the page from showing through transparent areas of the movie, while choosing Transparent Windowless allows the background of the page to show through transparent areas of the movie. These settings work only when you view your movie in Microsoft Internet Explorer version 4 or better.

Under HTML Alignment, pick a position for the embedded movie inside the browser window. Default uses the browser's default alignment, which is usually the same as Left.

Under Scale, choose the way in which the movie sits inside its boundaries as determined by the Dimensions fields. The Default (Show All) option preserves the original aspect ratio of the movie but may leave visible borders if the Dimensions fields don't match the size of the stage. The No Border option prevents visible borders from appearing around the movie by cropping the movie to fit its dimensions. The Exact Fit option prevents cropping but distorts the movie to fit its dimensions. The No Scale option prevents the movie from changing sizes if the viewer changes the size of the browser window.

> **The Big Picture**
>
> HTML alignment controls the position of the movie in the browser window, while Flash alignment controls the position of the movie inside its borders.

Finally, under Flash Alignment, determine the horizontal and vertical position of the movie inside its boundaries. Setting both lists to Center, for instance, positions the movie in the middle of its boundaries. These fields don't affect the general location of the embedded movie in the browser window—use the HTML Alignment list for that.

After you finish setting the options for the various files to publish, click OK to close the Publish Settings dialog box, and then choose File → Publish to publish your movie. As a shortcut, simply click the Publish button in the Publish Settings dialog box, and then click OK. When you upload your movie to the web, make sure that you send the HTML file as well as the SWF file.

The Least You Need to Know

- Use the Export Movie command to create a standalone Flash Player, which allows anyone with the right version to view your SWF file.

- Create stills of individual frames in your movie with the Export Image command.

- Use the Publish command to create an embedded Flash movie for the web.

- The Publish Settings dialog box enables you to determine what kinds of files Flash publishes.

- At the very least, an embedded movie requires a SWF file and an HTML file.

- Always test your embedded movie in a variety of browsers.

Part 4

Creating Shockwave Movies

You're bidding farewell to Flash for now, but don't worry about forgetting what you learned. You're about to use your skills with Flash MX to take the sting out of learning Macromedia Director 8.5. In no time at all, you'll be creating motion tweens and adding interactivity in the Rolls Royce of multimedia software, and you'll get your first taste of 3-D animation.

Chapter 15

Introducing Director

In This Chapter

◆ Working with the stage, score, and windows

◆ Creating all kinds of cast members

◆ Saving a Director project

Macromedia Director 8.5 is animation and multimedia software for creating Shockwave movies. In many ways, Director is a big brother to Flash. You'll find many similarities between Director and Flash, but you'll also discover some important differences. I hope to point out a few of each in this chapter, which introduces you to the interface, terminology, and drawing tools in Director.

To get started, pop the CD-ROM that comes with this book into your computer, and install the trial version of Macromedia Director 8.5. Then, launch the application, and away you go.

Exploring the Interface

Director doesn't share the same Macromedia MX interface that you used in Fireworks and Flash (as you can see in Figure 15.1), but don't let the initial dissimilarities fool you. There's a long, rectangular tool palette in the upper left corner of the screen that corresponds to the MX Tools panel. There's a stage that corresponds to the Flash MX stage and the Fireworks MX canvas. The stage is where you build your Shockwave movie. There's also a score at the bottom of the screen. The score corresponds to the Timeline panel in Flash MX. This is where you set up the action of your Shockwave movie.

Figure 15.1

Don't let the lack of panels and panel groups deceive you. The interface of Director 8.5 has much in common with Fireworks and especially Flash.

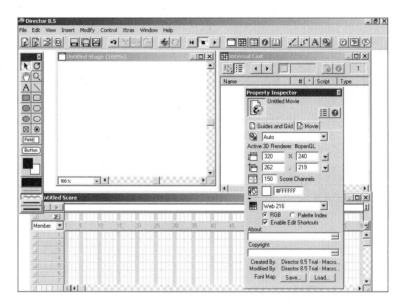

While Macromedia MX applications organize auxiliary functions into panels and panel groups, the Director interface opts for a more traditional, floating-window approach. You can think of each of the Director windows on your screen as a panel in Flash or Fireworks. Director windows provide commands and options for creating your movie, just like the panels do. You can open windows as you need them and close them when you don't, just like panels, by choosing from the Window menu. Aside from appearance, the only real difference between windows and panels is that you can drag the windows around the screen more easily and freely. You can also minimize, maximize, and close Director windows just like the windows in your computer's operating system.

When you launch Director for the first time, you see five windows: the Tool panel, the stage, the score, the Cast window, and the property inspector. The Tool panel, of course, gives you quick access to drawing commands and other movie-building goodies. The stage is where you create your movie, and the score is where you set up the animation.

The Cast window is another very important part of the interface. This is the window next to the stage that says Internal Cast. The Cast window works much like the Library panel in Flash, where Flash stores the symbols and sound effects that you use in your movie. You'll recall that, when you build a movie in Flash, you take instances of the symbols in the Library panel, arrange them on the stage, and control their behavior in the Timeline panel. The procedure in Director is almost exactly the same. Director stores its symbol-like objects—its *cast members*—in the Cast window. To create a Shockwave animation, you pull from the cast members in the Cast window, place their *sprites*, or their instances, on the stage, and control their behavior in the score.

You can view the cast members in the Cast window two ways: as graphical representations or in list form. The second button from the left at the top of the cast window is the Cast View Style button. This is the button with what appears to be a bulleted list as its icon. When this button is pressed in, the Cast window displays a text-only list of cast members. When this button is turned off, the Cast window displays thumbnail images of the cast members instead.

The property inspector in Director is an MX-style Properties panel by any other name. Select an item on the stage, and the property inspector lets you modify that item's properties, including size, location, color, angle of rotation, angle of skew, and so on.

Slide open the Window menu for a moment, and you find several other windows that don't currently appear on screen. (Director marks the active, visible windows with a check mark or a bullet.) I'll talk about many of these additional windows as their functions crop up.

Shop Talk

Cast members in Director are like symbols in Flash. These are the elements that you use in your movie. Sprites in Director are like instances in Flash. These are the objects that you manipulate on the stage.

The Big Picture

Macromedia FreeHand is another application that uses a Director-style interface of floating windows.

Setting Up the Stage

Go to the tool palette and grab the Arrow tool, which is the first tool on the left at the top of the palette. Click anywhere on the stage, and then look to the property inspector. As you can see in Figure 15.2, the property inspector reconfigures itself to give you options for modifying the characteristics of the stage.

Figure 15.2

When you select the stage, the property inspector gives you commands and options for modifying its characteristics.

These options appear under two tabs: Guides And Grid and Movie. Under the Guides And Grid tab, you can customize the way Director displays its optional visual aids. Guides are horizontal or vertical lines that you insert manually on the stage, as in Figure 15.3. Use guides as straightedges to help you line up the elements of your animation. To insert a guide, look under the Guides And Grids tab of the property inspector, and go to the icons marked New. Drag the left icon onto the stage for a horizontal guide, or drag the right icon onto the stage for a vertical guide. You can adjust the position of a guide by dragging it with the Arrow tool. To remove a guide entirely, drag it off the stage.

Animation Advice

To hide the guides on the stage, choose View → Guides, and a submenu slides out. Note that the Show Guides option has a check mark to the left of it. Select this option to remove the check mark and hide the guides. Restore the guides by repeating this procedure.

The grid is like a network of horizontal and vertical guides, as Figure 15.4 shows. Unlike with guides, though, you can't drag the lines of the grid with the Arrow tool. Turn on the grid by choosing View → Guides And Grid → Show Grid. Hide the grid by repeating the same command.

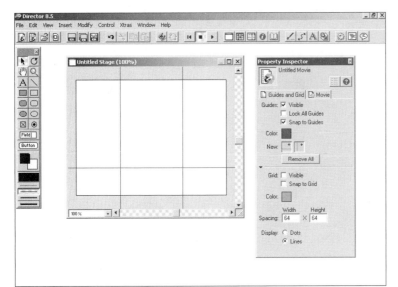

Figure 15.3

Adding guides to the stage is like laying a straightedge across a piece of paper. Guides help you to align the elements of your movie.

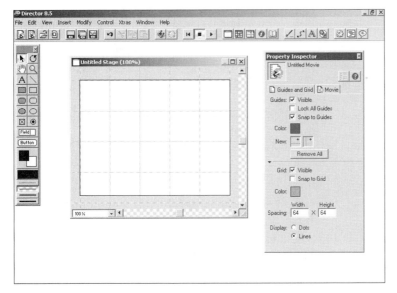

Figure 15.4

Turn on the grid by choosing View → Guides and Grid → Show Grid.

Click the Movie tab of the property inspector to change the physical characteristics of the stage. The Stage Size fields, which are the first pair of fields toward the top of the inspector, give the dimensions of the stage in pixels. To change the size of the stage, click the Arrow button to the right of the fields and pull a new set of dimensions from the menu that slides out (see Figure 15.5). The size of the stage's window changes automatically. You can also type width and height values directly into the fields.

Figure 15.5

Look under the Movie tab of the property inspector to change the physical characteristics of the stage.

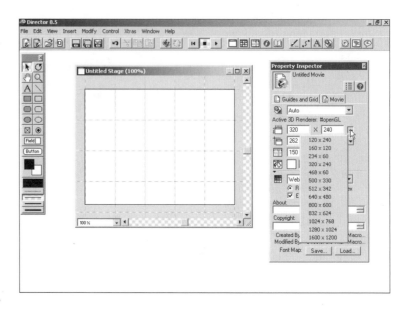

The Big Picture

Remember that guides and the grid are visual aids only. They don't appear in your final Shockwave movie.

Cut!

Don't double-click the color square to change the color of the stage. Double-clicking opens the color palette window, which enables you to adjust the colors in the palette manually. This is great when you want to create a customized palette for your movie, but it's not so great when you want to choose the color of the stage. To pick a stage color, click the color square and hold down the mouse button.

The next pair of fields controls the position of the stage on the screen. Again, type X and Y coordinates directly into these fields, or click the Arrow button to the right of the fields and choose a default setting from the menu.

An important step at the beginning of any Director project is to choose the movie's palette, or set of colors. The current palette appears in the dropdown list to the right of the last icon on the property inspector. By default, Director chooses the palette that corresponds to the system colors of your computer, either Windows colors or Mac colors. If you want to use a different palette, pull one from this list. The Web 216 palette is a good one to use, since it features only web-safe colors, or the 216 colors that Windows and Mac systems share when running in 256-color mode. When you choose the Web 216 palette, you help to ensure that Windows and Mac people see your movie exactly as you intend it to be seen, so pull Web 216 from the dropdown list.

If you want to change the color of the stage, find the paint bucket icon on the property inspector. To the right of this icon is a white square. Move the mouse pointer onto this square, and click and hold down the mouse button. A Color menu pops up. This menu contains all the colors in the current palette. If you choose a different palette for the movie, you get different color choices in this menu. Select a color for the stage, and release the mouse button.

Creating Cast Members

One of the main differences between Flash and Director is that, in Director, all the elements of the movie are cast members. If the same were true in Flash, all the elements of the movie would be symbols. You know from creating Flash movies that this isn't necessarily the case. When you work in Flash, you must specifically convert pieces of art into symbols. But in Director, as soon as you use one of the drawing tools or import an external file, you add a cast member to the cast window.

There are various kinds of cast members in Director. Among them are shapes, vector shapes, bitmaps, text, and external media files like QuickTime movie clips, sounds, and even SWF Flash movies. These external media files come from other software applications. To use them in your Shockwave movie, you simply import them into the Director cast window. I'll talk about importing external media files as cast members in Chapter 16. For now, let me focus on the cast members that you can create in Director.

Creating Shapes

A shape is a vectorlike cast member. The difference between a shape and a vector shape is that shapes are simpler and take up even less memory than vectors, which are already very memory efficient. The outlines of shapes aren't as crisp, though, which is the trade-off.

The Big Picture

I mentioned that the outlines of shapes aren't as crisp as the outlines of vectors. To be more precise, the outlines of shapes aren't anti-aliased, unlike the outlines of vectors in Director. Anti-aliasing is a common technique in computer graphics by which the computer tricks the human eye into seeing a smooth edge. In anti-aliasing, the computer gradually blends the colors of the contour of the image with the colors of the background.

Use the tools on the tool palette to create shapes. Table 15.1 gives a quick rundown of shape-drawing tools in Director.

Table 15.1   Shape-Drawing Tools in Director

Tool	What It Draws
Line	Straight lines
Filled Rectangle	Solid squares and rectangles
Rectangle	Hollow squares and rectangles
Filled Round Rectangle	Solid squares and rectangles with rounded corners
Round Rectangle	Hollow squares and rectangles with rounded corners
Filled Ellipse	Solid ellipses and circles
Ellipse	Hollow ellipses and circles

Give one of the shape-drawing tools a try. Select the Filled Ellipse tool, which is the sixth tool from the top on the left side of the tool palette. Move the mouse pointer onto the stage, position the crosshairs where you want to start drawing, hold down the mouse button, and drag. Adjust the size and shape of the ellipse as you go, and press Shift to change the ellipse into a perfect circle. Release the mouse button to finish.

If I'm right about Director, then you just added a cast member to your movie. There's a quick way to find out: Look at the Cast window. Sure enough, you find that Director has added a member to the cast called 1, ominously enough. If you look at the Cast window in graphical view, you see a miniature image of this cast member, along with a square icon in the lower right corner designating that the cast member is a shape.

Click the cast member in the Cast window, and go to the property inspector. The property inspector shows three tabs now (see Figure 15.6), all pertaining to the selected cast member. Under the Member tab, type a descriptive name for the cast member such as Filled Ellipse in the Name text box, and leave comments about the cast member in the Comments text box. Under the Shape tab, you can change the underlying shape of the cast member, and you can turn off the fill by deselecting the Filled check box. Under Cast, you find technical information about the cast member, including its size and the cast to which it belongs, which is currently the internal cast of the movie.

Animation Advice

To change the thickness of the outline of a shape, select its sprite and click one of the four thickness buttons at the bottom of the tool palette.

Now select the shape on the stage. This shape is a sprite, or instance, of the cast member. You can alter the properties of the sprite however you choose.

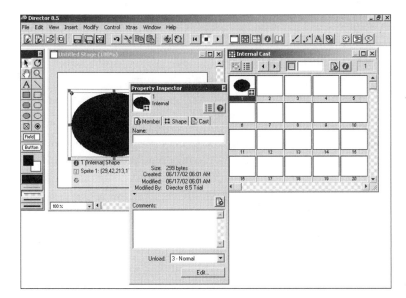

Figure 15.6

Select a cast member in the Cast window, and you can change the cast member's properties in the property inspector.

Go to the property inspector, which has changed to give you options for modifying the sprite, as Figure 15.7 shows. Look under the Sprite tab, find the left-facing paint bucket icon, and move the mouse pointer to its color square, which controls the foreground color of the sprite. (The right-facing paint bucket controls the background color—more on that later.) Hold down the mouse button on the foreground color square for the Color menu. Select a foreground color for the shape, and release. The sprite dutifully changes color.

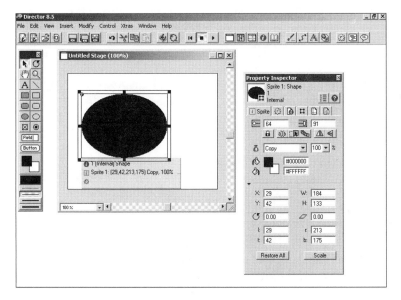

Figure 15.7

Then select a sprite on the stage, and you can change the sprite's properties in the property inspector.

Select the cast member again in the Cast window, and drag the cast member onto the stage to create a new sprite. Now, go to the property inspector and change the foreground color of this sprite to something different. The new sprite changes color, while the original sprite retains its original color. Just like different instances of the same symbol in Flash can have different properties, different sprites of the same cast member can have different properties.

Above the paint bucket icons is an inkbottle icon. The fields next to this icon control the sprite's *ink mode*, or the method that Director uses to present the sprite on the stage. (The ink metaphor may be slightly misguided here, since ink in Director doesn't behave like the ink in a fountain pen. Think of ink in Director as the appearance setting of the sprite instead of the sprite's color or texture.) The default ink mode is Copy, which makes the sprite into an identical version of the cast member. Choose a different ink mode by picking a new value from the dropdown list to the right of the inkbottle. The Transparency value, for instance, creates a transparent sprite. Set the ink mode to Transparency, and then pull a transparency value from the percentage list next door.

Shop Talk

A sprite's **ink mode** is the way in which Director presents the sprite on the stage. Think of the ink mode as the appearance setting of the sprite.

Combining ink modes, foreground colors, and background colors in shape sprites creates color effects. Choosing Blend as the ink mode causes Director to mix the foreground and background colors and color the sprite accordingly, while choosing Ghost causes Director to replace the foreground color with the background color on the sprite. Feel free to experiment with different settings for different types of sprites.

Creating Vector Shapes

While you can use the tools on the tool palette to draw simple shapes, you must open the Vector Shape window (see Figure 15.8) to draw full-fledged vector shapes. This window opens when you choose Window → Vector Shape from the menu.

Choose from the drawing tools on the left side of the window to create your vector. Table 15.2 gives a quick rundown of their functions.

Table 15.2   Vector-Shape Drawing Tools in Director

Tool	What It Draws
Pen	Straight and curved strokes
Filled Rectangle	Filled squares and rectangles

Tool	What It Draws
Rectangle	Squares and rectangles with strokes only
Filled Round Rectangle	Rounded-corner squares and rectangles
Round Rectangle	Rounded-corner squares and rectangles with strokes only
Filled Ellipse	Filled ellipses and circles
Ellipse	Ellipses and circles with strokes only

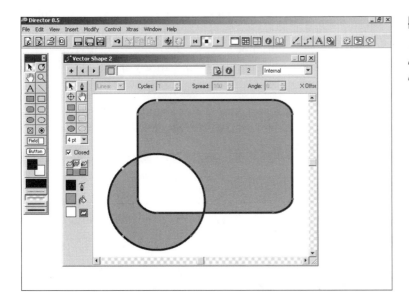

Figure 15.8

Use the Vector Shape window to create vector-shape cast members.

Director gets particular about vector shapes. If you start out with the Pen tool, for instance, you can only use the Pen tool in that vector shape. Director disables the rest of the tools. If you start out with one of the filled tools, Director lets you use filled tools only to add to the vector. (Overlapping fills cancel each other out.) If you start out with one of the nonfilled tools, you can only use nonfilled tools to add to the vector. In both cases, though, you can use the Pen to change the shape of the vector.

The three color squares at the bottom of the Vector Shape window control the stroke color, the fill color, and the background color of the vector shape, respectively. Hold down the mouse button on one of these color squares to choose the corresponding color. All the component shapes in your vector must use the same stroke, fill, and background colors.

Set the width of the stroke with the dropdown list immediately below the tools.

Use the three buttons under the stroke width list to control the fill of the vector. Clicking the first button hides the fills. Clicking the second button creates a solid fill. Clicking the third button creates a gradient fill, or a gradual shift between colors. Choose the colors of the gradient fill from the smaller color squares underneath these three buttons.

When you finish drawing your vector shape, simply close the Vector Shape window. Director automatically adds your new vector to the Cast window. Select its sprite to modify its properties. Choosing new foreground and background colors in the property inspector causes Director to blend the current colors of the vector with your new choices. Setting Background Transparent as the ink mode causes the background color of your vector shape to disappear. Once again, feel free to experiment with different combinations of colors and ink modes.

Animation Advice

To edit the style of a gradient fill, adjust the values of the fields along the top of the Vector Shape window.

To edit the original vector shape, double-click its cast member in the Cast window or a sprite of it on the stage.

Creating Bitmaps

Use the Paint window to create bitmap cast members (see Figure 15.9). Bitmaps, as you know, are raster graphics. Look on the left side of the Paint window, and you find a nice assortment of bitmap drawing tools, which Table 15.3 summarizes.

Figure 15.9

Want raster cast members?
Use the Paint window.

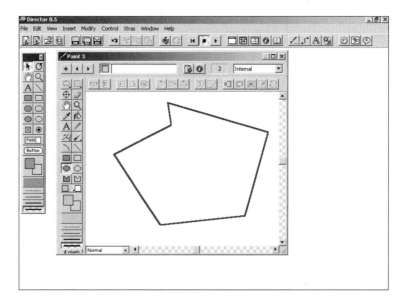

Table 15.3   Bitmap Drawing Tools in Director

Tool	What It Draws
Pencil	Pencil-style line of pixels
Air Brush	Airbrush-style line of pixels
Brush	Calligraphy-style line of pixels
Arc	Curved pencil lines
Line	Straight pencil lines
Filled Rectangle	Solid squares and rectangles
Rectangle	Hollow squares and rectangles
Filled Ellipse	Solid ellipses and circles
Ellipse	Hollow ellipses and circles
Filled Polygon	Filled multisided shapes
Hollow Polygon	Hollow multisided shapes
Eraser	Erases pixels
Paint Bucket	Fills enclosed regions with the foreground color
Text	Adds noneditable bitmap text

Unlike with the Vector Shape window, the Paint window lets you use different colors in your bitmap. You're not stuck with the same color combination for every tool. Set the foreground and background colors by holding down the mouse button on the foreground and background color squares.

Under the foreground and background color squares is a large rectangle with the current foreground color. Hold down the mouse button on this rectangle to choose a pattern for the foreground color instead of a solid shade. As you see when the pattern menu pops up, most of the patterns alternate the foreground and background colors, while a few are precolored textures.

Above the foreground and background color squares are smaller color squares for creating a gradient. Once again, a gradient in this context is a gradual shift between colors. Choose the component colors for the gradient by holding down the mouse button on these color squares. Hold down the mouse button on the middle icon to set the style of the gradient. To draw with a gradient, choose one of the filled drawing tools and set the dropdown list at the bottom of the Paint window to Gradient. This dropdown list controls the ink mode of the drawing tools. To paint with a gradient, select the Paint Bucket tool, set the ink-mode dropdown list to Gradient, and click enclosed areas in the bitmap.

The Big Picture

There are other ink modes besides Gradient in the ink-mode dropdown list. For instance, Reverse ink creates the opposite color in the Paint window, and Ghost ink suppresses the foreground color. Experiment with ink modes to create color effects.

Select areas of pixels with the Lasso and Marquee tools. These are the tools in the top row of the Paint window. The Lasso tool lets you draw a freeform shape around the pixels that you want to select, while the Marquee tool selects a geometric region.

After you select an area of pixels, you can apply transformations with the row of tool icons just above the drawing area. Table 15.4 gives you a quick rundown of their functions.

Table 15.4 Bitmap Transformation Tools in Director

Tool	What It Does
Flip Horizontal	Flips selected area from left to right
Flip Vertical	Flips selected area from top to bottom
Rotate Left	Turns selected area 90 degrees counter-clockwise
Rotate Right	Turns selected area 90 degrees clockwise
Free Rotate	Rotates selected area to your specification when you drag the selection's handles
Skew	Skews selected area when you drag the selection's handles
Warp	Distorts selected area when you drag the selection's handles
Perspective	Distorts selected area in perspective when you drag the selection's handles
Smooth	Smoothes contour of selected area
Trace Edges	Creates outlines of selected area
Invert	Inverts colors of selected area
Lighten	Lightens colors of selected area
Darken	Darkens colors of selected area
Fill	Fills selected area with foreground color
Switch	Changes all pixels with the current foreground color in the selected area to the destination color, or the second component color of the gradient

When you finish creating the bitmap, close the Paint window. Director adds your bitmap to the cast window and allows you to drag sprites of it onto the stage. Set the properties of the bitmap sprite with the property inspector. For instance, to hide the sprite's background color, set the ink mode to Background Transparent.

Inserting Text

The Text window allows you to create editable text cast members (see Figure 15.10). If you played with the Text tool in the Paint window, you know that, once you type the text, you can't get back in and edit it. Not so with a text cast member. You're free to edit everything about the text, from the dimensions of the object to its font, style, and formatting.

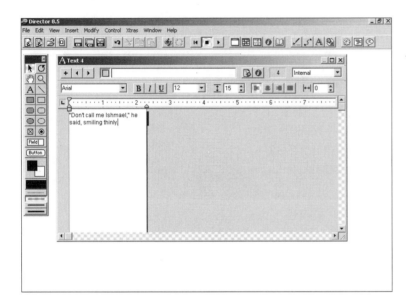

Figure 15.10

Use the Text window to create editable text cast members.

Choose Window → Text to open the Text window. Set the font, style, and size of the text with the controls at the top of the window. Set the width of the text cast member by dragging the margin of the rectangular area inside the window. Use your computer's keyboard to enter the text. When you finish, close the Text window, and drag a sprite of the new text cast member onto the stage.

To use the Text window to edit the text of the cast member, double-click the cast member in the cast window. To edit the text on the stage, double-click the text sprite with the Arrow tool. You can also change the width of the cast member by single-clicking the sprite with the Arrow tool and dragging the left or right handle.

CAUTION Cut!

Watch out! If you change the width or content of one text sprite, all the sprites of that particular cast member change accordingly. However, you can change the colors of one text sprite without affecting the other sprites of the same cast member.

Change the text color of a text sprite by selecting the sprite and choosing a new foreground color from the property inspector. Change the color of the rectangular field on which the text sits by choosing a new background color.

Saving Your Work

To save a Director project for the first time, choose File → Save from the menu. (In the future, if you want to save the project under a different file name, use File → Save As instead.) The Save Movie dialog box appears, as in Figure 15.11. Choose a location for the movie file, type a name for the file in the File Name text box, and click Save.

Figure 15.11

Save your Director movie as a DIR file with the Save Movie dialog box.

This procedure creates a DIR file, which is the Director equivalent of a Flash FLA file. The DIR is the editable version of your movie, the version that you keep in your archives. The version of the movie that you post on the web is the DCR file, the Shockwave movie, which corresponds to a Flash SWF. You use the Publish command to create Shockwave DCRs. I'll talk about this process in Chapter 19.

The Least You Need to Know

◆ Macromedia Director 8.5 is animation and multimedia software for creating Shockwave movies.

◆ The Director stage, score, cast members, and sprites correspond to the Flash stage, Timeline panel, symbols, and instances.

◆ Use the tools palette to add simple shapes as cast members.

◆ Use the Vector Shape window to create vector-graphic cast members.

◆ Use the Paint window to create raster-graphic cast members.

◆ Use the Text window to create editable text cast members.

◆ Save the editable version of your movie as a DIR file using the Save and Save As commands.

Building a Shockwave Movie

In This Chapter

◆ Importing the cast

◆ Creating sprites

◆ Setting up tweens

◆ Adding sound effects

It's time to build a Shockwave movie. Using what you already know about Flash, you'll find that working with Director isn't as bad as it might seem.

This chapter takes you through the process of movie making in Director step by step.

Importing the Cast

I mentioned in Chapter 15 that you can import a wide variety of external media files and use them as cast members in your Shockwave movie. Multimedia is one of the great strengths of Director. To give you a small sampling of the menu, as it were, I cooked up a little movie called *Wrong Way*. It doesn't feature alien life forms, space monkeys, flying saucers, or mailboxes, but it does mark the return of the frustrated robot. In this movie, the robot enters stage left and proceeds stage right, heedless of the sign that says Wrong Way, as Figure 16.1 shows.

Figure 16.1

In this movie, the robot learns the hard way to pay more attention to his surroundings.

This movie requires three graphics: the hill, the robot, and the sign. You could piece these images together in the Vector Shape or Paint windows, but drawing tools in Director aren't necessarily first class. It's almost always better to produce art in dedicated graphics programs such as Adobe Illustrator, Adobe Photoshop, Macromedia FreeHand, or Macromedia Fireworks and then import the files into Director for the animation treatment. In fact, that's just what I did. I created the art in external applications and exported three raster images: *hill.gif*, *robot.gif*, and *sign.gif*. You can find these files in the Chapter 16 folder of the CD-ROM that comes with this book.

To begin building the movie, launch Director, and click the blank stage with the Arrow tool. Then go to the property inspector, click the Movie tab, find the pair of fields that controls the dimensions of the movie, and type **550** in the first field and **400** in the second. These are the dimensions of a typical Flash movie, as you'll recall. It's a good, standard size. Why mess with success, right?

> **Animation Advice**
>
> If the floating windows in Director annoy or distract you, you're not alone. I hate the floating windows. When I'm trying to concentrate on a movie, I close all the windows that I'm not currently using, and I reopen them from the Window menu at need.

Choose Web 216 for the color palette of your movie. Then, hold down the mouse button on the property inspector's color square to choose a color for the stage. I picked a shade of blue, #99CCFF, to be precise, but you're a creative person. Pick whatever color you prefer.

Now, pop this book's CD-ROM into your computer, and choose File → Import from the Director menu. The Import Files dialog box appears, as in Figure 16.2. Navigate to the Chapter 16 folder on the CD-ROM. If you're using the Windows version of Director, hold down Ctrl, and select the files *hill.gif*, *robot.gif*, and *sign.gif*. Then, click the Import button. If you're using the Mac version of Director, you can't select multiple files at once, unfortunately. Add the files one at a time by selecting each and clicking the Add button, and then click Import.

Figure 16.2

Use the Import Files dialog box to add external media files like graphics, movie clips, and sounds as cast members in your Shockwave movie.

Director asks you if you want to import the first file as an animated GIF or as a bitmap image, by which Director means a nonanimated GIF in this instance. Since none of the three files are animated GIFs, choose the Bitmap Image option. You can also check the Same Format For Remaining Files checkbox if you prefer. If you don't, Director asks the same question for the other two images.

Click OK, and another dialog box appears, this one asking you to set the options of the image (see Figure 16.3). Here, you can choose the color depth of the image. The lower the color depth, the smaller the file size and therefore also the smaller the file size of the final movie. Since the image's color depth of 8 bits is already smaller than the stage's color depth of 24 bits, stick with the image's internal color depth. If the image's color depth had been higher than the stage's, I would have advised you to select the stage's color depth.

You can also choose how Director handles the GIF image's palette. Remember that GIF images have built-in color palettes. Director can import the GIF's built-in palette, which adds a little extra memory to your movie, or Director can remap the colors of the GIF's palette to match the palette of your movie, which is Web 216. Choose the Remap To option, and pull Web 216 from the list.

Figure 16.3

Choose options for an imported file with the Import Options dialog box.

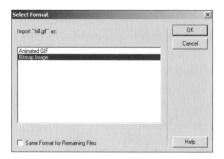

Notice that Director gives you an option for trimming excess white space from the image—a handy feature! Check this one. You can also check the Same Settings For Remaining Images option, since the other two images are also GIF files that you'll process the same way anyway. Again, if you don't check this option, Director simply asks you to set each image's options individually.

> ### The Big Picture
>
> Recall from working with Fireworks that the number of colors in a GIF image affects the size of the file. The more colors, the larger the file.

Click OK to proceed. Director imports the files and places them in the Cast window as full-fledged movie cast members, as Figure 16.4 shows. Notice also that Director took the liberty of naming your cast members according to their file names instead of giving them numbers. You're ready now to start building the movie.

Figure 16.4

When you import the images, Director adds them to the Cast window.

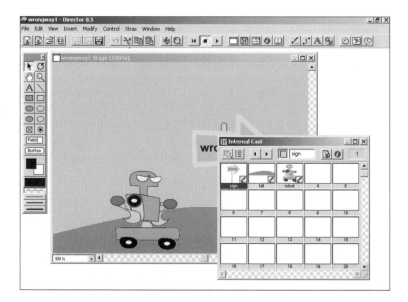

Making the Sprites

Cast members are like symbols in Flash. They don't appear in the actual movie. Instead, their sprites do all the dirty work, just like symbol instances in Flash.

Start with the sign, since this image is in the background, behind both the hill and the robot. Drag the sign from the cast window to the stage, and you add a new bitmap sprite to the movie, as Figure 16.5 shows.

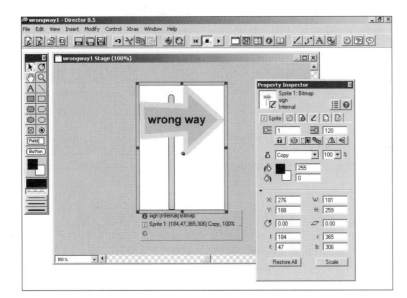

Figure 16.5

Drag the sign from the cast window to the stage, and you add a new bitmap sprite to the movie.

You can't help but notice that Director retains the white background of the GIF image, but you can fix this. Select the sprite, go to the property inspector, look under the Sprite tab, and set the ink mode to Background Transparent. The white background disappears without a trace, as in Figure 16.6.

Now, go back to the Cast window, and drag the hill onto the stage. Set the ink mode for this sprite to Background Transparent to get rid of the white background. Create a robot sprite, and clear away its background color, too. Arrange the sprites on the stage as in Figure 16.7.

Animation Advice

I find it helpful to use the graphic view of the Cast window rather than the list view.

Figure 16.6

Switch the ink mode from Copy to Background Transparent to eliminate the white background color of the sprite.

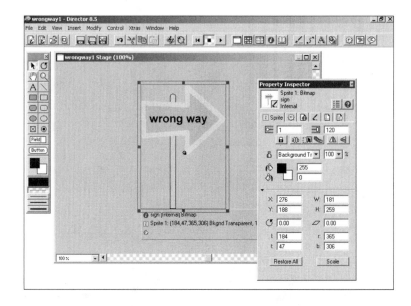

Figure 16.7

Add two more sprites, clear away their background color, and arrange them like this.

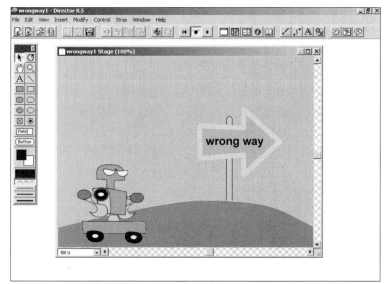

Working with the Score

Let me call your attention to the score, which is the version of the Timeline panel in Flash that Director uses. As you can see in Figure 16.8, Director has added three elements to the score, one for each of the sprites. These elements appear in Channels 1 through 3. A *channel* in Director is like a layer in Flash. Unlike Flash, though, where the layers stack from bottom to top, the channels in Director stack from top to bottom. That is, the uppermost channel contains the image that appears the farthest back in the background.

The numbers along the top of the score represent frames, just as in the Timeline panel. When you added the sprites to the stage, Director assigned 28 frames to each. This number 28 is arbitrary. You can easily change it. But to what? Time for some quick math.

Shop Talk

A **channel** in Director is like a layer in Flash. This is the row on the score that represents a sprite on the stage.

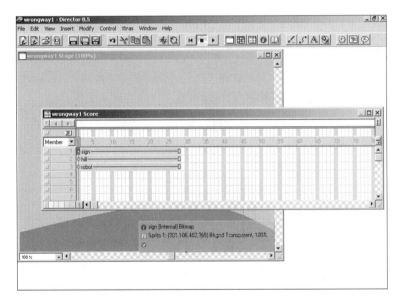

Figure 16.8

The sprites appear in the score, which works like the Timeline panel in Flash.

By default, Shockwave movies play at 30 frames per second, more than twice the frame rate of Flash movies. Assuming that you want to give the robot four seconds to cross the stage, you need a total of 120 frames for each sprite, since $4 \times 30 = 120$.

Right now, each sprite occupies 28 frames. There are two easy ways to change this value. One way is to click the last frame of the sprite, the one with the white rectangle. Hold down the mouse button, and drag this frame to Frame 120 on the score. Another way is to select the entire element by clicking anywhere in the blue region. Then go to the property inspector, look under the Sprite tab, and find the icon with the white rectangle, the one that resembles the ending frame. The current value in the field to the right of this icon is 28. Simply type **120** into this field, and press Enter or Return.

Pick the method that you prefer, and extend all three sprites to 120 frames each.

The Big Picture

In Director, the frame rate of the movie is also known as tempo.

Creating a Motion Tween

Now comes the easy part: creating the animation. Director gives you motion tween-ing, just like Flash, but I promise you that motion tweening in Director is going to seem much easier than it did before. Part of the reason is that you're more accus-tomed to the process after slogging through those Flash chapters. Part of the reason is that motion tweening is more intuitive in Director.

Case in point: Go to Channel 3, the robot channel, and click the frame in Frame 1, the frame with the white circle. If this frame reminds you of a *keyframe* in Flash, then you have this process licked already, because a keyframe is exactly what it is. With this keyframe selected, move the robot off the stage, as in Figure 16.9.

Figure 16.9

Select the keyframe in Frame 1 of Channel 3, the robot channel, and position the robot's sprite off stage left.

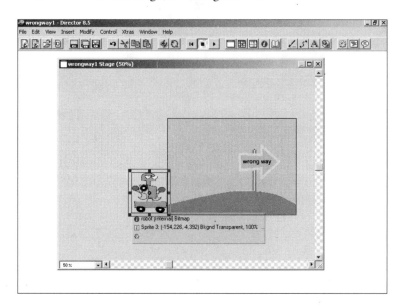

Now, look at the robot sprite on the stage. There's a handle in the center of the image. Move the mouse pointer to this handle, click it, hold down the mouse button, and drag the handle to where to you want the robot to end its motion tween, somewhere off stage right, as in Figure 16.10.

Believe it or not, there is no other step. That's all there is to creating a motion tween in Director. Drag the salmon-colored playback head across the score to see for yourself. The robot rolls blindly into danger.

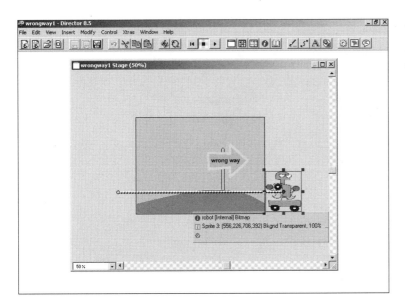

Figure 16.10

Drag the robot's motion handle off stage right.

You'll recall that, in Flash, you need to specify starting and ending keyframes to create a motion tween. Not so in Director. To get the sprite to move in a straight line, you just need a single keyframe. Director automatically adds the second keyframe to the last frame of the sprite.

Adjusting the Motion Path

You can add additional keyframes if you want the sprite to change direction during the course of its travels. To insert a new keyframe, select the sprite in the score, and position the salmon-colored playback head at the frame in which you want to add the keyframe. Then, choose Insert → Keyframe. With this keyframe selected, go to the stage, and drag the handle in the center of the sprite to its new ending position. Continue adding as many keyframes as you like to create more twists and turns in the sprite's motion path.

You can modify the motion path even more by selecting the sprite and choosing Modify → Sprite → Tweening. This calls up the Sprite Tweening dialog box, as in Figure 16.11.

Animation Advice

The Extreme setting of the Sprite Tweening dialog box adds its own kinks and twists to a motion path.

Drag the Curvature slider to the left, toward Linear, to make the sprite's changes in motion more angular. Drag the slider to the right, toward Extreme, to distort the motion path. You can also set the speed of the changes to Sharp or Smooth and ease the motion in and out.

Figure 16.11

Adjust the motion path of a sprite with the Sprite Tweening dialog box.

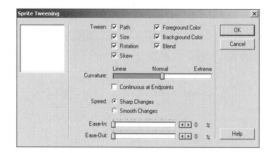

Previewing the Movie

To preview the movie in real time, choose Window → Control Panel. The Control panel gives you buttons for playing, pausing, and rewinding the movie, as Figure 16.12 shows. You can also change the movie's *tempo*, or frame rate, by typing a value in the field at the top right of the control panel.

Figure 16.12

Use the Control panel to play the movie in real time.

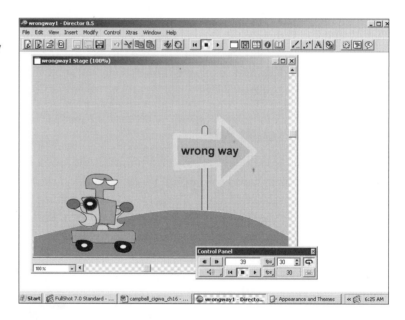

Before you continue, choose File → Save, and save this Director project as *wrongway1.dir*.

Tweening Other Properties

Like in Flash, you can tween other properties besides the X and Y coordinates of a sprite, including the size, angle of rotation, angle of skew, foreground color, background color, and blend. All you need are two good keyframes. First, select the starting keyframe in the tween, go to the property inspector, and set the properties for the sprite in this position. Then select the ending keyframe, go to the property inspector again, and set the properties for the sprite in this position. When you play back the movie, Director tweens the properties.

For instance, to tween the transparency of the robot sprite, select the first keyframe in Channel 3. Go to the property inspector, click the Sprite tab, and make sure that Background Transparent is the ink mode at 100%. Then select the last keyframe in Channel 3. On the property inspector, change the ink mode to Transparency, and type **0** in the Percentage field to the right. Play back the movie, and the robot gradually fades away. Select the ending keyframe again, and change the ink mode to Background Transparent at 100% to continue with this exercise.

> **The Big Picture**
>
> As in Flash, you can tween other sprite properties besides location as long as you have two keyframes.

There should be some sort of repercussion for the robot going the wrong way. Perhaps a collision or a steep drop is in order, but one that takes place offstage—this is an all-ages movie. The sign swaying back and forth a few seconds after the robot disappears might convey the idea that something dangerous has occurred at a level significant enough to cause seismic tremors or shock waves, especially if you add a sound effect to the movie, as you'll do in the next section.

For now, concentrate on creating the swaying motion. Start out by extending Channels 1 and 2 by nine seconds each, or 270 frames, since $9 \times 30 = 270$. Adding 270 frames to these channels makes Frame 390 the new ending frame. Select the sprite in Channel 1, go to the property inspector, and change the value of the ending frame to 390. Do the same for the sprite in Channel 2.

For the swaying motion to look realistic, set the *registration point*, or the point at which the transformation occurs, to the bottom of the signpost. Do this by double-clicking the sprite. The Paint window opens. Remember, the sign is a bitmap cast member. In the Paint window, select the Registration Point tool. This is the tool on the left in the second row from the top. A crosshairs appears in the Paint window. Drag the crosshairs to the bottom of the signpost, as in Figure 16.13, and close the Paint window.

> **Shop Talk**
>
> The **registration point** is the point at which a transformation occurs on a sprite.

Figure 16.13

To create a convincing sway-ing motion, set the registra-tion point of the sprite to the bottom of the signpost in the Paint window.

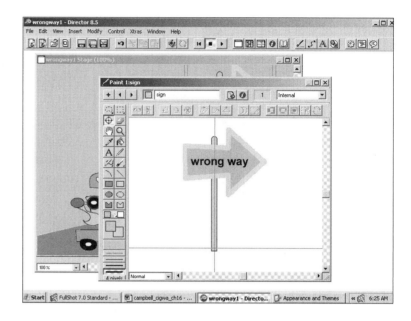

Unfortunately, changing the registration point causes the sign to change position on the stage. Drag the sprite back down to earth.

Now, select the sign sprite in Channel 1 of the score, and move the playback head to Frame 150. Choose Insert → Keyframe. Select the sprite again, move the playback head to Frame 155, and add another keyframe. Select the sprite a third time, move the playback head to Frame 160, and add another keyframe. Add two more keyframes the same way, one in Frame 165 and the last in Frame 170.

You now have multiple keyframes, which can mean only one thing: It's tweening time.

Select the keyframe at Frame 155, and go to the property inspector. Find the rotation field under the Sprite tab. This field is on the left, directly beneath the Y field. Change the value in this field to –10 to rotate the sprite 10 degrees counter-clockwise. Select the keyframe at Frame 165, and set the angle of rotation to 10. This rotates the sprite 10 degrees clockwise. You don't have to set the angle of rotation for the other keyframes, because the angle remains 0 degrees. Drag the playback head back and forth to test the tremor.

Not bad, but the wobble ends too soon, in my opinion. You can fix this by adding some more keyframes—a lot more. See Table 16.1 for a complete list of keyframes and angles of rotation.

Table 16.1   Keyframes and Angles of Rotation for Sign Sprite

Keyframe Position	Angle of Rotation
150	0
155	−10
160	0
165	10
170	0
175	−5
180	0
185	5
190	0
195	−2.5
200	0
205	2.5
210	0
215	−1
220	0
225	1
230	0
235	−0.5
240	0
245	0.5
250	0
255	−0.25
260	0
265	0.25
270	0

Play the movie all the way through from the Control panel. The wobble is better, but what this movie needs desperately is a sound effect. Before you jump to it, save this version of the movie as *wrongway2.dir* under File → Save As.

Adding Sound

Sound files qualify as external media files, which means that Director can import them into the Cast window. As you already know, once you get an external file into the cast, you can use that file in your movie.

The sound I have in mind is an explosion called *boom.mp3*. You can find this file in the Chapter 16 folder on the CD-ROM that comes with this book. To import this sound, choose File → Import, and navigate to the Chapter 16 folder. Select *boom.mp3*, and click Import. Director adds this sound to the cast window and calls it "boom" after its file name. To audition the sound, click the cast member, go to the property inspector, click the Sound tab, and press the Play button. The property inspector also tells you that this sound lasts about 7.5 seconds—an important piece of information.

Animation Advice

For Shockwave movies, the MP3 audio format is a good choice. It offers excellent compression and good sound quality.

Now all you have to do is create a sprite for the sound by dragging the cast member onto the stage. Notice that, when you do, Director doesn't add the sound to Channel 4, as you might expect. Instead, Director adds the sound to the first of two audio channels. To see the audio channels, click the Show/Hide Effects Channels button on the score. This button is the small one in the upper right corner of the score with up-arrow and down-arrow icons. Clicking it causes the score to expand, revealing the effects channels, two of which are for audio. As Figure 16.14 shows, the sound sprite you just added appears in Audio Channel 1.

Figure 16.14

Click the Show/Hide Effects Channels button to see the two audio channels in the score.

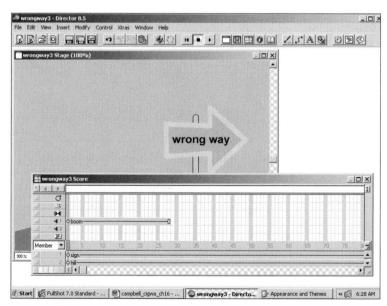

The sound sprite has a starting keyframe and an ending frame, just like the bitmap sprites in Channels 1 through 3. The starting keyframe determines when the sound plays. The ending frame determines when the sound stops playing.

You know from the property inspector that the sound lasts 7.5 seconds. Round that up to 8 seconds for good measure. An 8-second sound in a 30-frames-per-second movie means that, to hear the entire sound, you need 240 frames in the score, since $8 \times 30 = 240$. Click the sound sprite in the score, go to the property inspector, click the Sprite tab, and set the ending frame value to 241, since an ending position of 241 minus a starting position of 1 equals 240 frames.

> **The Big Picture**
>
> When you add sound with behaviors, as you will in Chapter 17, you have your pick of eight audio channels, not just two.

Now, move the sound sprite in the score so that the starting keyframe corresponds with the sign's first motion tween. The sign starts moving in Frame 150. So, click the sound sprite and move it by dragging it with the mouse. Be careful not to drag the starting or ending frames, or you'll wind up changing the length of the sprite. For best results, grab the sprite by the second or third frame. Drop the sprite at Frame 150, as in Figure 16.15.

Play the movie from the start. The sound effect adds some much-needed context.

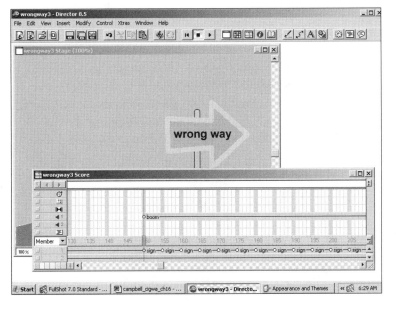

Figure 16.15

Move the sound sprite so that its starting keyframe corresponds with the first keyframe of the sign's motion tween.

You have two audio channels. You're using only one. Why waste a perfectly good sound track? Drag another sprite of the sound effect onto the stage. This time, Director adds the sprite to Audio Channel 2.

Click the second sound sprite, go to the property inspector, and set its starting frame to 153 and its ending frame to 390. This gives you just short of the full 240 frames, but that's all right, because the sound isn't quite eight full seconds long. Play the movie, and the explosion sounds much richer. Starting the second sound sprite just a few frames after the first adds to the richness.

Removing Excess Channels

Your movie keeps strict account of all the channels in the score, even the channels that you aren't using. To optimize the performance of your movie, strip out the channels that you don't need.

To do so, click a blank area of the stage with the Arrow tool, go to the property inspector, and look under the Movie tab. Find the field marked Score Channels, and enter the number of channels that you use in the score, not counting the audio or other effects channels. *Wrong Way* uses three channels, so type **3** in this field and press Enter or Return. Director removes the dead weight.

> **Animation Advice**
>
> Strip out unused channels in your movie before you create the Shockwave file. Since Director keeps track of all the channels in your movie, even unused ones, removing extraneous channels helps to improve performance.

If you decide to add to your movie afterwards, it's never a problem. Type a higher value in the Score Channels field. The maximum number of channels for any Director project is 1,000.

After you tidy up the score, choose File → Save As, and supply the file name *wrongway3.dir*.

Importing Flash Monkeys (and Movies)

Remember when I said that *Wrong Way* doesn't feature any space monkeys? I lied. Since Director is so good with borrowing external media files as cast members, I thought, why not bring Astro Ape into the equation? Besides overkill, overexposure, and lack of creative vision, what other reasons could there possibly be?

First thing's first: Fire the robot. This is a simple matter of selecting the robot cast member in the cast window and choosing Edit → Cut Cast Member (or select the cast member and press Delete). Notice that the robot's sprite remains in the score, even though this sprite no longer appears on the stage or in the cast window. Don't delete this sprite! You can use it.

Choose File → Import, and navigate to the Chapter 16 folder on the CD-ROM. Select the file *astroape.swf*, and click Import. This file is a short, 21-frame animation that cycles though Astro Ape's walking sequence. I've included the FLA of this movie on the CD-ROM if you want to open it and inspect it in Flash MX.

When you import the movie, Director adds it to the robot's old place in the cast window and redefines the robot's old sprite in the score. You don't even have to remake the motion tween or set the sprite's ink mode to Background Transparent. Director remembers the settings that you used for the robot sprite and applies them automatically to the new Astro Ape sprite, even though the sprites are two completely different formats.

> **CAUTION**
>
> ### Cut!
>
> If you want to add Flash movies to your Director project, make sure that you export your movies as SWF version 5 or lower. Director 8.5 can't import version-6 movies. SWF 6 is the most recent version, which Flash MX produces by default.

Adjust the position of the sprite in the first and last frames of the score if you like. Then, go to the Control panel and hit the Play button. The built-in animation of the SWF movie plays as Director tweens the position of the sprite. As simple as that, it is now Astro Ape that wanders blindly into serious trouble, as Figure 16.16 shows. This is multimedia at its finest. You know you're working with a quality piece of software when you can replace a static GIF cast member with an animated SWF movie without even breaking a sweat.

Save this movie as *wrongway4.dir* using the File → Save As command.

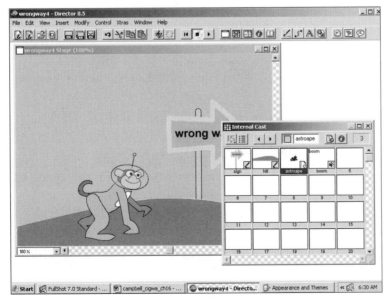

Figure 16.16

Recast your movie at the last minute by replacing the robot with Astro Ape. It's so easy to do, cast members ought to have a labor union to protect their rights.

The Least You Need to Know

- ◆ Use File → Import to import external files as cast members.

- ◆ The uppermost sprite in the score is actually the closest sprite to the background on the stage.

- ◆ Create a motion tween by dragging the handle in the middle of a graphic sprite to a new location on the stage.

- ◆ You can tween other sprite properties, including transparency, size, angle of rotation, and angle of skew.

- ◆ Preview a movie in Director by clicking the Play button on the Control panel.

- ◆ Add sound sprites to one of two audio channels in the score.

- ◆ Remove excess channels from your movie when you finish building the animation.

Chapter 17

Using Behaviors

In This Chapter

◆ Attaching behaviors to sprites

◆ Attaching behaviors to frames

◆ Creating interactive and branching movies

A behavior in Director is a ready-made action that you attach to a sprite or a frame in the score. Use behaviors to control the playback of the movie, create clickable elements, add complex motion paths, and play sounds, among many other things.

This chapter explores a few common applications of behaviors for adding interactivity and character to your movie.

Speaking the Lingo

Behaviors in Director are actually Lingo scripts. *Lingo* is a computer language for creating and controlling Director movies, much like the relation of ActionScript to Flash movies, only Lingo is more powerful and also more complex. (The boxed version of Director ships with a telephone-directory-size volume all about writing Lingo scripts.) Building movies visually by dragging cast members onto the stage and manipulating keyframes and properties is fine for straight-up-the-middle Director projects, but for more advanced, interactive projects like games and shopping carts, Lingo is the only way to go. Professional Director animators spend more time in the script window than on the stage and in the score.

Figure 17.1 shows part of a Lingo script for the relatively simple action of pausing the movie at the current frame. As you can see, the coding is more involved than you might guess it would be. Fortunately, you don't have to write a line of Lingo to use behaviors in Director, and you won't use the script window for more than a quick look or two in this chapter. When you add a behavior to a sprite or frame, Director automatically attaches the necessary Lingo scripts to your movie. As you'll soon see, these scripts appear as cast members, just like the visual and audio components.

Shop Talk

Lingo is a programming language for creating and controlling Director movies.

Figure 17.1

Even a seemingly simple task like pausing the movie at the current frame requires some sophisticated Lingo scripting.

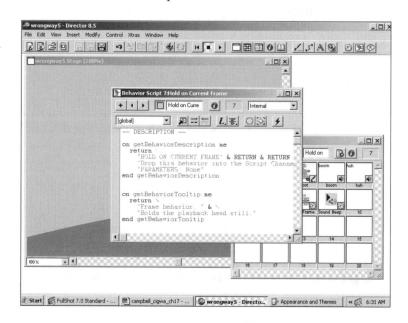

Behaviors are a quick way for visually oriented, computer-phobic designer types to get a good return from their Director investment. Keep in mind, though, that behaviors are, in essence, prepackaged code. There's only so much you can do with behaviors before you have to bite the bullet and produce customized scripts of your own.

If you aspire to be the great Director author of our time, Lingo is in your future, although coming to terms with the Lingo beast is a daunting prospect for most. For this reason, many web animators prefer cutting their teeth on ActionScript in Flash first. While ActionScript isn't as powerful or as flexible as Lingo, it's generally more straightforward and easier to learn. After you get used to the process and rhythm of writing computer code to control animation, Lingo is a logical and less painful next step.

Attaching Behaviors to Sprites

I mentioned earlier that you can attach behaviors to sprites or frames. Both methods have their advantages. Attaching a behavior to a sprite is useful when the action corresponds to a particular sprite at a particular time in the movie.

Let me show you what I mean by way of an example. Launch Director and choose File → Open. Navigate to where you saved *wrongway3.dir*, the version of the movie with the robot and the sound effect. Select this file, and click Open. Director loads the movie and its cast. Click the sprite in Channel 3, the Robot Channel, to select the entire range of frames. Then, drag the salmon-colored playback head to Frame 45, and choose Insert → Keyframe. Keep this keyframe selected in the score.

To attach a behavior to this sprite, choose Window → Library to call up the Library window in Director (see Figure 17.2). Unlike Flash, where the library stores symbols, the Director library stores behaviors. Hold down the mouse button on the icon in the upper left of the Library window, and a menu of behavior categories slides out. Pick a category, and then scroll through the list of behaviors that appears in the window.

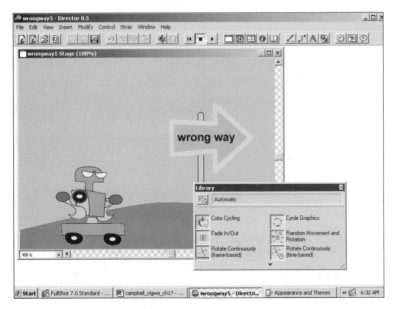

Figure 17.2

Use the Library window to choose from ready-to-go Lingo behaviors in Director.

CAUTION

Cut!

The Library window in Director isn't the same as the Library panel in Flash. The Library panel shows the symbols in the current Flash movie. The Library window in Director shows Lingo behaviors.

The behavior I have in mind for the robot sprite at Frame 45 is Play Sound. There's a classic *Huh?* sound effect in the Chapter 16 folder of the CD-ROM that fits this robot perfectly. When the robot reaches Frame 45, the confused utterance of *Huh?* would do nicely.

Before you attach the behavior, then, bring in the sound effect as a cast member. Choose File → Import, navigate to the Chapter 16 folder, select the file *huh.mp3*, and click Import.

Now, go to the Library window, click the icon in the upper left corner, and choose the category Media → Sound. Six behaviors appear in the Library window: Play Sound, Pause Sound, Stop Sound, Sound Beep, Channel Volume Slider, and Channel Pan Slider. You want the robot to say *Huh?* at Frame 45, so drag the Play Sound icon onto the selected robot sprite on the stage.

When you release the mouse button, the Attach Behavior Options dialog box appears, as in Figure 17.3. This dialog box tells you that Director must attach the behavior to a complete sprite. Currently, only Frame 45 of the complete robot sprite is selected. Now, you don't want to attach the sound to every version of the sprite in the movie, just the one at Frame 45, so select the Split Sprites Before Attaching option. This option causes Director to insert a completely new robot sprite just in Frame 45, and this unique sprite will have a Play Sound behavior. The sprites in the other frames will not.

Figure 17.3

If you want the behavior to affect a sprite only in a particular frame, choose the Split Sprites Before Attaching option in the Attach Behavior Options dialog box.

Click OK to continue, and a Parameters dialog box opens, as in Figure 17.4. This dialog box enables you to customize the behavior to suit your needs.

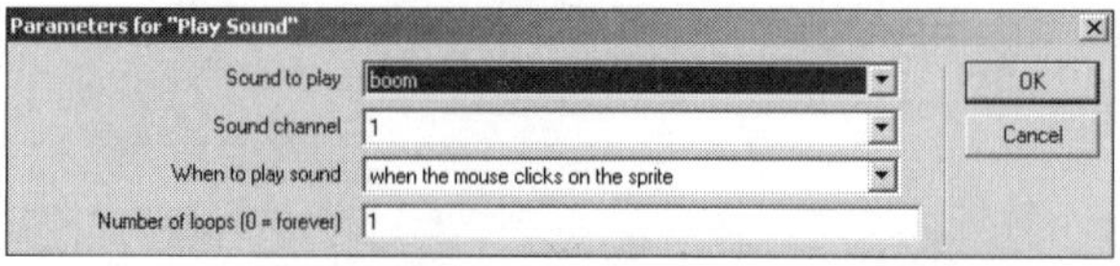

Figure 17.4

Customize the Play Sound behavior with the Parameters dialog box.

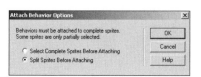

Choose to play the sound called *Huh?* by pulling this sound from the first dropdown list. You can use sound Channel 1 for this effect, since there is currently no sound on this channel—the explosion on the first audio channel doesn't come in until Frame 150. Pull down the Sound Channel list, though, and notice that there are actually eight audio channels instead of the two that appear on the score. Using Lingo and behaviors, you get more options for your movie than you would normally have. But choose the first sound channel anyway.

> ### The Big Picture
> If you know Lingo, you can write your own behaviors.

Under When To Play Sound, choose the option for when the sprite first appears. Take this to mean when the sprite appears in Frame 45, since that's the position of the selected sprite on the stage.

Under Number of Loops, keep the default value of 1. If you want the robot to say *Huh?* a couple of times, type a different value here.

Click OK to attach the behavior to the sprite. The Play Sound behavior appears in the Cast window. Double-click this cast member to call up the behavior inspector (see Figure 17.5), and click the Script Window button, the third from the right, to view the Lingo script for this behavior. Close both windows after you've had a quick peek at the code.

Open the Control panel and play the movie. Sure enough, when the playback head hits Frame 45, the Play Sound behavior you added kicks in.

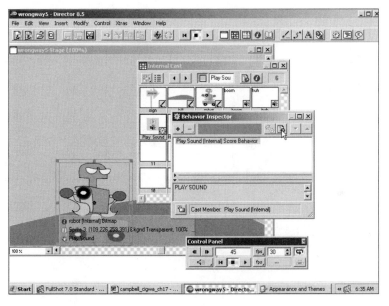

Figure 17.5

When you double-click a behavior in the Cast window, the behavior inspector appears. Click the Script Window button, the third one from the right, to view the Lingo script for the selected behavior.

Attaching Behaviors to Frames

If attaching a behavior to a sprite makes sense when you want to tie the behavior to a particular sprite, then attaching a behavior to a frame makes sense when you want to tie the behavior to a particular frame of the movie.

The score in Director has a special channel, the Behavior Channel, reserved for frame behaviors. This channel appears just above Channel 1 in the score. Instead of a number, the Behavior Channel has a white note card or script icon.

Attaching behaviors to frames is straightforward. Simply drag a behavior from the library window into a frame of the Behavior Channel.

> **Cut!**
>
> Not all behaviors work as frame behaviors. If Director won't let you drag a behavior into a frame of the Behavior Channel, attach the behavior to a sprite instead.

Here's an example. Go to the Library window and choose the Navigation category. Scroll the behaviors list until you see the one called Hold On Current Frame. This behavior causes playback to pause at the frame in which you attach it. Drag the Hold On Current Frame icon to Frame 45 of the Behavior Channel. Director adds Hold On Current Frame to the cast and inserts an icon in the Behavior Channel at Frame 45, as Figure 17.6 shows.

Figure 17.6

Attach a behavior to a frame, and Director inserts an icon in the Behavior Channel of the score.

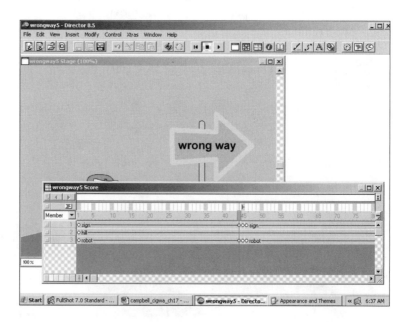

Play back the movie again from the start. The movie pauses at Frame 45, just in time for the robot's sprite behavior.

Adding Interactivity

Pausing the movie at Frame 45 is fine, but your audience has no way of getting around this roadblock, at least not yet. By adding a few more behaviors, you can give your audience the ability to advance the movie beyond Frame 45, thereby making them personally responsible for whatever fate befalls the robot.

What about making the sign clickable? When an audience member clicks the sign, the movie continues. That sounds like a reasonable enough strategy. Here's how to implement it.

The Big Picture

Any sprite on the stage is potentially clickable in Director, unlike in Flash, where you must specifically designate a symbol as a button.

Since you want to tie the clicking behavior to the sign, you want to attach the behavior to the sprite, not a frame. So, proceed as you did when you attached the behavior to the robot sprite. Select the sprite in Channel 1 of the score, position the playback head at Frame 45, and choose Insert → Keyframe. With this keyframe selected, go to the Library window, which should still show the Navigation category. If it doesn't, pull the Navigation category from the menu.

Scroll through the Navigation behaviors until you come to the one called Go To Frame X Button. This behavior turns its sprite into a clickable element that, when clicked, advances the playback head to whatever frame you choose. This is exactly the action you want. When the audience member clicks the sign, the movie can jump past the Hold On Current Frame behavior at Frame 45.

Drag Go To Frame X Button to the sign sprite on the stage. Once again, Director informs you that it must split the sprite if you want the behavior to apply to the sprite in Frame 45 only. Choose Split Sprites Before Attaching again, and click OK. In the Parameters dialog box that appears, Director asks to what frame the movie should jump after the click. Type **46** into this field, since Frame 46 is the frame that immediately follows the one with the roadblock. Click OK to attach the behavior to the sprite.

Before you play back the movie, attach one other behavior to this sprite. It would be nice if the movie responded with a sound effect to confirm the click. In the Library window, choose the Media → Sound category again, and drag the Sound Beep behavior to the sprite.

Now play the movie from the start. The action stops at Frame 45, according to the behavior in the Behavior Channel. But the sign sprite at Frame 45 is clickable. Clicking it causes the movie to advance to Frame 46, but where's the beeping sound?

Certain behaviors get fussy when you mix them with certain other behaviors on the same sprite or frame. In most cases, to correct this problem, all you need to do is change the order in which the behaviors happen. By default, Director executes the behaviors in the order in which you added them. So, on the sign sprite, the Go To Frame X Button behavior happens first, followed by the Sound Beep behavior. By this configuration, though, the Sound Beep behavior gets lost in the shuffle.

Select the keyframe at Frame 45 in Channel 1. This is the keyframe that corresponds to the sign sprite to which you attached the behaviors. Now go to the property inspector, and click the tab with the gear icon, the Behaviors tab. The property inspector shows both behaviors of the selected sprite. To change the order of the behaviors, select Sound Beep, and click the Up-Arrow button. Sound Beep now executes first, as Figure 17.7 shows. Play back the movie from the beginning, and you find that the behaviors behave. Save this version of the movie as *wrongway5.dir*.

Animation Advice

If multiple behaviors on a sprite don't function properly, try changing the order in which the behaviors execute.

Figure 17.7

Change the order in which multiple behaviors happen on the property inspector.

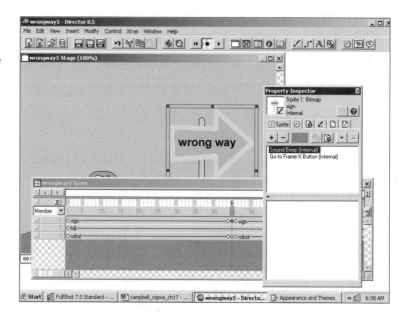

Using Markers

As of now, your audience has only one choice: to send the robot the wrong way. For the sake of decency, you should give the audience the option of turning the robot back. Building a separate branch of the movie that shows the robot turning around and exiting stage left will do the trick.

You'll recall from Chapter 13 that organizing a Flash movie into scenes is a convenient way to control the branches of an interactive movie. Director doesn't offer scenes, but it does give you *markers*, which are like flags on the score that indicate the beginning of a particular section of the movie. Using behaviors, you can cause the movie to jump to a marker and play out the branch that it indicates. The beauty of jumping to markers instead of specific frames is that, while frame numbers may change if you modify your movie, you can simply drag the marker to a new position in the score without having to edit the behavior.

Shop Talk

A **marker** is an element on the score that indicates the start of a particular section or branch of the movie.

Markers appear in the Markers Channel of the score. The Markers Channel is the uppermost channel in the window, above the Behaviors Channel and all the other effects channels. To add a marker, drag the playback head to the desired frame and choose Insert → Marker. Type a name for the marker in the Markers Channel, and press Enter or Return. To reposition the marker in the score, drag its arrow icon to the left or right. To remove the marker, drag it off the score.

For now, create a marker at Frame 391 of the current movie. This is where you'll build the branch that shows the robot turning around and going back. Drag the playback head to Frame 391, and choose Insert → Marker. Type **Robot goes back** as the marker name, as in Figure 17.8.

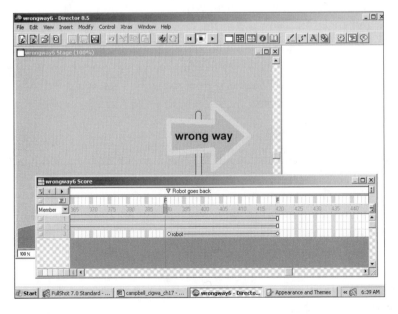

Figure 17.8

Drag the playback head to Frame 391 and choose Insert → Marker to mark the start of a new branch in the movie.

Now, build the branch. You want the sign and the hill to appear in this segment, so drag the ending frames of Channels 1 and 2 to Frame 420. This gives the robot a one-second exit.

Go to the Cast window, and drag the robot into Frame 391 of Channel 3 to add a new robot sprite to the stage. Click the Sprite tab of the property inspector, and set the ink mode to Background Transparent. Also, click the Flip Horizontal button. This is the second button from the right under the ending frame field. While you're at it, type 420 in this field to extend the new sprite to Frame 420.

Go back to Frame 45 in Channel 3. Select this frame, and copy down the X and Y values of this sprite from the property inspector. Select the keyframe in Frame 391, and supply these X and Y values in the appropriate fields. This ensures that the new robot sprite appears in the same position as the old one.

Next up: Create the motion tween. Drag the handle in the middle of the robot sprite off stage left.

You now have an alternate branch of the movie that shows the robot turning away from danger. To prevent this branch from playing after the explosion happens, set up a behavior in Frame 390 that causes the movie to jump back to Frame 1.

Go to the Library window, choose the Navigation category, and drag the Play Frame X behavior to Frame 390 in the Behavior Channel. Type 1 in the field of the Parameters dialog box, and click OK. Now, when the movie hits Frame 390, playback jumps automatically to Frame 1.

All you have to do now is give the audience a way to jump to the alternate branch. Clicking the robot should suffice. Adding the beep to register the click is a good idea, too. Remember, though, that you should add the beep first, since adding it second caused problems the last time.

 Animation Advice _____

The beep that the Sound Beep behavior uses is the default beep of the operating system on which the movie is playing. You can change the beep by choosing a new default beep sound from your operating system's Control panel. Keep in mind, though, that this change works only on your computer. When you view your movie on another computer, that computer's default beep sound is the one you hear.

Position the playback head at Frame 45 in the score, and select the robot sprite on the stage. Drag the Sound Beep behavior from the Cast window to the sprite. Now, tackle the jumping action. Go to the Library window, and drag the Go Next Button behavior from the Navigation category to the sprite. The Go Next Button behavior makes the robot clickable. Clicking the sprite causes the movie to jump to the next marker in the score, which just so happens to be the Robot Goes Back marker at Frame 391.

Play the movie from the start. Playback stops at Frame 45. If you click the sign, the movie jumps to Frame 46, and the robot goes the wrong way. An explosion is heard. The sign shakes. When the movie hits Frame 390, a frame behavior causes playback to jump to Frame 1, and the fun starts again.

The Big Picture

You can create transitions between frames by double-clicking a frame in the Transition Channel of the score. This channel is immediately above the first Audio Channel. When you double-click a frame in this channel, the Frame Properties: Transition dialog box appears. Choose the category of transition from the list on the left, and select a Transition behavior from the list on the right. You get options like Dissolve, Wipe, and Push. Transitions come in handy when you want to switch scenes. To apply a transition to an individual sprite, look under the Animation → Sprite Transitions category of the Library window.

If you click the robot instead of the sign when the movie pauses, playback jumps to the Robot Goes Back marker at Frame 391. This marker indicates a branch of the movie in which the robot turns around and rolls off the stage to the left, and the movie loops automatically to Frame 1.

You have an interactive, behavior-enhanced movie on your hands. Save your work as *wrongway6.dir*.

Making Fun

This chapter really only scratched the surface of behavior possibilities. Now that you have a better feel for the process, explore some of the other behavior categories in the Library panel, and have some fun with the robot in Frame 45. For instance, attaching the Random Movement and Rotation behavior to the robot sprite in Frame 45 gives the poor guy something else to say *Huh?* about, as you can see in Figure 17.9. Find this behavior under the Animation → Automatic category of the library. Incidentally, notice under this category that there's a Sway behavior. The next time you need a Wrong Way sign to react to a seismic tremor, you can simply apply this behavior to the sprite instead of creating the sway action by hand, as you did in Chapter 16. Since building the sway manually was labor-intensive, you can appreciate the timesaving aspect of Lingo behaviors.

Figure 17.9

The best way to learn behaviors is to goof off with them, such as attaching the Random Movement and Rotation behavior to the robot sprite in Frame 45 to create a no-gravity zone.

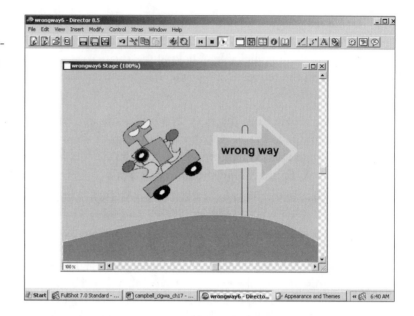

To remove a behavior after you've tried it out, select the sprite, go to the property inspector, click the tab with the gear icon, and select the behavior in the list. Click the Minus button and choose Remove Behavior from the menu that slides out, or simply press the Delete key. Then go to the Cast window, select the cast member that corresponds to the behavior, and choose Edit → Cut Cast Member.

The Least You Need to Know

- Behaviors are prewritten Lingo scripts.

- The Library window in Director contains categorized behaviors for many different purposes.

- Attach a behavior to a sprite when you want an action to apply to a particular sprite at a particular frame in the score.

- Attach a behavior to a frame when you want an action to apply to a frame of the movie, not to any single sprite.

- When you attach a behavior to a frame, the behavior appears in the Behavior Channel.

- Whether you attach a behavior to a sprite or a frame, the behavior appears in the Cast window.

- Use markers to indicate the beginning of a certain scene, event, or branch of your movie.

Creating 3-D Animation

In This Chapter

◆ Exploring characteristics of 3-D graphics

◆ Adding 3-D cast members

◆ Controlling 3-D sprites with animation behaviors

◆ Tweening 3-D sprites

I'm going to go out on a limb here and make a value statement. Three-dimensional graphics are cool. They look cool, they behave in cool ways, and the essential idea behind them is cool.

Director 8.5 is cool, too, because it allows you to import 3-D graphics as cast members, create certain kinds of 3-D cast members of your own, and build simple animations in the 3-D world using nothing more than the same commands and tools that you've been using.

This chapter introduces you to the fascinating world of virtual space as it pertains to Director and Shockwave.

Entering a 3-D World

Three-dimensional graphics and two-dimensional graphics are very different things. Perhaps most important, 3-D graphics contain much more information about the subjects they depict. When you look at a 2-D graphic, you get essentially one point of view on the subject of the image. The computer doesn't know what the other side looks like, because this information isn't in the image file. As far as the computer is concerned, the subject doesn't have another side. A 2-D graphic is like a slide in this sense. When you flip the slide over, you don't see the backside of whatever is in the picture. You see an inverted version of the front of the slide.

In 3-D graphics, the computer understands exactly what the subject looks like, because the 3-D graphics file contains information about the subject's width, height, and depth, not just its width and height. This means that the computer can display the subject not just from one point of view, but from every conceivable point of view in three-dimensional space. You can look down on the image from above. You can go around behind it. You can see it from underneath. In fact, you have an infinite number of points of view, no two of which are exactly the same. For this reason, a 3-D graphic is more like a sculpture than a slide. You can walk around the image, as it were, and see it from a different angle.

Let me hit you with some terminology at the top of the chapter. A *world* is a computerized 3-D environment. It has the properties of width (X), height (Y), and depth (Z) as opposed to the width and height of 2-D graphics. The objects that exist in this environment are called *models*. These are the sculptures I was talking about earlier. You can view 3-D models from every conceivable angle.

The *camera* is the point of view from which you see the model. You can position the camera anywhere in the world. When the camera is underneath a model, you see the model from below, as if you're looking up at it. When the camera is above a model, you see the model from above, as if you're looking down at it. When you move the camera around the model, you see the model's sides.

Shop Talk _____

In 3-D graphics, the **world** is a computerized 3-D environment. A **model** is virtual 3-D representation of an object. The **camera** is the point of view from which you see the model. The **light** is the source of illumination in the 3-D world.

The *light* is the direction and color of the source of illumination in the world. Just like you can't see anything when you turn out the lights and pull the blinds in an actual 3-D space, you can't see your models in virtual 3-D space if you don't define a light source.

That's enough vocabulary to start. It's time to launch Director!

Creating 3-D Text

To work with 3-D in Director, you need a 3-D model, and the easiest way to create a 3-D model in Director is to make 3-D text.

With a new movie open and ready to go, choose Window → Text. The text window opens. Choose a font from the dropdown list at the top of the window, and set the font size to something large like 96. Then, type **Aa** in the text area, as in Figure 18.1. Then, in the Cast Member Name field to the right of the arrow buttons, type **Aa** also.

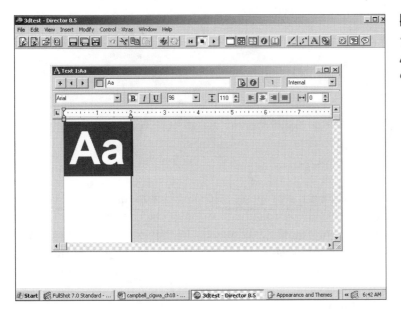

Figure 18.1

To create 3-D text, you need a text cast member. Create one in the Text window.

Close the text window to add this new text cast member to the cast window. Create a sprite by dragging the cast member onto the stage.

Select the sprite on the stage, and go to the property inspector. Click the Text tab, which is the fourth tab from the left, the one with the red T icon. Don't click the 3D Extruder tab just yet. This is the tab with the blue T icon. You'll use the extruder soon enough.

Under the Text tab, look for the Display list, and set this list from Normal to 3D Mode. The text sprite acquires three dimensions, as Figure 18.2 shows.

The Big Picture

After you create a block of 3-D text, you can still edit it as text. To do so, double-click the 3-D text sprite with the Arrow tool.

Figure 18.2

Select the sprite, go to the property inspector, and change the Display list under the Text tab from Normal to 3D Mode. The text sprite acquires three dimensions.

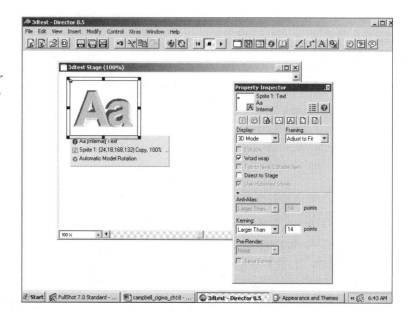

Using the 3D Extruder

Now click the 3D Extruder tab on the property inspector (see Figure 18.3). The first row of fields on the property panel controls the position of the camera. That is, these values determine the point of view on the 3-D model. To change the view, type new values into these fields. Making the X value smaller shifts the camera to the right, while making the X value larger shifts the camera to the left. Making the Y value smaller shifts the camera down, while making the Y value larger shifts the camera up. Making the Z value smaller moves the camera closer to the model, while making the Z value larger moves the camera farther away.

Shop Talk

The **front face** is the front of a letter in 3-D text. The **back face** is the back of the letter, and the **tunnel** is the region that connects the two faces.

The next set of three rows controls the degree of rotation of the camera. Type values in these fields to rotate the camera along the X, Y, and Z axes, respectively.

Three-dimensional letters have a front face, a back face, and a tunnel by default. The *front face* is the front of the letter. The *back face* is the back of the letter. The *tunnel* is the region that connects the two faces. It extends backward into the Z-axis. If you want to turn off any of these components, uncheck the checkboxes under the camera rotation fields.

Figure 18.3

Use the 3D Extruder tab on the property inspector to set up the 3-D properties of the text.

Drag the Smoothness slider to determine the smoothness of the text. Dragging the slider to the left makes the text more angular and less complex. Dragging the slider to the right gives the text rounder, more flowing curves.

Drag the Tunnel Depth slider to set the depth of the tunnel. Dragging the slider to the left makes the tunnel shallower and therefore brings the back face of the text closer to the front. Dragging the slider to the right makes the tunnel deeper, sending the back face of the text farther away.

If you want the text to appear with a beveled edge, choose Miter or Round from the Bevel Edge list. The Miter setting gives you a hard bevel, while the Round setting gives you a softer, more rounded look. Set the degree of the bevel by dragging the Bevel Amount slider to the right of these fields.

Under Director Light, choose the direction of the light source from the list, and choose the color of this light by holding down the mouse button on the Directional color square. You can also choose colors for the ambient and background light by holding down the mouse button on the appropriate color squares. Ambient light is the diffuse light of the 3-D world. To see its effects, choose a bright ambient

Animation Advice

The width and height of a texture graphic should be the same, and these values should be powers of 2: 2, 4, 8, 16, 32, 64, 128, 256, and so on. Textures in 3-D video games are often 256 by 256.

light color, and make the directional light black. Background light is the light coming from behind the camera.

The shader determines the surface appearance of the text. Set the general color of the surface with the Diffuse color box, and set the color of the highlights with the Specular color box. Keep in mind that a brightly colored directional light changes the color of the surface of the text, just like shining a brightly colored light on a real 3-D object changes its color.

You can also add a texture to the surface of the text. A texture is nothing more than a raster graphic. When you add a texture to a 3-D model, the computer prints the content of this raster image across the surface of the model. In the Chapter 18 folder of the CD-ROM that comes with this book, you'll find four texture files: *oil.bmp*, *water.bmp*, *marble.bmp*, and *wood.bmp*. To use one of these on your 3-D text, choose File → Import, navigate to the Chapter 18 folder, and select a texture. Director adds the texture file to the Cast window. Then, on the property inspector, choose Member from the Shader Texture list, and type the name of the cast member in the field to the right. For instance, if you imported *wood.bmp*, type **wood** in the field. Figure 18.4 shows exactly this texture on the text.

Figure 18.4

If you import a raster graphic of, say, wood grain as a cast member in your movie, you can apply this graphic to 3-D text as a texture.

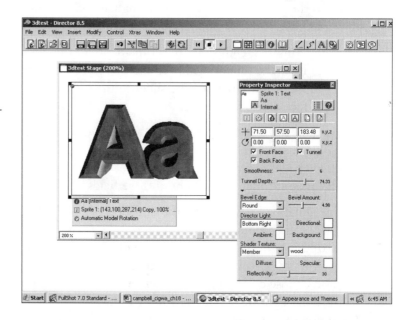

With an image editor like Fireworks or even the built-in Paint window in Director, you can create your own texture bitmaps.

Using the Shockwave 3D Window

The Shockwave 3D window gives you visual control over the camera of a 3-D cast member (see Figure 18.5). When you open this window, you can forget about typing values in the Camera Position and Camera Rotation fields of the property inspector.

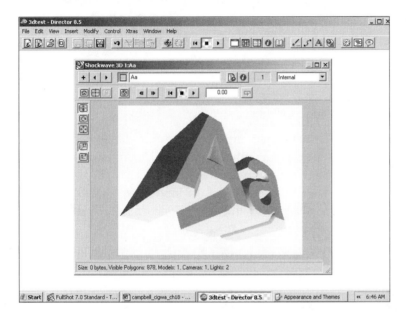

Figure 18.5

With the Shockwave 3D window, you can manipulate the camera of a 3-D cast member with ease.

Select your 3-D cast member in the cast window, and then choose Window → Shockwave 3D. There's a column of five buttons along the left side of the window. These are the camera controls. The first button, Dolly Camera, changes the Z-position of the camera in relation to the 3-D object. To use this tool, click the Dolly Camera button, and then move the mouse pointer into the editing window. Hold down the mouse button, and drag the mouse toward you to dolly the camera away from the object. Drag the mouse away from you to dolly the camera toward the object.

The second button is Rotate Camera. Click this tool, move the mouse pointer into the editing window, hold down the mouse button, and drag the mouse to rotate the camera around the 3-D object. To rotate the camera in relation to the Y axis, click the fourth button before you use the Rotate Camera tool. To rotate the camera in relation to the Z axis, click

> **Cut!**
>
> You can't change the light, shader, or texture from the Shockwave 3D window, so don't close the property inspector just yet.

the fifth button. The third button is Pan Camera. Using this tool pans the camera left, right, up, or down.

After you finish modifying the camera settings, click the second button in the row of buttons along the top of the editing window. This is the Set Camera Transform button. If you want to scrap your changes and start over, click the first button, Reset Camera Transform. To restore the camera to its default setting, click the fourth button from the left, Reset World.

When you're ready to return to Director, simply close this window.

Importing 3-D Models

Using Director, you can build 3-D text quickly and easily. Unfortunately, Director doesn't come with interface tools for creating other types of 3-D images. If you want to feature other 3-D graphics in your Shockwave project, use dedicated 3-D modeling software to build the model, export the model in W3D format, and then import the *W3D* file into Director.

Shop Talk

W3D is a proprietary file format, owned by Macromedia, for web-optimized 3-D graphics.

There's only one catch. Most 3-D modeling software is more expensive than many people are willing to pay. Maya from Alias|Wavefront and 3ds max from Discreet, two of the most popular systems, cost several thousand dollars each.

There is another alternative. ShapeShifter3D from Tabuliero is a smaller, less sophisticated, and much less expensive piece of software designed to work specifically with Director 8.5. A free trial version of ShapeShifter3D appears on the CD-ROM that comes with this book. I'll use ShapeShifter3D to discuss the basic concepts of 3-D modeling in Chapter 20. In the meantime, there are a few simple 3-D models in the Chapter 18 folder of the CD-ROM: *cube.w3d*, *orb.w3d*, *tube.w3d*, and *shape.w3d*. I created these with ShapeShifter3D, and they're ready to import into your movie.

Choose File → Import, navigate to the Chapter 18 folder, and select any combination of these sample 3-D models. Director brings them into the cast window when you click Import. Use the Shockwave 3D window to edit the camera position for these models, and modify the lighting with the property inspector. Look under the 3D Model tab, which is the tab to the left of Guides and Grid, as Figure 18.6 shows.

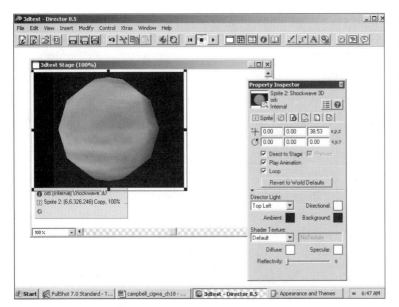

Figure 18.6

Adjust the properties of an imported 3-D model under the 3D Model tab of the property inspector.

Exploring 3-D Behaviors

You have at least one 3-D cast member. At least one 3-D sprite sits on the stage. It would be reasonable to assume that you want to animate this sprite.

I won't lie to you. While Director is capable of sophisticated 3-D animation, you need to use Lingo, and lots of it, to achieve the desired effects. However, as a substitute, Director also supplies a modest set of 3-D animation behaviors. Behaviors, as you know, are prewritten Lingo scripts, and the 3-D behaviors in Director give you and your audience the ability to manipulate basic features of the 3-D sprite, like the position of the camera or the location of the model in the context of its world.

To see the 3-D actions, open the Library window under Window → Library. Choose the 3D → Actions category to start.

> ### The Big Picture
>
> For sophisticated 3-D animation in Director, Lingo is the way to go. However, Director also allows you to import animations that you create in your 3-D modeling software.

Assigning Actions and Triggers

Most 3-D behaviors have two components: an action and a trigger. The *action* is what happens to the 3-D sprite during the animation, such as changing the position of the camera. The *trigger* is what causes the animation to start playing, such as holding down the left mouse button. In most cases, your audience controls how the animation plays out: The direction in which an audience member drags the mouse determines how the camera rotates, and so on.

Shop Talk

An **action** is what happens to a 3-D sprite during an animation. A **trigger** is what causes the animation to start playing.

While the action and trigger are actually separate Lingo scripts and separate cast members, your 3-D behavior as a whole won't work unless you add both components.

There are a few exceptions. The Automatic Model Rotation behavior is one of them. This behavior rotates the 3-D model without any user input, so you don't need to specify a trigger. Try attaching this behavior to your 3-D sprite right now.

Find the Automatic Model Rotation behavior in the Library window under the 3D → Actions category. Then, drag this behavior onto the 3-D sprite on the stage.

The Parameters dialog box appears, as in Figure 18.7. Set the speed of the rotation by dragging the top slider, and choose the axis around which the model should rotate from the list. Click OK to attach the behavior, and click the Play button on the control panel to see the animation.

Figure 18.7

Set the parameters of the Automatic Model Rotation behavior when you drag this behavior onto a 3-D sprite.

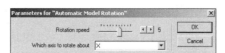

If you want to modify the parameters of this behavior, select the sprite, and look under the Behaviors tab of the property inspector. The Behaviors tab is the one with the gear icon. Select the Automatic Model Rotation behavior from the list, and pull different values from the dropdown sliders and menus.

Animation Advice

When you work with actions and triggers, it's easier if you assign the action first.

Before you continue, remove this behavior by selecting it in the property inspector and clicking the minus button. You don't want to stack too many 3-D behaviors on the same sprite right now while you're trying to learn their effects. While you're at it, you can also go to the Cast window, select the Automatic Model Rotation cast member, and choose Edit → Cut Cast Members.

Now, apply a behavior that requires an action and a trigger. Start with the action. Find the Drag Model to Rotate behavior in the Library window under 3D → Actions, and drag this behavior onto the 3-D sprite. The Drag Model to Rotate behavior requires the user to drag the model with the mouse for rotation to happen, as opposed to the Automatic Model Rotation behavior, which animated the model without prompting.

In the Parameters dialog box that appears (see Figure 18.8), set the sensitivity of the mouse with the first slider. A low value dulls the mouse response, while a high value makes the mouse hyperkinetic. In the field below the slider, type the name of the group to which this behavior applies. You can use any name that you like here. The group name doesn't have to be the same as the cast member's, but why risk confusing yourself? Keep it simple! Use the name of the cast member as the name of the group.

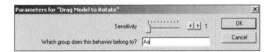

Figure 18.8

Different behaviors have different parameters. Define the group to which the behavior applies for Drag Model to Rotate.

Click OK to set the action. Now, set the trigger. Choose the 3D → Triggers category from the Library window. Scroll down the list to see your options. Since dragging implies the mouse button already, it makes sense to use the mouse button as the trigger of the behavior. Drag the Mouse Left behavior from the Library window to the 3-D sprite. A different Parameters dialog box appears, as in Figure 18.9.

Figure 18.9

Set the Mouse Left behavior as the trigger for the Drag Model to Rotate action with this version of the Parameters dialog box.

Determine how the trigger works by pulling a value from the first dropdown list. If you want to require a *modifier key* like Shift, Ctrl (Windows), or Command (Mac), choose this from the second dropdown list, and enter a second modifier key if you prefer in the third field. For instance, to require the visitor to

Shop Talk

A **modifier key** is a key that the user must press in conjunction with the click of the mouse button.

click the mouse button and hold down Shift+R, set the second dropdown list to Shift, and type **R** in the third field.

Finally, choose the group and the action that you want to trigger. The fourth drop-down list contains all the possibilities. For the purposes of this example, choose the Rotate on X And Y option, and don't specify any modifier keys. Click OK to set the behavior.

Play the movie to test out this new behavior. The model doesn't rotate automatically this time. You need to drag the model with the mouse to activate the animation.

To modify the parameters of these behaviors, select the 3-D cast member and go to the Behaviors tab of the property inspector.

Attaching Multiple Behaviors

By assigning different trigger behaviors to different actions on the same 3-D sprite, you can enhance the performance of your 3-D animation.

For instance, assume that you want to give your audience the ability to rotate a 3-D model along the X and Y axes as well as the Z axis. You already assigned the left mouse button to control the X and Y rotation. What you need now is another trigger to control the Z rotation. A modifier key to the left mouse button sounds like it could work, so that the user presses this key while dragging to switch to the Z-rotation behavior.

> **The Big Picture**
>
> You can attach multiple actions and triggers to the same 3-D sprite.

Drag the Mouse Left behavior from the cast window onto the 3-D sprite. The Parameters dialog box returns. This time, choose Shift as the modifier key, and pull Rotate on Z from the Select a Group and Action dropdown list. Click OK to set the behavior.

Play the movie, and drag the model without holding down Shift. This allows you to rotate the model on the X and Y axes. Hold down Shift and drag to rotate the model on the Z axis.

You can also set up the same trigger to cause multiple actions. Go to the library panel again, and this time drag the Dolly Camera action to the 3-D sprite. In the Parameters dialog box that opens, specify a low number like 1.00 in the first field to slow down the speed of the dolly action. Otherwise, you'll rapidly zoom past the model when you test the behavior! Also, be sure to specify the same group that you did when you assigned the Drag Model to Rotate behavior. If you don't, Director will assume that you want to dolly the camera in a different 3-D sprite.

Now, drag the Mouse Left behavior from the Cast window to the sprite once again. Set the action to Move Camera In, and don't supply a modifier key.

Play the movie. When you drag the model, you also trigger the Dolly Camera behavior, since you set up both animations to happen when the user clicks the mouse button.

Want to dolly back and rotate the model along the Z axis when the user holds down Shift and clicks? Drag the Mouse Left cast member to the 3-D sprite yet again. Set the modifier key to Shift, and set the action to Move Camera Out.

Animating the 3-D Sprite

In essence, 3-D sprite is a sprite like any other. Just as you can set up a motion tween with a bitmap, vector shape, shape, or text, you can also set up a motion tween for a 3-D sprite.

To do so, proceed as you would with any other sprite. Select the 3-D sprite on the stage, and drag its motion handle to a new location. The motion handle for a 3-D sprite appears in the upper left corner, not the middle. Tweak the properties of the motion path by selecting the 3-D sprite and choosing Modify → Sprite → Tweening.

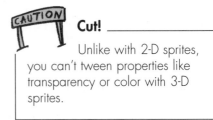

Cut!

Unlike with 2-D sprites, you can't tween properties like transparency or color with 3-D sprites.

You can combine 2-D and 3-D sprites in the same animation. In fact, you don't have to do anything different. Simply drag a 2-D cast member from the cast window to the stage, as in Figure 18.10.

Unfortunately, a 2-D cast member can't enter the virtual world of a 3-D sprite. Think of the 3-D sprite as a window, not an open door. Your 2-D cast members can look inside, but they can't go in. Apart from that, they're quite compatible. Two-dimensional sprites and three-dimensional sprites have no problems whatsoever sharing the same stage, which brings up another good reason to be a digital director instead of a Hollywood one: No prima donnas.

Figure 18.10

Two-dimensional and three-dimensional sprites can peacefully coexist on the same stage.

The Least You Need to Know

- Three-dimensional graphics are like sculptures in the sense that you can look at them from every conceivable point of view.

- Director allows you to create 3-D models from text cast members.

- You can import 3-D models saved in the Macromedia W3D format to the cast.

- Use the Shockwave 3-D window to set the default view of the camera.

- Use the property inspector to set the light, shader, texture, and other properties of a 3-D sprite.

- Three-dimensional behaviors in Director allow you to create simple animations with the model in a 3-D world.

- You can set up motion tweens with 3-D sprites.

- You can mix 2-D and 3-D sprites on the same stage.

Publishing Your Shockwave Movie

In This Chapter

◆ Creating a standalone projector

◆ Controlling looping in a projector

◆ Publishing an embedded movie

◆ Setting publishing options

You battled through the windows and tools of the Director interface. You made a small quantum leap in terms of understanding the strengths and limitations of the 3-D capabilities in Director. Now you want to get your Shockwave movie out there. But how?

You have a couple of choices. One is to create a projector, or a self-contained Shockwave movie that requires no additional software to play. Another is to create an embedded movie, which gives you a smaller file size but requires that your audience view your movie in a Shockwave-equipped web browser.

This chapter takes you through the steps of creating both kinds of finished movie files.

Creating a Projector

A *projector* is a self-contained, standalone movie for offline viewing. When you create a projector file, you combine the cast and score of your movie with the software components for playing it back. Double-click on a projector file, and the movie opens in its own window on your desktop, as in Figure 19.1. Your audience doesn't need the Shockwave Player plug-in to view your movie. In fact, your audience doesn't even need a web browser. To distribute your work, you can place the projector file on a CD or floppy disk, or, less commonly, you can attach it to an e-mail.

Figure 19.1

When you double-click a projector file, your movie opens and plays in its own window.

The main disadvantage is that projector files tend to be large, usually a couple megabytes at minimum. Therefore, projectors work best when download time isn't a factor, like when you plan to hand out CDs or floppy disks of your movie. If you plan to distribute your work by e-mail, it makes sense to create a projector file only if you and your recipients have high-speed Internet connections.

Shop Talk

A **projector** is a self-contained, standalone movie that contains the animation as well as the necessary playback software. Projector files tend to be large, and they work only on a specific platform, either Windows or Mac.

Another disadvantage to projectors is that they're not cross-platform compatible. If you create a projector with the Windows version of Director, your projector file plays on Windows systems but not on Mac systems. If you create a projector with the Macintosh version of Director, your projector file plays on Mac systems but not on Windows. Unfortunately, Director doesn't enable you to convert a Mac projector to a Windows-compatible one or a Windows projector to a Mac-compatible one.

Preparing Your Movie

When you play your movie in Director, the movie automatically loops when it reaches the last frame. This isn't the case in a projector file. When the movie reaches the last frame, the movie stops, and the projector's window automatically closes. If you want your movie to loop during playback in the projector window, you have to add a behavior like Play Frame X to the last frame of your movie.

As an example, launch Director, and open the file *wrongway6.dir*, which you saved to your hard drive in Chapter 17. Go to the score after the movie opens, and drag the salmon-colored playback head to Frame 420, the last frame of the movie. To cause the movie to loop back to Frame 1, drag the Play Frame X behavior from the Cast window to Frame 420 in the Behaviors Channel. Type **1** in the field of the Parameters dialog box that appears to send the playback head to Frame 1. This creates what programmers call a loop. No matter which branch of the movie plays, the last frame causes the movie to jump back to the first frame. Choose File → Save to update *wrongway6.dir*.

It goes without saying that, if you want the projector window to close automatically at the end of your movie, don't set up a loop.

Making the Projector File

To create the projector file, choose File → Create Projector. The Create Projector dialog box opens, as in Figure 19.2.

Figure 19.2

Use the Create Projector dialog box to save your movie as a standalone projector file.

Select the Director project that you want to save as a projector, and then click the Add button. To create a projector from *wrongway6.dir*, then, choose this file from the dialog box, and click Add.

Click the Options button, and the Projector Options dialog box appears, as in Figure 19.3. Under Playback, check the second option if you want the movie to continue playing when the projector window isn't active—that is, when the person who is viewing the movie opens another program. If you don't check this option, the movie pauses when the viewer switches to another program and restarts when the viewer clicks on the projector window again. I'll talk about the first option under Playback later on in this chapter.

> ### The Big Picture
>
> You can build multiple movies into the same projector file. I'll talk more about this process in the next section.

Figure 19.3

Set the options for the projector file in the Projector Options dialog box.

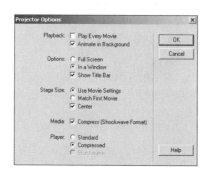

Under Options, determine whether you want the projector to play full screen or in a window on the desktop. Check the Show Title Bar option to display the file name of the movie at the top of the projector.

Under Stage Size, select the Use Movie Settings option for now. I'll talk about the second option shortly. If you want to center the stage on the screen, check the option for this. Otherwise, the stage appears at its default position from the Stage Location fields of the property inspector.

> ### Animation Advice
>
> If you want to get the best possible quality for your movie, don't choose the Compress (Shockwave Format) option under Media, and don't compress the player. As you might expect, these extravagances increase the file size of your projector. Of course, if you're distributing your movie on a CD, you can afford weighty projector files.

Check the Compress (Shockwave Format) option under Media. Doing so reduces the file size of your projector.

Under Player, choose Compressed to reduce the file size of your projector. If you choose Standard, the movie starts playing faster, but the projector file is larger.

Click OK to close the Projector Options dialog box. Then, click OK in the Create Projector dialog box, and the Save Projector As dialog box appears. Specify a file name such as wrongway6 in the File Name field, and click OK. Director packs your movie and everything required for playback into the projector file.

To test your projector, minimize Director for the time being, and find the folder that contains the DIR version of wrongway6. You should find the projector file in the same location. Double-click this file to play it. To stop playback, close the projector window.

Notice that the projector file for this short movie is 1.69MB. Most of the weight in this file comes from the built-in playback software. You can improve on the size of your movie considerably by publishing an embedded Shockwave movie instead, as you'll see in the second part of this chapter.

Packaging Multiple Movies

One advantage to building a projector file is that you can include more than one movie in the same projector. You can set up the movies to play one after another in the same projector window.

Give this a try with the movies *wrongway3.dir* featuring the robot and *wrongway4.dir* featuring Astro Ape. Choose File → Create Projector to open the Create Projector dialog box. Select *wrongway3.dir* and click the Add button. Then, select *wrongway4.dir* and click the Add button. Use the Move Up and Move Down buttons to change the order in which the movies play if you prefer.

Click the Options button for the Projector Options dialog box. Under Playback, check the Play Every Movie option. This causes the projector window to play all the movies in the projector file, one after the other. Under Stage Size, select the Use Movie Settings option to use the original stage size of each movie in the projector, or select the Match First Movie option to resize the stages of subsequent movies to match the stage size of the first. It so happens that *wrongway3.dir* and *wrongway4.dir* have the same size stage, so it doesn't matter which option you choose in this case.

Click OK on the Projector Options dialog box, and click Create on the Create Projector dialog box. Give this projector file a name like wrongway34, and click OK. When you test the projector, the first movie plays in its entirety, followed by the second movie. You can't even tell that there's a change. When the second movie finishes, the projector window closes.

Cut!

Be careful about looping when you include multiple movies in your projector file. If one of your movies loops, the projector will never get to the next movie on the list.

Looping Multiple Movies

Recall that you used the Go to Frame X behavior to loop a single movie in a projector. Using the Go to Movie X behavior, you can loop a series of movies in a projector.

Here's an example. Load *wrongway3.dir*, and set the score to the last frame, Frame 390. Drag the Play Movie X behavior from the Navigation category of the Library window to Frame 390 of the Behaviors Channel. In the dialog box that appears, type the name of the movie to which you want to jump. In this case, type **wrongway4** and press Enter or Return. Choose File → Save to update the movie.

Now load *wrongway4.dir*, and attach the Play Movie X behavior to its Frame 390. Type **wrongway3** in the Parameters dialog box this time, and press Enter or Return. Save your changes.

Choose File → Create Projector, and add the movies *wrongway3.dir* and *wrongway4.dir*, as before. This time, though, after you click the Options button, uncheck the Play Every Movie option, because you don't need it. The behaviors you added to the movies themselves control the looping perfectly.

The Big Picture
When you include multiple movies in a projector but don't specify the Play Every Movie option in the Projector Options dialog box, the projector plays the first movie only. Behaviors in the first movie must call the other movies if you want to show them in the projector window.

Finish creating the projector. When you test it, notice what happens. The first movie plays until it reaches Frame 390. The behavior in Frame 390 tells the projector to jump to the movie called wrongway4, which the projector conveniently finds in the package that you created. This new movie plays from start to finish. When it reaches its own Frame 390, another behavior tells the projector to jump back to the movie called wrongway3, and so on and so on and so on, until the computer crashes, the world ends, or the user closes the projector window.

Publishing an Embedded Movie

The alternative to creating a large standalone projector file is to make a much smaller embedded Shockwave movie. An *embedded Shockwave movie* sits inside a web page. When a browser equipped with the Shockwave Player plug-in loads this web page, the movie plays.

Embedded Shockwave movies are smaller than projector files because the movie file itself contains only the animation. You don't need to build playback software into an embedded movie—the Shockwave Player plug-in supplies this automatically. As a result, though, you can't view an embedded Shockwave movie outside of a web browser. The movie doesn't open in its own, independent window as it does with a projector file. Instead, the movie always appears inside a browser, as in Figure 19.4.

Creating an embedded movie is the best way to distribute your work on the web. The file size of the movie is much more reasonable, and you don't have to worry about Mac and Windows incompatibility issues. The only snag is that your viewers must also have the Shockwave Player plug-in for their browser of choice.

While I'm on the subject, take this opportunity to install the latest Shockwave Player plug-in for your browser and platform at www.macromedia.com/downloads. If you don't, you could run into problems when you test your embedded Shockwave movies.

Got Shockwave on your system? Good! Load the movie *wrongway6.dir* into Director and prepare to embed.

Shop Talk _____

An **embedded Shockwave movie** is a Shockwave movie that sits in a web page. This type of movie is smaller than a projector, since it relies on the browser's Shockwave Player plug-in to provide the playback software.

Cut! _____

If your default web browser doesn't have the latest version of the Shockwave Player plug-in, you won't be able to view your own embedded movies!

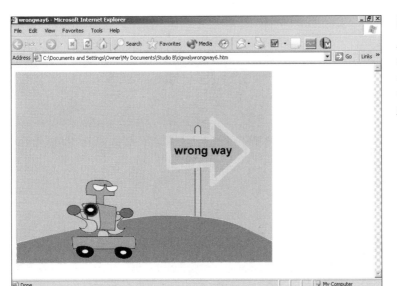

Figure 19.4

An embedded Shockwave movie is smaller in size because it leverages your web browser's Shockwave Player plug-in.

Adjusting Publishing Settings

Use the Publish command to create an embedded Shockwave movie. Before you do, though, review the publishing settings under File → Publish Settings. The Publish Settings dialog box appears, as in Figure 19.5.

Figure 19.5

Review the publishing settings for your embedded Shockwave movie with the Publish Settings dialog box.

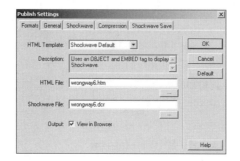

Start with the Formats tab. From the HTML Template list, select the kind of web page in which you want to embed your movie. The Detect Shockwave template is a good choice. This template contains code that detects the presence or absence of the Shockwave Player plug-in. If the browser that loads this page doesn't have the right version of the plug-in, the browser prompts the user to download and install the correct version.

If you plan to build your own page for the embedded movie with a tool like Macromedia Dreamweaver MX, you can choose not to create an HTML template by pulling No HTML Template from this list.

If your movie contains 3-D content, you can choose 3D Content Loader as the HTML template. This template includes an extra DCR file called *3D_progbar.dcr*, which displays the download progress of the 3-D movie. Make sure to store this DCR file with your movie's DCR file.

The rest of this dialog box contains fields for the file names of the various components. In general, it helps if you use the same name for every component, so keep the Director default options.

To view your movie in a web browser immediately after you publish it, check the View In Browser option under Output.

Altering Movie Characteristics

Under the General tab, determine the dimensions of the embedded movie. Choose Match Movie from the Dimensions list to make the embedded movie the same size as the stage in Director. Otherwise, choose either Pixels or Percentage of Browser Window, and specify the exact size in the fields beneath the list.

> **The Big Picture**
>
> Embedded Shockwave movies loop automatically by default. However, it's not a bad idea to add frame behaviors to your movie to control looping anyway. Building the loop into your movie ensures that your movie plays back correctly, even if you embed it in a page that doesn't give a looping value or turns looping off.

By default, Director makes the background color of the web page the same color as the stage. If you want the page to have a different background color, hold down the mouse button on the Page Background color box, and choose a new shade from the color menu that appears.

Controlling Playback and Appearance

Under the Shockwave tab, set up the properties of the embedded movie. Check the features in the Playback area that you want the user to be able to control by opening the Shockwave Player plug-in's Context menu. If you don't want to give the user control over a particular feature, uncheck it.

From the Stretch Style list, determine the way in which the movie stretches if the dimensions of its place on the page don't match the actual dimensions of the movie. (If you picked the Match Movie option from the Dimensions list under the General tab, choose No Stretching from the Stretch Style list, since the movie doesn't have to stretch to fit the page.) After you choose a stretch style, pull values from the Stretch Position fields to align the movie horizontally and vertically in its area of the page.

The Background Color color box determines the color of the movie area on the page. If your movie doesn't fill the entire area, this color appears as a border around the movie.

Under the Compression tab, set up the levels of compression for bitmap and audio cast members. In general, JPEG compression for images is best. Select the JPEG option under Image Compression, and then set the level of compression with the slider. Dragging the slider to the left makes the images smaller but of poorer quality. Dragging the slider to the right makes the images larger but better looking. JPEG quality 80 takes some of the sting out of your image files while retaining most of the quality.

> **Animation Advice**
>
> Standard image compression works well when your movie contains relatively little color information. You could probably get away with standard compression on all versions of *Wrong Way*, since these sprites have large areas of flat color. Whenever you use photorealistic images in your movie, though, go with JPEG compression.

To compress the audio in the movie, check the Compression Enabled box under Shockwave Audio, and then choose a level of compression from the list. Remember from your work with Flash that the lower the bit rate of the sound, the smaller the file, but the poorer the quality. A bit rate of 64 kbps suffices for movies with a few sound effects. Spoken word or music tracks almost always require higher bit rates. If your audio is in stereo, converting it to mono helps to reduce the final file size of the movie. To do this, check the Convert Stereo to Mono option.

It's important to note that Director doesn't compress MP3 sound files. Since the sound effects that you used in *wrongway6.dir* are MP3s, it doesn't matter what level of compression you specify under this tab.

When you finish, click OK on the Publish Settings dialog box, and choose File → Save to update your movie.

Publishing the Movie

Choose File → Publish to create the embedded movie. Using the file names that you specified under the Formats tab on the Publish Settings dialog box, Director creates a DCR file for the movie and an HTML file for the page that embeds it. If you checked the View in Browser option under the Formats tab, Director also automatically launches your default web browser and loads the newly created page so that you can see your embedded movie in its new natural environment.

I promised you that the embedded movie would be much smaller than the projector version, and it looks like I'm able to keep that promise. My DCR file weighs in at 145K, which is on the heavy side for the web, but it's certainly better than the 1.69MB projector. Of course, a comparable Flash movie would be much smaller still.

The bottom line is, these files are ready for the web. Upload them to your site for immediate consumption.

The Least You Need to Know

- Two options for publishing your movie include creating a projector file and embedding the movie.
- When you create a projector, you get a standalone, platform-specific movie.
- You can add multiple movies to the same projector file.
- Use behaviors to control looping in multiple-movie projectors.
- When you embed your movie, you get a smaller movie file that plays only in a web browser.
- Under Publish Settings, you can determine which features of the movie the user can control.
- Embedded movies work better than projectors on the web.

Part 5

Where to Go from Here

Web animation is just a piece of the tapestry of computer animation, and computer animation these days is all about 3-D. This part uses Shockwave 3D as your ticket into the fascinating world of 3-D graphics and animation. You'll build a few simple 3-D models of your own before you're through, and you'll learn how the pros use 3-D animation to enhance your favorite entertainment media.

Chapter 20

Exploring 3-D Modeling

In This Chapter

◆ Using ShapeShifter3D

◆ Drawing primitives

◆ Creating your own 3-D objects

◆ Defining materials

This chapter introduces you to 3-D modeling by way of Tabuliero ShapeShifter3D, a software tool for creating 3-D graphics specifically for Director 8.5. While ShapeShifter3D isn't as advanced as high-end modeling software like 3ds max or Maya, it still provides a solid introduction to the same concepts and techniques that the big boys use.

You can find a trial version of ShapeShifter3D on the CD-ROM that comes with this book. After you install the modeling software, launch it from Director by choosing Xtras → ShapeShifter3D.

Looking Around

Take a moment here to familiarize yourself with the ShapeShifter3D interface (see Figure 20.1). The menu bar at the top of the window works different from the menus in most applications these days. When you select a menu like File, Edit, or Select, the menu doesn't slide down. Instead, menu items appear in the white bar directly below the menu. When you open the File menu, for instance, the choices include New, Open, and Merge. But if you click Edit, the options in the white bar change to Undo, Redo, Delete Selected, and so on.

Figure 20.1

Use ShapeShifter3D to create simple 3-D models for use in Director 8.5.

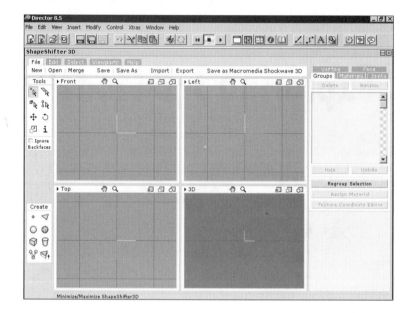

On the left side of the window are two sets of icons: Tool icons and Create icons. Use the Tool icons to select and transform the objects you draw with the Create icons.

The four boxes in the middle of the window are the viewports. These show your 3-D model from various perspectives. The default configuration is Front view and Left view in the first row, followed by Top view and the 3D composite in the bottom row. If you want to use a different configuration, click the Viewports menu, and choose a new layout from the icons that appear in the white bar.

The tabs on the right side of the window organize commands for creating and modifying the model. In this respect, the ShapeShifter3D tabs are like the palettes in Director, only you can't drag the tabs around the screen. They stay exactly where they are. Try clicking through the tabs, and notice that each one gives you a different set of buttons and options.

Defining a 3-D Object

The best way to get comfortable with the software is to take it for a test drive. In this section, you'll create a few simple 3-D objects.

Drawing a Primitive

A *primitive* is a basic 3-D shape. ShapeShifter3D provides four primitives: the sphere, the geosphere, the box, and the cylinder. You can modify a primitive after you draw it, and you can combine different primitives of various sizes to create more complex models.

Start off by drawing a sphere. Click the Sphere icon in the Create group on the left side of the screen. This is the icon on the left in the second row. When you select the Sphere tool or any primitive tool for that matter, the mouse pointer changes into a crosshairs.

> **Shop Talk**
>
> A **primitive** is a basic 3-D shape, while a **wireframe** is the structure of a 3-D object.

Bring the crosshairs into the Front, Left, or Top viewport. Then, hold down the mouse button, and drag the mouse. Go slowly at first so that you can see what happens.

No matter which viewport you choose, your sphere appears in all four. The Front viewport shows your sphere as if you were standing directly in front of it, looking at it from eye level. The Left viewport shows your sphere from the left side, and the Top viewport shows your sphere from the top. The 3D viewport gives you a composite representation of the sphere.

Draw a medium-size sphere, and then release the mouse button. The structure or *wireframe* of the sphere appears in red in the Front, Left, and Top viewports, meaning that the sphere is selected. The actual color of the sphere is the version that appears in the 3D viewport.

To change the position of the sphere in its world, click the Move icon in the Tools group. The Move tool is the left icon in the third row. Move the mouse pointer onto the selected sphere in any of the first three views, hold down the mouse button, and drag. Notice that the sphere automatically changes position in

> **The Big Picture**
>
> When you select an element in ShapeShifter3D, the element appears in red.

the other viewports, according to the direction that you drag the object. You can also type values in the X, Y, and Z fields that appear under the tools when you choose the Move tool. Enter coordinates for the selected object, and then click the Move button. To prevent the object from moving in a particular direction, click the X, Y, or Z buttons. These buttons lock the object at its current position along the X, Y, or Z axes, respectively.

To zoom in or out in a viewport, click the viewport's magnifying glass icon. The mouse pointer changes into a magnifying glass. Move the mouse pointer into the viewport, and hold down the mouse button. Drag away from you to zoom in on the viewport, or drag toward you to zoom out. Notice that the other viewports remain as they were. Reset the viewport to its default magnification by clicking the Reset View button, which is the icon with the R, to the right of the magnifying glass. To exit zoom mode, click the magnifying-glass icon again.

To pan a viewport, click the viewport's hand icon. When you drag the mouse, you push the viewport in the same direction. Once again, the other viewports remain unaffected. Use the Reset View button to return to the default pan setting, and exit panning mode by clicking the hand icon again.

At any time, you can change the angle of the 3D viewport by moving the mouse pointer into it, holding down the mouse button, and dragging. Return the 3D viewport to its default angle by clicking its Reset View button.

Experiment with moving the sphere and changing your views of it. When you're satisfied with the controls, go to the right side of the window, and click the Groups tab if it isn't already selected. You will find an entry for Sphere01 in the list—this is the object you created. You can give the object a different name if you prefer by selecting the current name and clicking the Rename button. Clicking the Delete button removes the object from the 3-D world entirely.

Now, select the sphere icon again under Create. Notice that two fields appear beneath the set of icons: Stacks and Slices. The values in these fields control the complexity of the object's wireframe, with a maximum value of 16 each. By default, ShapeShifter3D gives you 6 stacks and 12 slices.

Animation Advice

You can create unusual geometric shapes by experimenting with the number of stacks and slices in a sphere.

For your new sphere, type **16** in both fields, and draw the object in a viewport of your choice. Move the new sphere as required so that the two objects don't overlap, and compare their appearance. I think you'll agree that the sphere with 16 stacks and 16 slices looks more realistic than the one with 6 stacks and 12 slices. Check out Figure 20.2 to compare a sphere with 16 stacks and 16 slices to one with only three of each.

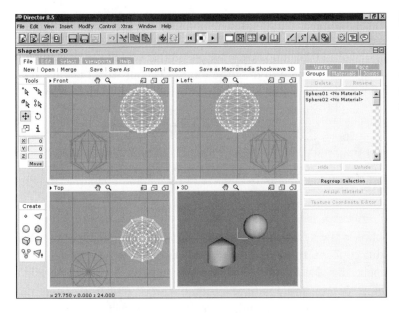

Figure 20.2

The sphere on the top has 16 stacks and 16 slices, while the sphere on the bottom (if you can even call it a sphere) has only three of each.

Now look to the right of the Sphere icon under Create, and click the Geosphere icon. Move the mouse pointer into one of the drawing views, and create a geosphere. The main difference between a sphere and geosphere is the method of construction, as you see when you compare the wireframe of the geosphere with that of the regular sphere (see Figure 20.3). A geosphere is less complex than a regular sphere, but it doesn't look as smooth.

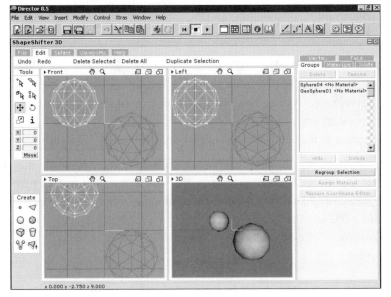

Figure 20.3

Notice the difference in the wireframes of the sphere (top) and geosphere (bottom).

> **The Big Picture**
>
> The main difference between a sphere and a geosphere is the method of construction.

Try out the Box and Cylinder primitive drawing tools. These tools work on a similar principle: Position the mouse pointer in one of the drawing views and drag the mouse. If your world begins to get too crowded, don't forget the Delete button under the Groups tab. You can also look under the Edit menu and click the Delete Selected option to get rid of an unwanted object.

Modifying the Wireframe

The wireframe of a primitive consists of vertices and faces. *Vertices* are points that represent positions in 3-D space, while a *face* is the triangular area between any three vertices. To help you visualize this concept, think of a good old-fashioned two-dimensional sheet of paper. Take a pen, and plot a point anywhere on the page. This point is a vertex. Now add two more points, and you have a total of three vertices. Connect the three vertices with lines, and you get a triangular face. To make a rectangle, you need two faces. Turn them up so that they point in opposite directions, and press their flat edges against each other.

> **Shop Talk** _____
>
> **Vertices** are points that represent positions in 3-D space. A **face** is the triangular area between three vertices. Oddly enough, faces are one-sided objects.

A 3-D primitive, even a sphere, is nothing more than a series of triangular faces arranged in such a way as to create the desired shape. It stands to reason that, by selecting faces or vertices in ShapeShifter3D and changing their properties, you can change the shape of the object that they form.

Select the Edit menu, and click the Delete All option to clear the world. Then, click the Sphere icon under Create, and draw a small sphere. Now, under Tools, select the left tool in the first row, the Select Vertex tool. Bring the mouse pointer into any of the drawing views, and click an empty area of the screen. The wireframe changes from red to white, indicating that nothing is currently selected.

Look at the wireframe, and you should see a number of round points. These are the vertices. With the Select Vertex tool, click a vertex in the wireframe. The vertex turns red. Now, grab the Move tool, and move the vertex to a new position in 3-D space. The faces that share this vertex change size (see Figure 20.4). By holding down Shift, you can select multiple vertices one at a time, or you can drag the Select Vertex tool and pick up several at once.

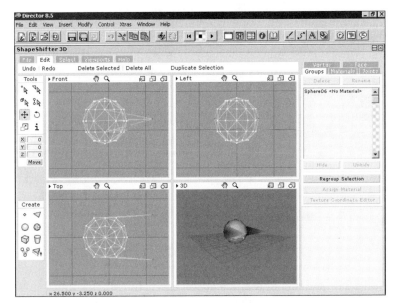

Figure 20.4

Select a vertex and move it, and the faces that share the vertex change size.

Now choose the Select Faces tool, which sits to the right of the Select Vertex tool. Using this tool, you can manipulate individual faces in the primitive. Click inside a face to select it, and then use the Move tool to reposition it, as shown in Figure 20.5. Once again, you can hold down Shift or drag the Select Faces tool to select multiple faces. By choosing the By Vertex option under the Tools group, you can click a vertex with the Select Faces tool and automatically select all the faces that share the vertex.

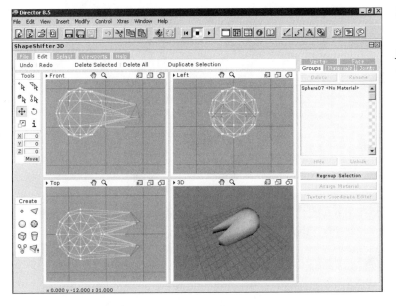

Figure 20.5

Use the Move tool in conjunction with the Select Faces tool to move a face.

You can do more with faces than move them. To change the angle of the selected faces, use the Rotate tool, which sits to the right of the Move tool. To make the selected face larger or smaller, use the Scale tool, which sits underneath the Move tool.

Use the Extrude tool under the Create group to extract the selected area from an object. Try extruding the top of a sphere. Click the Delete All option under the Edit menu, and then draw a new sphere. Grab the Select Faces tool, and check the By Vertex option. Click the uppermost vertex in the Front viewport to select the top of the sphere.

Animation Advice

Use the **Extrude** tool to draw out a particular section of a wireframe.

Now grab the Extrude tool. This is the tool on the right in the bottom row of the Create group. Move the mouse pointer into the Front viewport, hold down the mouse button, and drag away from you. The top of the sphere moves away, but it doesn't separate from the rest of the object. Instead, you get a cylindrical column on the top, as shown in Figure 20.6.

Figure 20.6

Extrude the top of a sphere to create a cylindrical column.

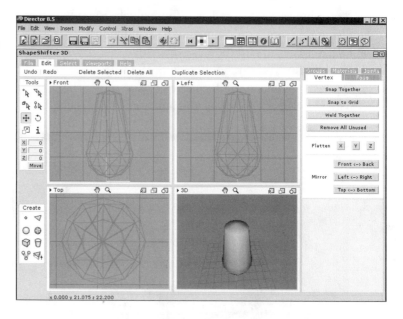

Here's an interesting trick. Delete the current shape, and draw a new sphere. Select the top, just like before, and grab the Extrude tool, but this time push the top of the sphere into the middle of the object instead of moving it away from the object. This creates a bowl-like effect, as Figure 20.7 shows.

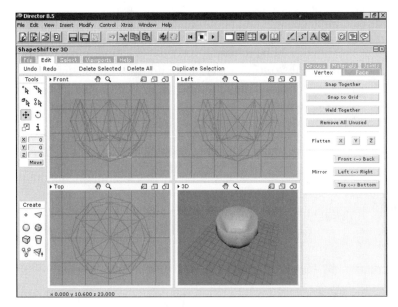

Figure 20.7

By extruding the top of a sphere into the middle of the object, you create a bowl-like effect.

Use the Select Groups tool, which is the icon under the Select Vertex tool, to select the entire collection of vertices and faces that make up an object. You can use the Rotate and Scale tools on groups just as easily as you can with faces. For instance, by scaling a sphere, you can flatten it to create a saucer shape, as in Figure 20.8.

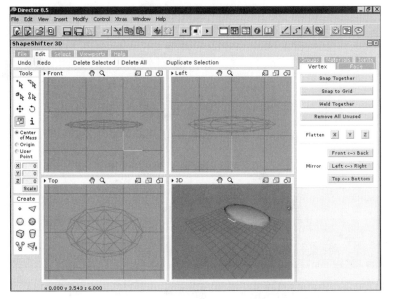

Figure 20.8

Create a saucer shape by flattening a sphere with the Scale tool.

Creating Your Own Objects

Drawing primitives is a great way to add basic shapes to your 3-D model, but you can also plot your own vertices and define your own faces to build more sophisticated objects. This procedure takes practice to master, and to do it justice requires a book of its own, but I can show you the basics, at least, and leave the experimenting to you.

Let me direct your attention to the first row of icons under Create. From left to right, these are the Create Vertex tool and Create Face tool. Before you use them, clear out your 3-D world by clicking the Delete All option under the Edit menu.

> **The Big Picture**
>
> A face contains exactly three vertices in ShapeShifter3D.

Select the Create Vertex tool, and move the mouse pointer into the Front viewport. Click the mouse button and release to plot a vertex. Add two more, and you have enough to define a face. Remember, in ShapeShifter 3D, a face contains exactly three vertices.

To define the face, grab the Create Face tool. Position the mouse pointer on top of one of the vertices you just plotted, and click. Now move the mouse pointer counter-clockwise to the next vertex, and click again. Continuing in a counter-clockwise direction, click on the third vertex, and a triangular face appears in the Front viewport. You should also be able to see the face in the 3D viewport, as in Figure 20.9.

Figure 20.9

Plot three vertices with the Create Vertex tool, and you can use the Create Face tool to define a new face.

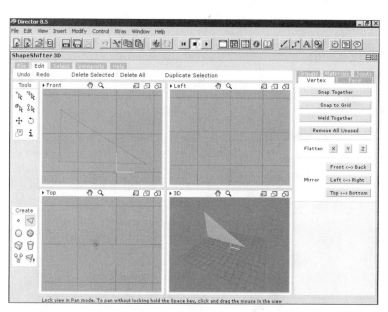

When you drag the mouse in the 3D viewport to change the camera's angle, you notice something extremely peculiar. The face seems to disappear from the opposite side. This happens because individual faces are one-sided objects. (Faces are one-sided to conserve the amount of memory in the final file.) To create a face that appears to have two sides, you must actually position two single-sided faces back to back, with one side facing one way and the other side facing the opposite way. To do this, select the face (if it isn't already selected), look under the Edit menu, and click the Duplicate Selection option. Then, look under the Vertex tab on the right side of the window, and click the Front To Back button, since you're working in the Front viewport. If you were working in the Left viewport, you'd click Left To Right instead, or Top To Bottom in the Top viewport. These buttons flip the selected vertices so that they face the opposite side, while your duplicate vertices face the original side. The effect is that of a two-dimensional, two-sided object (see Figure 20.10), but you need two sets of three vertices—in other words, two single-sided faces—to make it happen.

Cut!

If you create a face and the face doesn't seem to appear, you probably didn't click the vertices in counter-clockwise order. When you select the vertices in clockwise order, the resulting face faces the opposite way. To see the face, Try rotating the camera of the 3D viewport.

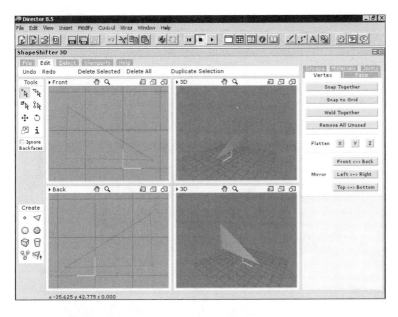

Figure 20.10

Because faces are one-sided, you must add the face's mirror image to create the effect of a 2-D object in 3-D space.

So much for the one-sidedness of faces. It's time to get down to business. The goal of your mission is to create a 3-D pyramid, so click the Delete All option again, and grab the Create Vertex tool.

Move the mouse pointer into the Top viewport. Recall that this viewport shows you what your model looks like from directly above. Before you start plotting vertices, imagine what a pyramid looks like from above—it has a pointed tip, but its base is square. Looking down on the pyramid, you don't see the tip, but you see the square shape of the base.

Animation Advice

All the faces in a solid 3-D object should face outward. You don't need to define faces for the interior of the object, since you can't see inside the object anyway.

In the Top viewport, plot four vertices for the four corners of the pyramid's base. Now, grab the Create Face tool. Each face consists of exactly three vertices, so create one face from the top left, top right, and bottom right vertices, and create a second face from the bottom left, top left, and bottom right vertices, as in Figure 20.11. If the square base appears on top of the grid in the 3D viewport, select both faces in the Top viewport, and click the Top to Bottom button under the Vertex tab. Remember, this is the base of the pyramid, so the underside needs to be visible.

Figure 20.11

Create two faces side by side to make the square base of a pyramid.

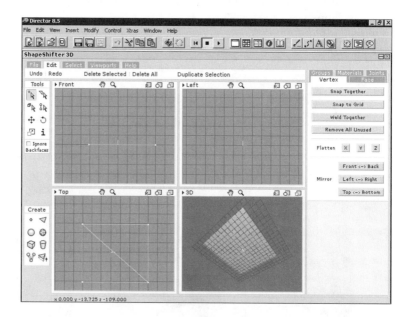

Now, you need the top of the pyramid. Visualize the object again—you can see the pointed tip when you look at the pyramid from the front, so take the Create Vertex tool and, in the Front viewport, plot a new vertex at the location of the tip. Notice that the new vertex also appears in the Top viewport in the center of the base.

To create the sides, grab the Create Face tool, and go back to the Top viewport. Make the north side by defining a face from the top left vertex, the middle vertex, and the top right vertex. Make the east side from the vertices in the top right, middle, and bottom right. Make the south side from the vertices in the bottom left, bottom right, and middle, and make the west side from the vertices in the top left, bottom left, and middle. Remember to select the vertices in counter-clockwise order. If you don't, the faces appear inverted. When you finish, you get a 3-D pyramid, as in Figure 20.12. Spin the pyramid around in the 3D viewport to make sure all the faces show.

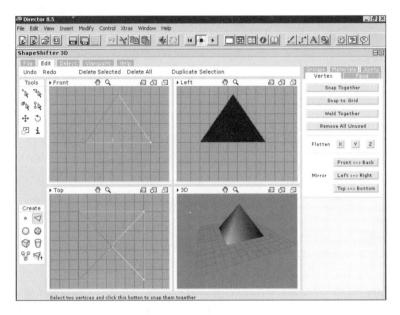

Figure 20.12

Plot a vertex for the top of the pyramid, and create four faces for the sides by borrowing the vertices of the base.

Assigning Materials

In ShapeShifter3D, a *material* is a collection of settings for the appearance of a 3-D object. You create a material under the Materials tab on the right of the window, and then you assign the material to an object. You can use the same material for multiple objects.

To start, clear the 3-D world by clicking Delete All under the Edit menu, and draw a new primitive shape or two. Then, look under the Materials tab, and click the New button. ShapeShifter3D adds a material called Material01 to the list, and a number of controls appear, as in Figure 20.13. The first four

Shop Talk

A **material** is a collection of settings and parameters that determines the appearance of a 3-D object.

buttons control the light of the material: Ambient, Diffuse, Specular, and Emissive. In ShapeShifter3D, ambient light is the nonspecific illumination coming from the 3-D world. Diffuse light is the general color of the material's surface, while specular light is the color of the material's highlights, or the reflected light from the material's surface. Emissive light is the color that the material radiates or gives off. Setting the emissive light to black means that the material doesn't give off any light of its own, although it still reflects light, just like this book isn't glowing of its own accord (or at least it shouldn't be), yet you can still read it as long as there is a source of light in the room for it to reflect.

Figure 20.13

Use the Materials tab to create a collection of appearance settings for your 3-D objects.

To set the color of a light, click a button. ShapeShifter3D gives you three new fields for the color definition: R (red), G (green), and B (blue). Adjust the values in these fields to mix the color manually, or click an area of the color spectrum to grab the values for that particular shade. Click OK to set the color, or click Cancel to keep the existing color.

The Shininess field describes the reflectivity of the material's surface, where 0% is dull and 100% is highly reflective. Supply a value in this field.

The Blend field determines the opacity or transparency of the material, where 100% is completely opaque and 0% is utterly transparent. When you apply a transparent material to a 3-D object, the object itself becomes transparent.

Finally, the Texture field shows the texture image that the material uses, if any. Remember that a texture is just a raster graphic that wraps around the

> **The Big Picture**
>
> You can create a vast number of shades by mixing different quantities of red, green, and blue light.

surface of a 3-D object. To choose a new texture for the material or replace the current texture, click the Choose button, and navigate to the texture image. If you want to remove the texture altogether, click the None button.

As you define the appearance of the material, the sample sphere to the left of the light buttons changes appearance accordingly. Keep your eye on the sphere to get just the right effect from the material you're creating. Also, to change the name of the material to something more helpful than Material01, click the Rename button.

When you're satisfied with the results, click the Groups tab, and select the entry for one of your primitive objects. Apply a material to this object by clicking the Assign Material button. Then, choose the material that you want to assign, and click OK. The composite image in the 3D viewport acquires the material, although the other three viewports retain their nonmaterial wireframes, as shown in Figure 20.14.

> **The Big Picture**
>
> In 3-D modeling, if you place an object inside a transparent object, the interior object becomes visible, just like you would expect. The Blend setting of the container object doesn't affect the transparency of the interior object.

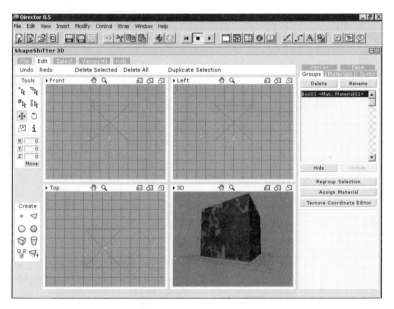

Figure 20.14

Assign materials to objects in your 3-D model. The 3D viewport shows the results.

You can edit a material at any time by going back to the Materials tab, selecting a material, and adjusting the settings.

Exporting the Model

Look under the File menu, and click the Save As Macromedia Shockwave 3D button to export your model in the Director W3D format. The Export Macromedia Shockwave 3D Options dialog box appears, as in Figure 20.15.

Figure 20.15

Use the Export Macromedia Shockwave 3D Options dialog box to save your model in W3D format for use in Director.

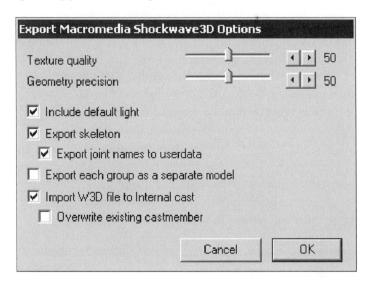

The first two options in this dialog box affect the size of the W3D file. Drag the Texture Quality and Geometry Precision sliders toward the right to give you the best looking model but also the largest in terms of file size. Drag the sliders to the left to reduce the quality of the model while keeping the file size down. Remember, your model will end up in a Shockwave movie that your viewers must download from the web, so finding the right balance between file size and image quality is no less important here than it is for animated GIFs or Flash movies.

Cut! _____

If you choose to export your model with the Shape-Shifter3D default light, you can't modify the lighting in Director.

Uncheck the Include Default Light option if you want to set the lighting for the model in Director. If you keep this option checked, you won't be able to modify the model's light. However, if you uncheck this option, the model appears pitch-black in Director at first, much like a darkened room. Until you set the light from the 3D Model tab of the property inspector, you won't be able to see into the 3-D world.

If you have more than one group in the current model, you can export each one as a separate W3D file by checking the option for this. Leave this option unchecked if you want all the objects to remain in a single 3-D model.

Check the Import W3D File to Internal Cast option to bring your models into the Director Cast window automatically. Otherwise, you can import your W3D files manually by choosing File → Import from the Director menu.

Click OK to choose the file name and location of the W3D file, and then click the Save button. You can continue to work in ShapeShifter3D, or you can close the window and return to Director.

The Least You Need to Know

- ◆ A primitive is a basic 3-D shape like a sphere, box, or cylinder.

- ◆ The wireframe or structure of a 3-D shape consists of vertices and faces.

- ◆ Vertices are points in 3-D space, and a one-sided face is the area between three vertices.

- ◆ By changing the positions of faces and vertices in a wireframe, you change the shape of the object.

- ◆ Use the Extrude tool to lift out a portion of a wireframe.

- ◆ A material is a collection of appearance settings for a 3-D object.

- ◆ Export 3-D models from ShapeShifter3D directly into the Director Cast window.

Animating a 3-D Model

In This Chapter

You learned in Chapter 20 the basics of creating a 3-D model from vertices and faces. This chapter introduces you to the tools and techniques for creating sophisticated animation from 3-D models.

The subject of 3-D animation is a fascinating one. To cover it with any depth requires at least a book of its own. Hopefully you'll let me slide if I touch on only the most essential points in this humble chapter.

If what you find here interests you, there's a wealth of free information on the web. Browse to www.google.com and search for 3-D animation to begin your journey. But consider this a fair warning: Once you start, you won't want to stop.

Building the Bones

Move over, Dr. Frankenstein! One of the most common techniques for animating a 3-D model is to build a skeleton of bones and joints into the wireframe.

The skeleton of a 3-D model looks exactly the way you'd expect, as Figure 21.1 shows. The bones extend through the portion of the model that moves, just like your forearm bone extends the length of your forearm. The joints at the ends of the bone determine which way the bone can move, much like your elbow. As the skeleton moves, the 3-D model deforms. That is, its default appearance changes, just as it does when you flex your arm.

Figure 21.1

One of the most common techniques for animating a 3-D model is to build a skeleton of bones and joints into the wireframe.

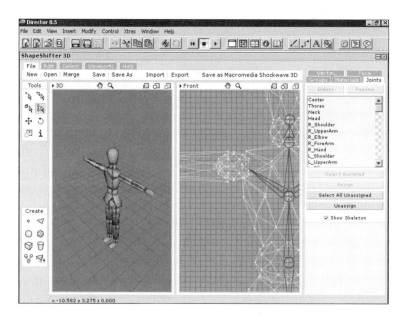

To achieve more realistic movement, 3-D animators use two kinds of joints: parent joints and child joints. In the context of your arm, a parent joint is like your shoulder. When this joint moves, the entire bone structure of your arm moves with it. A child joint, by comparison, is like your elbow. Its bone moves in relation to the position of the upper arm. The wrist is a child joint twice over. It's a child of the elbow joint, which in turn is a child of the shoulder joint. A great way to conceptualize this idea is to think of the lyrics to that screwy old song about which bones are connected to which other bones.

> ### The Big Picture
>
> The adult human body has 206 bones and 230 joints.

The skeletons of 3-D models are often quite complex. Even a simple structure for a human body without fingers or toes requires about 27 joints. A typical 5-fingered hand uses 15 to 19 joints alone. If your character needs to bend, you need a flexible spine—more joints. Adding mutations like wings, prehensile tails, and multiple heads also increases the complexity of the skeleton.

You can add a system of bones and joints to your 3-D models in ShapeShifter3D with the Create Joints tool under the Create group. This is the tool on the left in the bottom row of icons. Click once with the Create Joints tool to add a parent joint to the model. To add a child joint, first select its parent joint with the Select Joints tool, the tool on the right in the second row of icons under Tools. With the parent joint selected, switch to the Create Joints tool and place the child joint. When you save the W3D file for use in Director, make sure that you check the Export Skeleton option. To manipulate the skeleton in a Director project, though, you need to write Lingo code. Director doesn't provide behaviors for bone animation.

Another way to add bone animation to a Shockwave movie is to create the animation in your modeling software. When you import the animated model into Director, you can play back the animation with a few lines of Lingo. ShapeShifter3D doesn't come with animation tools, but higher-end packages like 3ds max and Maya do.

Morphing

With *morphing*, you change the shape or appearance of a 3-D model over time. This process is something like shape tweening in Flash, only morphing is much more powerful and precise. One of the best examples of 3-D animated morphing is also one of the first: Arnold Schwarzenegger's adversary in the film *Terminator 2* (1991) changes repeatedly from actor Robert Patrick into a puddle of liquid metal.

In shape tweening, you'll recall that Flash takes the art in one keyframe and gradually transforms it until it matches the art in the next keyframe. The principle in 3-D animation is the same, only the modeling software takes the model in the first keyframe and creates a series of morphs, or intermediate models, to attain the final model in the second keyframe.

Shop Talk

Morphing is the process of changing one 3-D model into another over time.

Remember that you used shape hints to encourage Flash to tween the shapes a certain way. Shape hints establish a correspondence between a point on the first shape and a point on the second shape so that, when the shape tween plays, the shape hint on the first shape moves toward the corresponding shape hint on the second shape. Computer animators use a similar procedure, associating vertices on the first model with vertices on the second model. As you know from Chapter 20, when you change the position of a vertex, the faces that share the vertex also change. You also know that complex models have an abundance of vertices from which to choose. By creating correspondences between vertices on the two models, 3-D animators achieve very precise control over exactly how the morph plays out.

Animators create facial expressions for 3-D characters with a combination of bone animation and morphing. Bone animation supplies the position of the hard parts of the face: the jaw, neck, and head. Morphing approximates the muscle movements of the face, which is the key to creating realistic expressions. A character who drops his jaw when frightened isn't nearly as effective as a character who drops his jaw, bulges his eyes, and ruffles his brow.

Animating the Camera

It's easy to get stuck in a 2-D rut when you approach 3-D animation for the first time. Beginning animators tend to think in terms of moving the model itself. But a 3-D model exists in the context of a world, and your view of the model depends on the position of the camera in this world. Just like a movie director plays with the movement and position of the camera to enhance the effect of a scene or the performance of an actor, 3-D animators manipulate the virtual camera to create a fully realized animation.

Camera animation is relatively easy, much easier than bone animation or morphing, and you don't need modeling software to do it. Think back to the behaviors you added to your 3-D text in Chapter 18. Virtually all of them created the impression of motion by manipulating the location of the camera in the 3-D world. Your model itself wasn't moving—the camera was. One of the main advantages to this technique is that the camera is an essential component of the 3-D model by default. The camera comes pre-installed, in other words. You already have it at your disposal. You don't need to build a skeletal structure of bones and joints to manipulate the camera, and you don't have to create correlations between vertices. All you have to do is determine where to point it and when.

Animation Advice

Don't underestimate the effectiveness of camera animation. The camera represents the point of view of the audience. By changing this point of view, you can convey subtle differences in mood or tone or enhance the content of the animation. Looking down on a frightened character makes the character seem more frightened, while looking up at a heroic character makes the character seem more heroic.

Most 3-D animation relies on a combination of camera movement and model manipulation. Nowhere is this truer than in the 3-D video game industry. The characters on the screen are often 3-D objects with bone animations for running, jumping, crouching, shooting, and everything else. The player's perspective of the game is the point of view of the camera. When the player looks closer to examine a clue or retrieve a weapon, the camera zooms in, and when the enemy deploys a surprise attack, the camera zooms back out dramatically. Without the movement of the camera, most 3-D games aren't nearly as exciting.

In first-person scenarios, where the image on the screen represents only what the player's character sees, the position of the camera is a crucial part of the game. Here, the role of the camera is to limit the amount of information that the player receives at any given time. The less the player sees in a potentially hostile environment, the more challenging the game becomes. To survive, the player must glance over his or her shoulder for trouble or look closely at every detail in the area for clues—all simple camera manipulations, once you have the 3-D model.

Another common application of camera animation is the flythrough shot that establishes the topography of a setting or environment in a movie. These are the bird's-eye views of the fiery mountains or evil fortresses, where the camera starts in the distance and comes in quickly, giving the audience a quick tour of the premises before ducking into an open window or going through a door, where the computer-generated sequence ends and the live action begins. There may be little or no model manipulation in a flythrough at all. That is, the camera may be the only moving element in the scene. The camera simply shows off the complexity and level of detail built into the model.

Exploring the Hardware

With a typical desktop computer, you can create 3-D text in Director and simple models in ShapeShifter3D. More involved 3-D animation requires more expensive equipment, much of it tailor-made to the rigors of 3-D.

Processor speed and RAM are vital components in a 3-D animation workstation. The best systems have at least a gigabyte of RAM and not one but two microprocessors. The reason for all this firepower is that 3-D graphics are mathematically intense, and animating them requires extraordinary computational gymnastics. A gig of RAM and dual processors don't give a computer the ability to perform different kinds of calculations, but they do allow a computer to perform typical calculations much faster. While you can run 3-D animation software on any computer that meets baseline requirements, you often find yourself sitting around waiting for something to happen on slower systems.

Cut!

Overheating is a common problem for 3-D animation hardware. Make sure that your computer has sufficient cooling: fans, heatsinks, and even thermal compounds.

Shop Talk

A **graphics card** is a miniature computer inside your computer that assists the CPU in displaying graphics.

The computer's graphics card is an equally important consideration. A *graphics card* is a miniature computer with only one function: displaying images. By taking on much of the display processing, the graphics card frees up the computer's CPU for other operations. The more work that the CPU can farm out to the graphics card, the faster and more reliable your graphics display becomes. Standard graphics cards for desktop computers aren't usually a good match for 3-D modeling and animation. More expensive graphics cards designed for computer gaming, even 3-D gaming, aren't optimal, either. The best option is a workstation-class graphics card, which, as you might expect, is also the most expensive option. These graphics cards can take on the greatest share of the processing workload, and they can even handle two monitors at once.

Finished 3-D animations ready for 2-D playback, or rendered animations, as they're called, make for extremely large files, so ample hard drive space is helpful for storage. A 40GB hard drive is fine to start, but 3-D animators often prefer more elbowroom. Setting up multiple hard disks in a storage array called a RAID—a Redundant Array of Inexpensive Drives—can improve the performance of the disks as well as safeguard the data they contain.

Some animators who work in broadcast media prefer SCSI hard drives to IDE hard drives. SCSI, pronounced "skuzzy," stands for Small Computer System Interface, and IDE stands for Integrated Drive Electronics. Your computer more than likely uses IDE hard drives, which are less expensive to manufacture and install. A top-of-the-line IDE drive can attain speeds of 7,200 or 10,000 rotations per minute, while SCSI hard drives can hit 10,000 or even 15,000 rotations per minute. Faster hard drives mean smoother playback, which is why animators in broadcasting use them. You don't want awkward stalls or hiccups when you output your animation. Of course, the cost of SCSI hard drives is significantly higher than IDE. A 36GB SCSI drive at 15,000 rpm costs almost twice as much as a 120GB IDE drive at 7,200 rpm. Given that the best IDE drives rival SCSI drives in performance at a considerable reduction in cost, many pros have chosen not to bother with SCSI at all.

Unlike other kinds of creative pros, more 3-D animators tend to work on Windows platforms than Mac platforms, if they even work on Windows at all. Linux with its legendary stability is a favorite among animators, although the improved stability of Windows NT, 2000, and XP demonstrates that Microsoft can compete in the high-end animation arena. All the major 3-D animation software comes in Windows versions. Most of it comes in Linux versions as well, and some packages come in Mac OS X versions.

Silicon Graphics, Inc., manufactures a line of highly recommended 3-D modeling and animation workstations. Silicon Graphics workstations use a variant of the UNIX operating system called IRIX, which many 3-D animation packages support, in concert with MIPS processors—the same chips in Sony PlayStation 2 and other consumer electronics. These are the machines behind the 3-D animation in movies like *Spider-Man*, *Stuart Little*, *Evolution*, and *Hollow Man*.

 Animation Advice

SCSI hard drives are potentially faster than IDE hard drives, but their cost is substantially greater. Improvements in IDE technology have minimized the practical advantages of SCSI drives, so, unless you need broadcast-quality playback speed in certain applications, IDE hard drives work fine.

Exploring the Software

Given the rather steep hardware requirements, the real magic behind 3-D animation is the software. The explosion of interest in 3-D animation in the last year or so has led many software companies to slash prices drastically. Now, for the first time, dedicated amateurs can learn and work on the same applications responsible for their favorite games and movie sequences, all for the price of about 60 DVDs.

There are at least a dozen professional packages on the market. In this section, I'll say a few words about the top five for animators: 3ds max, Maya, LightWave, Softimage|3D, and Softimage|XSI.

The most widely used 3-D modeling and animation software is 3ds max from Discreet, although 3-D animators tend to prefer nearly every other package to this one. While 3ds max finds work in film and TV, its core industry is 3-D gaming, with credits like *Max Payne* and *Tomb Raider II*. It runs on Windows 2000 and Windows 98 with at least 128MB RAM, and Discreet recommends dual Pentium III processors.

The Big Picture

Animators use 3-D animation software to create games, effects for movies, and simulations for scientific and technological applications.

Alias|Wavefront Maya is probably the darling of 3-D animation software, with impressive film credits like *Spider-Man*, *Lord of the Rings*, and *Enemy at the Gates*, and gaming credits like *Gran Turismo 3* and a good chunk of the PlayStation 2 catalog. For its high profile, Maya is also one of the most competitively priced animation packages. It also has one of the most rigorous hardware qualifications. Only a few, very specific hardware platforms and configurations receive the Alias|Wavefront seal of approval, all with at least 128MB RAM. Maya runs on a wider variety of operating systems than its competitors, though, including Mac OS X, IRIX, and Linux, in addition to Windows 2000, NT, and XP Professional. Incidentally, Alias I Wavefront is a subsidiary of Silicon Graphics, Inc., animation workstation makers extraordinaire.

NewTek LightWave 3D also works extensively in film, with credits ranging from Oscar-nominated *Jimmy Neutron, Boy Genius* to dinosaur-infested *Jurassic Park III* to cow-infested *O Brother Where Art Thou?* LightWave 3D is also the package of choice for TV production, with credits on *Babylon 5, Justice League, The X-Files, Smallville,* and countless commercials. This software runs on Mac OS X and Windows 98, ME, 2000, or NT with 128MB RAM or Mac OS 9 with 384MB RAM.

Avid Technology Softimage I 3D specializes in character animations for film and TV. This package has the high honor of providing all the computer-generated characters in *Star Wars Episode 2*. Softimage I XSI, its younger, bigger brother, boasts the world's first nonlinear animation system. The latest releases of 3D and XSI offer features especially for the 3-D gaming industry in a bid to reclaim some of the territory surrendered to 3ds max. Both Softimage packages run on Windows 2000, NT, XP Professional, IRIX, and Linux operating systems with 128MB RAM.

Animation Advice

If you're looking for software that's more advanced than ShapeShifter3D but not quite as advanced as the major professional packages, you might try Curious Labs Poser, a 3-D character modeler, or Corel Bryce, a 3-D landscaper. Both packages enable you to animate your models. James Dean Conklin, the technical editor for this book, recommends the following as cheap and fun: GroBoto from Braid Media Arts, Organica from Impulse Inc., Inspire from NewTek, and Amorphium from Electric Image, all of which run on the Mac.

Which of these five is the best? That race is too close to call. Individual animators have their personal favorites, and perhaps they reserve their most worshipful praise for Maya more so than 3ds max, but the bottom line is this: With enough work, persistence, and practice, all of them can help you achieve just about anything you can imagine in 3-D animation.

In many cases, the application's renderer is the deciding factor in a 3-D animator's purchase. The renderer is the component that translates the 3-D animation into a finished, playable 2-D animation. Obviously, the renderer is an important consideration—you don't want to invest a serious chunk of change in the animation software only to output mediocre-looking results. The LightWave 3D built-in renderer earns top honors in speed as well as quality, making LightWave 3D perhaps the best all-around package for independent 3-D animators and small studios. Softimage I 3D and Softimage I XSI ship with variations of the high-end mental ray renderer from mental images. (Note the all-lowercase styling of the company and product name.) This renderer is known for its exceptional photorealistic output. The game *Myst* was rendered in mental ray.

The most widely used renderer in film is RenderMan from Pixar. RenderMan is a standalone application. It doesn't come with 3-D animation features of its own, nor does it ship with any of the 3-D animation software I've been discussing. Instead, animators import their 3-D files into RenderMan and output a final, rendered piece. When you see 3-D animation on the big screen, you can bet money that you're looking at the handiwork of RenderMan. RenderMan and Maya work together regularly. In fact, many Maya animators prefer rendering in RenderMan, since the general opinion among working pros is that the built-in renderer of Maya doesn't achieve the same level of excellence as the rest of the package. RenderMan isn't a good choice for beginning or quasi-pro 3-D animators, however, because it's still built for and marketed to production studios. RenderMan requires professional installation and upkeep. Unlike its collaborator Maya, it hasn't entered the volume market, at least not yet.

Bringing 3-D Animation to the Web

Publishing bandwidth-intensive 3-D animation on the web is no mean feat. The Macromedia Shockwave 3D format (W3D), which you explored in Chapter 18, is one of the most promising solutions, not only because W3D provides good compression, but also because the Shockwave installed-user base is so high. The built-in audience that comes with the Shockwave Player plug-in coupled with the good name of Macromedia has encouraged manufacturers of 3-D animation software to develop exporters to W3D format. Maya, 3ds max, LightWave, and Softimage|XSI all support W3D.

You know from experience that Director by itself doesn't give you as much 3-D animation as you might like, especially if you don't want to write Lingo. Developing 3-D animation in your modeling software allows you to work around many of the Director limitations in this regard. Export your finished animation to W3D format, and then import the W3D file into the Director Cast window. For your visitors to interact with your 3-D movies, though, there's no getting around that Lingo requirement, unless you just want to dolly the camera.

Not even strong software support eliminates the problem of file size. It isn't uncommon for Shockwave 3D animations to weigh in at 2 or 3MB, which is about 2 or 3MB too large for most web surfers unless they really, really want 3-D content. Until high-speed connections are the rule rather than the exception, you'll find Shockwave 3D on the web in small doses, just hinting at the format's possibilities (see Figure 21.2).

Figure 21.2

Explore new worlds with Maya on the web via Shockwave 3D. Oh, the possibilities!

The Least You Need to Know

♦ Adding a skeleton of bones and joints to a 3-D model is a common method of animation.

♦ Morphing is the technique of changing one 3-D model into another over time.

♦ Animators create facial expressions by a combination of bone animation and morphing.

♦ High-end 3-D animation requires more sophisticated hardware than typical desktop applications require.

♦ Animators use 3-D animation software to create games, add effects to movies and TV, and build simulations.

♦ Shockwave 3D is one of the most promising solutions for bringing 3-D animation to the web.

♦ Most 3-D animation is still too large in terms of file size for mass consumption on the web.

Appendix A

Making Web Animation Accessible

Online connectivity has become an important part of day-to-day life for people all over the world. More than likely, you own at least one e-mail account, and you probably own more than one. You probably also shop for books, CDs, DVDs, car rentals, and airline tickets on the web. You may have filed your taxes electronically. By 2004, you might be able to cast your vote for president over the Internet, almost certainly by 2008.

Being connected is so much a part of business and pastime in this information age that not being connected is a cause for concern. I don't just mean the digital divide—that widening gulf between the technological haves and have-nots. I mean also the anatomical and psychological assumptions that our technology seems to make. Computers favor people who can look at flickering screens for hours and hours at a time, who have the use of both hands, and who can hear "You've got mail." Computers don't like you so much if you have vision or hearing impairments, dyslexia, epilepsy, carpel tunnel syndrome, back problems, or cognitive disabilities.

For the same reason that businesses need to install wheelchair ramps, and buttons on elevators need to have Braille labels, electronic information needs to provide comparable levels of access to those with disabilities. In the United States and many other countries, it's the law. Section 508 of the USC Rehabilitation Act requires that all federal agencies make their electronic and information technology accessible to everyone, regardless of disability. The Feds can't do business with you if you don't comply. Imagine the scramble at the software companies, service providers, and computer manufacturers when those words came down in 1998.

The web is nothing if not electronic information, but the nature of the web presents interesting challenges where accessibility is concerned. The web is almost purely visual, for one. The very popularity of the web comes from its graphical approach. How can image-laden, text-filled websites provide access to people who can't read the screen?

Special software and hardware can meet the website halfway. For the visually impaired, there are screen readers, which convert electronic text into spoken words. For those with vision and hearing impairments, there are also Braille readers. A microphone headset and voice-recognition software can eliminate the need for a mouse or keyboard. For equipment like this to work, the website needs to provide text-based descriptions for all images and text-based links for all purely graphical ones. This is the concept of text equivalence. As long as there is comparable text-based content, screen readers and the like can provide comparable access to the information on the site.

Web animation must also meet accessibility challenges. The World Wide Web Consortium (W3C) proposes a number of accessibility recommendations for digital content creators, including web animators. Be sure to visit www.w3c.org/WAI for more information on this important topic. I summarize the most relevant guidelines for animators here:

- Animators should provide synchronized alternate equivalent content to audio and video. This often takes the form of text captions or spoken-word narration tracks that play in sync with the animation.

- Text captions should transliterate the audio of the animation, including sound effects. Text captions must play in sync with the animation.

- Spoken-word narration should describe key visual elements in the animation, including character actions, setting, and changes of scene. Narration must play in sync with the animation. If you have to pause the animation so that the narration can catch up, so be it.

- Make sure that your animation doesn't strobe, flash, blink, or flicker. Flickering can induce seizures in people with epilepsy.

◆ Interactive controls, such as buttons in your movie, must also be accessible. That is, use text captions or spoken-word narration to describe the interactive controls and their functions, and provide alternate ways to activate the controls besides pointing and clicking. For instance, in Flash, you can assign the Key Press event to a button in addition to the Release event. This allows your audience to substitute a hotkey for the mouse.

Making Accessible Flash Movies

Flash MX enables you to create more accessible movies than in previous versions of Flash, and the Flash Player 6 plug-in for Microsoft Internet Explorer on Windows coordinates with several kinds of screen readers to present your accessible content. Unfortunately, the Flash Player 6 plug-in for Netscape on Windows doesn't provide the same level of accessibility, nor do the plug-ins for any browsers on the Mac.

Standard text objects in Flash MX have automatic text equivalence. That is, supported screen readers can access the text without any special effort on your behalf. In addition, by filling out a few text fields, you can assign text equivalence to the following objects:

◆ Dynamic text objects, or text objects whose content changes during the course of the movie

◆ Input text fields, or fields in which the viewer can type, like the text fields on a web page

◆ Instances of button symbols

◆ Instances of movie-clip symbols

◆ The movie itself

Use the Flash Accessibility panel (see Figure A.1) to assign text equivalence to these objects. The Accessibility panel opens when you choose Window → Accessibility.

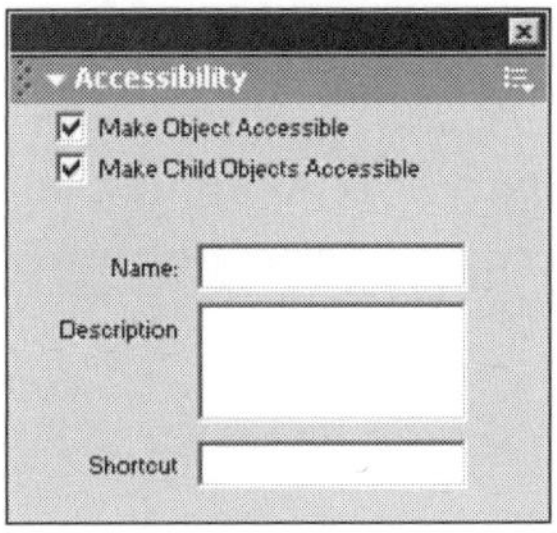

Figure A.1

Use the Accessibility panel to assign text equivalence to certain types of objects in your Flash movie.

Select an object on the stage with the Arrow tool. (To select the movie object, click a blank area of the stage.) If you can assign text equivalence to this object, the Accessibility panel provides the appropriate fields. In the Name field, type a name for the object. Most supported screen readers say this name aloud. In the Description field, provide a thorough description of the object according to the W3C's recommendations. In the Shortcut field, enter the keyboard shortcut that corresponds to this object.

The top of the Accessibility panel gives you additional options for the selected object. Check the Make Object Accessible option (or the Make Movie Accessible option, in the case of the movie itself) if you want screen readers to find the object and read its equivalent text. Unchecking this option hides the object from screen readers. Check the Make Child Objects Accessible option if you want screen readers to find accessible objects inside the selected object and read their equivalent text. (A *child object* is an object that belongs to another object.) By unchecking this option for the movie itself, you hide all its accessible objects, since all the objects inside the movie are children of the movie object.

Not all accessible objects provide the same fields and options, as Table A.1 shows.

Table A.1 Accessibility Fields and Options by Object

Object	Name	Description	Shortcut	Make Object Accessible	Make Child Objects Accessible
Dynamic text		✓		✓	
Input text	✓	✓	✓	✓	
Button	✓	✓	✓	✓	✓
Movie clip	✓	✓	✓	✓	✓
Movie	✓	✓		✓	✓

Keep in mind that only Flash Player 6 movies support this level of accessibility. If you publish your movie to an earlier version of the Flash Player, screen readers won't be able to use the equivalent text.

For Flash MX accessibility tips, examples, and an up-to-date list of supported screen readers, visit www.macromedia.com/software/flash/productinfo/ accessibility/.

What's on the CD-ROM

The CD-ROM that comes with this book isn't just a unique fashion accessory. It also contains everything you need to create web animation with this book.

Exploring the Contents

The CD-ROM is organized into folders and files, just like the hard drive of your computer. There are two main folders: BookExamples and 3rdParty.

The BookExamples folder contains the source files for building the animations in each chapter as well as the animation files themselves at each stage of production, in case you want to cheat or skip ahead a few steps.

The SoftwareLibrary folder offers the following pieces of trial-ware and free samples:

- **Macromedia.** Here are the trial versions of Fireworks MX, Flash MX, and Director 8.5.

- **Apple.** This folder contains the installer for the free QuickTime 6 player.

- **Tabuleiro.** Find the trial version of ShapeShifter3D 1.5 in this folder.

Launching the CD

Turn on your computer, place the disc in the CD-ROM tray, and then close the tray. On a Windows system, the main menu of the CD should appear momentarily. If it doesn't, choose Start > Run from the Windows desktop and type the drive letter of your CD-ROM device plus a colon character (:), and then type **\Start/exe.** For instance, if drive letter D is your CD-ROM device, type **D:\Start.exe**. Click OK or press Enter to launch the CD.

On a Macintosh system, the CD-ROM doesn't launch automatically. If you use a Macintosh, follow the instructions in the next section, "Browsing the CD."

Browsing the CD

You can also easily view and explore the directory structure of the CD. On a Windows system, double-click the My Computer icon on the desktop. (If you're using Windows XP, you may have to click the Start button to find the My Computer icon.) This calls up a window of icons for the devices on your computer. Left-click the icon for your CD-ROM drive, and choose Explore from the context menu. Double-click the CD icon to launch the CD, or double-click the folder icons to see what's inside.

On a Macintosh system, an icon representing the CD should appear on your desktop shortly after you insert the disc. Double-click this icon to see the CD contents. The CIGWA icon launches the disc. Browse the disc yourself by double-clicking the folders.

Installing Fireworks

Macromedia Fireworks MX is an image editor for web graphics. You use Fireworks to create animated GIFs in this book, but the software has many other uses that you should feel free to explore. You work with Fireworks in Part II of this book.

Find your trial version of Fireworks MX in the 3rdParty/Macromedia/Fireworks folder. Double-click the installer icon in this folder to install Fireworks on your system.

The installation procedure itself is painless. A series of dialog boxes appears on the screen, giving you different installation options. Feel free to customize the installation if you prefer. When in doubt, choose the default settings. The entire installation takes about 10 minutes.

Your trial version is fully functional for a period of 30 days, which starts after you successfully complete installation.

Installing Flash

Macromedia Flash MX is an animation tool for creating SWF files. You use Flash in Part III of this book.

Your trial version of Flash is in the 3rdParty/Macromedia/Flash folder. Double-click the installer icon to install Flash on your system. Then, simply follow the instructions in the dialog boxes that appear.

Like with Fireworks, your trial version of Flash lasts for 30 days.

Installing Director

Macromedia Director 8.5 is a multimedia development tool. Let me rephrase that: It's *the* multimedia development tool. You use Director to build Shockwave movies in Part IV of this book.

Find your trial version of Director in the 3rdParty/Macromedia/Director folder. Double-click the installer icon, and follow the instructions that appear on screen.

This trial version is fully functional for 30 days.

Installing QuickTime

Apple QuickTime 6 is software that plays digital media files like movie clips. If you have QuickTime version 4 or better on your system, you can import a greater variety of audio files for your animations in Flash MX.

The 3rdParty/Apple/ folder contains installer software for the free QuickTime 6 player. To install QuickTime on your system, double-click this icon, and follow the instructions that appear on screen.

If you already have QuickTime version 4 or better on your system, you don't need to install QuickTime 6 unless you want to upgrade.

Installing ShapeShifter3D

Tabuleiro ShapeShifter3D is an Xtra for Director 8.5 that allows you to create basic 3-D models. (An Xtra is a plug-in by any other name.) You use ShapeShifter3D in Part V of this book.

The 3rdParty/Tabuleiro/ folder contains the installer for this Xtra. To install ShapeShifter3D, double-click this icon and follow the on-screen instructions.

After installation, locate the files *ShapeShifter3D.x32* and *ShapeShifter3D.dxr* (Windows) or *ShapeShifter3D* and *ShapeShifter3D.dxr* (Mac). Copy these files to the Director Xtras folder on your hard drive. The next time you launch Director, you will be able to open ShapeShifter3D from the Xtras menu. Macintosh users should allocate at least 40MB RAM to the Director 8.5 trial version, or ShapeShifter3D won't run.

Your trial version of ShapeShifter3D doesn't expire, but it only allows you to export 3-D models with 500 faces or less, which is more than enough for learning the basics.

Glossary

ActionScript   The scripting language in Flash for creating interactive movies.

ambient light   In 3-D modeling, the nonspecific light of the 3-D world.

anchor point   An element that defines the shape of a vector graphic.

angular blending   In a shape tween, blending that retains the hard edges of the component shapes.

animation symbol   In Fireworks, a symbol that has built-in animation.

anti-aliasing   A technique in computer graphics for making rough or jagged edges appear smooth.

audio channels   In Director, the channels of the score that can contain audio cast members.

audio cues   Sound-based hints that reinforce the clickability of a button.

back face   The reverse side of a 3-D letter in Director.

background light   In Director 3D, the light that comes from behind the camera.

banding   A characteristic of overcompressed graphics files in which gradients (or gradual blends of color) appear as discrete layers of color.

behavior   In Director, a ready-made Lingo script for a sprite or frame.

bitmap   Another name for a raster graphic.

bone In 3-D modeling, an area between two joints in the skeletal structure of a model.

branching movie An interactive movie with multiple threads, the order of which the audience determines.

button actions In Flash, ActionScripts that a button triggers.

camera In 3-D graphics, the point of view into a 3-D world.

canvas The area in which an animator creates an animated GIF in Fireworks.

cast members In Director, the collection of elements in a movie.

channel In Director, a region of the score that represents a sprite on the stage.

diffuse light In 3-D modeling, the general color of a material's surface.

distributive blending In a shape tween, blending that creates shapes with rounder, more abstract corners.

dithering A technique to improve the number of colors in a GIF image by tricking the human eye into seeing composite shades.

down state The appearance of a button when a viewer clicks it.

embedded movie A movie that plays inside a web browser.

emissive light In Director, the color of the light that a material radiates or gives off.

event synchronization In Flash, the sound setting that ties a sound to a particular event in the animation.

face In 3-D modeling, the triangular area expressed by three vertices. Faces are one-sided objects.

fill In vector graphics, the interior region of a shape.

fixed-width text object A container for text with defined margins.

frame In Flash and Director, the smallest unit of time in an animation. In Fireworks, a single, static image in an animated GIF.

frame actions In Flash, ActionScripts that a frame in the timeline triggers.

frame-by-frame animation In Flash and Director, an animation technique in which each frame of a sequence contains a different piece of art.

frame delay In animated GIFs, the amount of time that a frame remains on screen.

front face   The forward side of a 3-D letter in Director.

graphics card   A hardware component that takes over many of the display tasks of a computer's CPU.

group   In Flash, a collection of vector shapes that acts as a single object.

hit state   The clickable region of a button.

illustration program   A software application for creating and editing vector graphics.

image editor   A software application for creating and editing raster graphics.

ink mode   In Director, the method for drawing a sprite in a movie.

instance   A graphic that refers to a symbol.

interactive movie   A movie that relies on audience participation to determine how the timeline of the movie plays out.

joint   In 3-D modeling, a point at which a model deforms.

keyframe   In Flash and Director, a frame that marks an event in a movie.

layer   A transparent, stackable drawing surface in graphics applications.

light   In 3-D modeling, the source of illumination in a 3-D world.

Lingo   Scripting language in Director for interactive movies.

marker   In Director, a point on the score that indicates the beginning of a particular section of a movie.

mask layer   In Flash, a layer whose artwork acts like a window on the layers underneath.

material   In 3-D modeling, a collection of appearance settings for a 3-D object.

model   An object or collection of objects in a 3-D world.

mono, monaural   A sound with a single audio channel.

morphing   In 3-D modeling, the technique for changing one 3-D model into another over time.

motion guide layer   In Flash, a layer containing the path that a moving object should follow.

motion tween   In computer animation, the process of moving a symbol instance or sprite from one position on the stage to another.

movie   In Flash and Director, an animation.

multimedia   The ability or capacity of a file format to include various types of files.

onion skinning   A computer animation technique that shows multiple frames simultaneously.

over state   The appearance of a button when the viewer hovers over it with the mouse pointer.

pixel   A very small, colored square picture element.

player   A software application that displays a particular kind of movie file.

plug-in   An optional piece of software that extends the functionality of another piece of software.

primitive   In 3-D modeling, a basic 3-D shape.

projector   In Director, a self-contained, standalone movie.

raster graphic   A computer image composed of pixels.

registration point   The point at which a graphical transformation occurs.

render   In 3-D modeling, to export a model or animation for 2-D playback.

scale   To change size.

scene   In Flash, a collection of frames and layers that represents an animation sequence.

score   In Director, the area where an animator sets up the action of a movie.

shader   In Director 3D, the control that determines the surface appearance of 3-D text.

shape   In Director, a very simple, vectorlike graphical cast member.

shape hints   Corresponding points on either shape in a shape tween. During the tween, Flash moves the shape hint on the starting shape toward the corresponding shape hint on the ending shape.

specular light   In 3-D modeling, the color of a material's highlights, or the color of the light that reflects off the material's surface.

sprite   In Director, an instance of a cast member on the stage.

stacking order   The order in which elements sit on top of each other in a layer.

stage   In Flash and Director, the area in which an animator builds a movie.

start synchronization   In Flash, a sound setting much like event synchronization, only this setting prevents the sound from playing if another instance of the same sound is already playing in the movie.

stereo   A sound with two audio channels, left and right.

still   A static image of a single frame in an animation.

stop synchronization   In Flash, the sound setting that stops playback of an event sound or start-synchronized sound.

stream synchronization   In Flash, the sound setting that ties the playback of a sound to the animation timeline.

streaming   A characteristic of some media formats by which the presentation of content begins before the entire media file has downloaded.

strobing   Leaving afterimages. Strobing is a common problem in animated GIFs.

stroke   In vector graphics, the outline or contour of a shape.

symbol   In Flash, the definitive version of an image, from which an animator creates and modifies instances.

tempo   In Director, the frame rate of the movie.

texture   In 3-D modeling, a raster graphic that covers the surface of a 3-D model.

tunnel   The connecting structure between the front and back faces of a 3-D letter in Director.

tweening   The process of calculating the correct in-between frames given a starting frame and an ending frame.

up state   The default appearance of a button.

variable-width text object   A container for text with no predetermined right margin.

vector graphic   A computer image expressed in terms of the shapes that the image contains.

vertex, vertices   In 3-D modeling, a point or points in 3-D space.

viewport   In ShapeShifter3D, a window that shows a particular perspective of a 3-D model.

visual cues   Graphical hints, such as a change of color or size, that reinforce the clickability of a button.

weight   In vector graphics, the thickness of a stroke.

wireframe   In 3-D modeling, the structure of a 3-D model, consisting of vertices and faces.

world   In 3-D modeling, a virtual 3-D environment.

Index

U-V

W-X-Y-Z

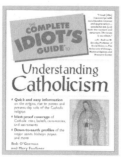

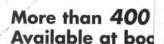